Local Economic and Employment Development (LEED)

Designing Local Skills Strategies

Edited by
Francesca Froy, Sylvain Giguère
and Andrea-Rosalinde Hofer

ORGANISATION FOR ECONOMIC CO-OPERATION AND DEVELOPMENT

The OECD is a unique forum where the governments of 30 democracies work together to address the economic, social and environmental challenges of globalisation. The OECD is also at the forefront of efforts to understand and to help governments respond to new developments and concerns, such as corporate governance, the information economy and the challenges of an ageing population. The Organisation provides a setting where governments can compare policy experiences, seek answers to common problems, identify good practice and work to co-ordinate domestic and international policies.

The OECD member countries are: Australia, Austria, Belgium, Canada, the Czech Republic, Denmark, Finland, France, Germany, Greece, Hungary, Iceland, Ireland, Italy, Japan, Korea, Luxembourg, Mexico, the Netherlands, New Zealand, Norway, Poland, Portugal, the Slovak Republic, Spain, Sweden, Switzerland, Turkey, the United Kingdom and the United States. The Commission of the European Communities takes part in the work of the OECD.

OECD Publishing disseminates widely the results of the Organisation's statistics gathering and research on economic, social and environmental issues, as well as the conventions, guidelines and standards agreed by its members.

This work is published on the responsibility of the Secretary-General of the OECD. The opinions expressed and arguments employed herein do not necessarily reflect the official views of the Organisation or of the governments of its member countries.

ISBN 978-92-64-06662-5 (print)
ISBN 978-92-64-06664-9 (PDF)

Series: Local Economic and Employment Development (LEED)
ISSN 1990-1100 (print)
ISSN 1990-1097 (online)

Photo credits: Cover © Martin Mistretta/Digital Vision/Getty Images.

Corrigenda to OECD publications may be found on line at: *www.oecd.org/publishing/corrigenda*.

About the Authors

Pieter Bevelander is associate professor at MIM, Malmö Institute of Migration, Diversity and Welfare, a senior lecturer at the School of IMER, Malmö University, Sweden and research fellow at IZA, Bonn, Germany. His main research field is international migration and different aspects of immigrant integration. His latest research topics include the socioeconomic and political impacts of citizenship acquisition of immigrants and minorities in host societies and the attitudes of the native population towards immigrants and other minority groups. He has reviewed and published for several international journals as well as co-editing together with Don DeVoretz the recent publication *The Economics of Citizenship* (2008).

Per Broomé obtained his Master of Arts from the University of Lund in 1969. He has a career in organisational development and management consultancy. He has been on the board of The Swedish Association of Human Resource Management and president of a management consulting company. He has been engaged in, and headed research projects since the late 80's. He is extensively published in the field of population economics and organisational demographics with a special focus on age, immigration and ethnicity. He is currently research coordinator at Malmö Institute for Studies of Migration, Diversity and Welfare (MIM), Malmö University.

Randall Eberts is President of the W.E. Upjohn Institute for Employment Research, an independent non-profit research organisation that conducts and supports research on policy-relevant employment and regional economic issues. His current research examines the role of local partnerships in workforce and economic development. Mr. Eberts also works closely with the federal and state governments to develop management tools that use statistical analysis to help improve the performance of workforce programmes. He received his PhD in economics from Northwestern University.

Francesca Froy is the coordinator of activities on employment, skills and local governance within the Local Economic and Employment Development (LEED) Programme at the OECD. A policy analyst, she implements studies on Designing Local Skills Strategies, Managing Accountability and Flexibility, Skills for Competitiveness and Integrating Employment, Skills and Economic Development. She co-edited the OECD publications *From Immigration to*

Integration: Local Solutions to a Global Challenge and *Flexible Policy for More and Better Jobs*. Prior to joining LEED she worked in Brussels evaluating European projects and programmes, and helping to manage the DG Employment and Social Affairs initiative IDELE (identification and dissemination of local employment development). A practitioner by background, she has worked for a number of years in both the Public Employment Service and a municipal government in the United Kingdom. She has a BSC in Anthropology from University College London and an MA in cultural theory (the Body and Representation) from the University of Reading.

Sylvain Giguère is Head of the Local Economic and Employment Development (LEED) Division at the OECD. He manages a team of 25 economists, analysts and support staff based at both the OECD Headquarters in Paris and the OECD LEED Centre for Local Development in Trento, Italy. A Canadian national, Mr. Giguère joined the OECD in 1995 and developed a policy research agenda to provide guidance on how public policies can be better co-ordinated and adapted to local conditions to improve economic and social outcomes. This work has produced a broad range of policy lessons, from labour market policy to economic development, published widely. He studied economics at University of Quebec in Montreal and Queen's University (Kingston, Ont.) and holds a PhD in economics from University of Paris 1 (Sorbonne).

Lisa Grossman began her public policy career at MDRC, a non-profit social policy research organisation, where she studied community college access and retention for low-wage workers. She was co-principal investigator for the first qualitative study of MDRC's Opening Doors project, and more recently worked on projects to improve employment and health outcomes for individuals with disabilities. She has also worked for the National Governors Association Center for Best Practices as a Senior Policy Analyst and for the City University of New York's School of Professional Studies in Program Development. She currently works as a Contract Specialist for the US Navy. She has a Masters of Public Administration from the New York University Wagner School, and a Bachelor of Arts degree from Williams College.

Andrea-Rosalinde Hofer is a Policy Analyst at the OECD LEED Trento Centre for Local Development. She has managed several country reviews and pioneered capacity building activities in the areas of local governance and entrepreneurship. Before joining the OECD in 2004, Andrea undertook research and managed local policy development projects on decentralisation, local governance and public administration reform at the University of Federal Armed Forces in Munich, and at the United Nations (UNDP and UNODC). She has published on local governance in transition economies, policy frameworks for local entrepreneurship support, the role of universities in local economic development, and the impact of migration on skills and business sector development. Andrea holds a MA degree in Political Science and an MSc degree in Agricultural Engineering/Rural Development; she is pursuing doctoral studies on the impact of local governance on local economic development.

Cristina Martinez-Fernandez (PhD UNSW, Doc Salamanca) is a Policy Analyst on Local Governance and Employment at the OECD Centre for Entrepreneurship, SMEs and Local Economic Development (CFE) "LEED" Programme where she investigates skills development in SMEs, the skills requirements of the green economy and implications for entrepreneurship and innovation. Cristina also manages the OECD/LEED Initiative on "Employment and Skills Strategies in Southeast Asia" (ESSSA). Previously she was an Associate Professor at the Urban Research Centre, University of Western Sydney in Australia, where she lead the research programme on Urban and Regional Dynamics which includes the study of demographic processes and policies and strategies that influence urbanisation. She has published more than 100 journal papers, research reports and book chapters.

Rhonda Phillips, a professor in the School of Community Resources and Development at Arizona State University, works to expand the reach of community-based education and research initiatives for enhancing quality of life. Community investment and well-being comprise the focus of Rhonda's research and outreach activities. Rhonda has worked on several indicator projects and is a member of the Arizona Community Indicators Project Committee for Community Health and Well-Being. She has authored or edited seven books, including *Introduction to Community Development*; *Concept Marketing for Communities*; and *Community Development Indicators Measuring Systems*.

Zhang Rufei received his Master Degree (1987) from the Tongji University, Shanghai. A native Chinese, he worked for the Shanghai Municipal Urban Planning Institute and held increasingly senior positions over eight years in the Institute, including chief of the department responsible for development controls in Shanghai, and project director for updating Shanghai's Long Term Development Plan. In 1998, Mr. Zhang joined Chreod Ltd, a Canadian consulting firm, as the company's managing director and principal representative in China. Mr. Zhang's consulting work has largely been on capital investment projects, market research for foreign investors, and on development research and infrastructure planning for central and municipal governments in China, and for international agencies including the World Bank, International Finance Corporation, the Asian Development Bank, OECD, CIDA and GTZ.

Foreword

The issue of skills has attracted significant attention from the LEED Directing Committee in recent years. In 2005, the OECD LEED Programme completed a project on "Skills Upgrading for the Low-qualified" to identify effective practices in training workers who are trapped in low-skilled and low-paid employment. The report identified a series of governance failures, emphasising a need for government to shift their priorities from labour market integration to up-skilling in their policies, and highlighting the need to adopt mechanisms that have been implemented effectively at the local level within national policy interventions. More recently, LEED has been seeking to understand how local policy makers can more broadly address the skills issues affecting their localities, through balanced local skills strategies.

The recent economic downturn has shown more than ever the value of investing in skills. In their response to rising unemployment, governments have seen education and training as means of keeping vulnerable workers economically active, while improving their productivity and building the long-term prosperity of local communities. It is more and more likely that jobs will demand higher skills levels in the future, as low-skilled jobs are lost and redefined in the current restructuring process. But to achieve higher skills levels, a joined-up approach will be necessary between employment agencies, economic development bodies and local employers.

Planning and managing skills development is becoming more complicated. What firms are increasingly seeking is not just skills, but talent. Talent is all about aptitude – not just having the right knowledge and skills, but also being able to apply them effectively. This is important, as it means that it is no longer enough just to train people in job-specific tasks. Workers also need strong generic skills – the ability to analyse, communicate, innovate, problem-solve, and take risks where needed. For localities wishing to build a pool of talent, investing in education and training systems for the young is no longer sufficient. Attention also needs to be paid to adult skills.

Making sure that local people can access training and learning throughout their working lives is one key area for action. However demographic change and rising mobility means that some localities are having to attract and retain talent from elsewhere, which requires openness, tolerance and the management of diversity. At the same time, disadvantaged groups in the labour market can bring valuable knowledge and competences to employers if they are more effectively integrated, as can low-skilled workers, if they are properly nurtured and developed. Because this policy area involves such a diverse set of issues, it needs to be managed through a balanced approach, with local policy makers maximising the synergies between different interventions and negotiating trade-offs.

In the coming years, local policy makers will need to become much more creative and innovative in building their local skills base. This book summarises the latest practices across OECD and non-OECD countries and assesses the obstacles faced to success. It is my hope that its key messages will be as useful to governments as they will be to local practitioners seeking to excel in this increasingly important policy area.

Sergio Arzeni

Director, OECD Centre for Entrepreneurship, SMEs and Local Development

Table of Contents

List of boxes

List of tables

List of figures

Executive Summary

In order to prosper in today's economy, local communities increasingly need to ensure that they adequately invest in education and skills. Higher-level skills, such as the ability to analyse and process complex information, be creative and communicate effectively, are all increasing in importance in the context of the knowledge-based economy. In addition, the recent economic downturn has shown more than ever the value of investing in skills as a means of retaining employment in difficult times. It is more and more likely that future jobs will demand higher skills levels, as low-skilled jobs are lost and redefined in the current restructuring process.

At the same time, modern production techniques are characterised by rapid skills obsolescence. As business needs evolve, demands are placed on local vocational education and training systems to adapt, which can be difficult when their management is centralised, as is the case in many OECD countries. An ageing population threatens to produce shortages of both labour and skills in many localities, particularly rural areas. When people retire their skills and experience are not so easy to replace. A further factor leading to the increasing importance, but also increasing complexity, of human resources issues is rising mobility. International immigration has more than tripled in OECD countries over the last twenty years (OECD, 2007). Some localities lose skills in this process, while others gain. While sending regions across the developing world are building strategies to cope with the loss of skills to emigration, receiving regions are investing significant resources in ensuring that the skills brought by newcomers are recognised and adapted to their new context.

These competing demands and concerns present a major challenge to local communities seeking to develop local skill strategies and invest in their future labour force. With limited resources, local policy makers need to establish priorities to ensure that concerted local action can have a real impact on the labour market. However, what should the local priorities be? The attraction and integration of new talent? The retention of existing skilled workers? The education and training of future generations of young people in the needs of the local labour market? The integration of disadvantaged groups who are currently outside the labour force? Or "upskilling" the current labour force and working with employers to move towards more knowledge-intensive forms of production? While national policy will have a role to play, much of the responsibility for a number of these actions will fall squarely on the shoulders of local and regional agencies.

Their task is not an easy one. In order to make the right decisions, and effectively balance interventions, policy makers need to have a detailed understanding of the skills supply and demand in their local labour force – what is known as the local "skills ecology". They also need to have some foresight as to the likely industrial sectors and types of employment opportunities which will dominate in years to come. Such information is difficult to collect, and even more difficult to analyse effectively. Once priorities have been set, local agencies need to have the power to influence education and training policy (which, as noted above, is often managed nationally) and effective ways of working in partnership, given that skills are a cross-cutting issue faced by policy makers in fields as diverse as education and training, employment, economic development, social development and entrepreneurship.

The OECD LEED Programme has been looking at cases of localities in Africa, the Americas, Asia, Australasia and Europe that have developed a joined-up strategic approach to raising skills at the local level. This publication reviews the results of this research, highlighting state of the art practice and ways of overcoming the various obstacles and challenges to success.

The first part of this publication includes two international overviews of local practice in skills development. Chapter 1 looks at the key elements which have proved important in the development of balanced local skills strategies in advanced economies. Local stakeholders clearly realise that it is no longer enough just to invest in the formal education and training system, and are turning towards a more diverse range of strategies to increase the supply of skills in their localities. Increasingly, strategies centre on three particular themes: attracting and retaining talent, integrating disadvantaged groups into the workforce development system and upgrading the skills of the low-qualified. While many new initiatives are being experimented with in each of these three areas, it is important that different interventions are brought together in a balanced overall strategy, which maximises synergies and ensures that no member of the local population is left behind.

In developing countries local development strategies are often hindered by the loss of skills through emigration. Chapter Two reviews the approaches that are being undertaken in Albania, Ecuador, El Salvador, Ghana, Nigeria, Nicaragua, Mexico, Romania, and Sierra Leone to better manage migration to help rebuild local economies and better harness skills gained overseas. Governments can respond to emigration defensively, that is, through restriction of international mobility and reparation for loss of human resources and capital, or strategically by collaborating with host countries and localities, resourcing diaspora, recruiting international labour, and stimulating return migration. Today it seems that defensive policies are on the decline and strategic international collaboration is on the increase. Activities which stimulate private sector development, at the same time as transferring skills and know-how back home, show particular promise for putting sending regions onto a more sustainable economic development path. However, activities in this area are currently small scale and *ad-hoc*, and limited by low capacities within local governments in many developing countries.

Case studies

It is useful to look into certain strategies in more detail to understand how they fit with the local economic context. In the second part of the publication, we review six case studies, looking at cutting edge examples of skills development strategies from Australia, China, Sweden and the United States. These case studies highlight three themes in particular: the advantage of developing an integrated approach to workforce development, the importance of upgrading worker skills, and the need to better manage migration.

Developing an integrated approach to workforce development

Chapter 3 provides an analysis of the Shanghai Highland of Talent Initiative, which is a good example of a city-wide skills strategy to help adapt a local labour force to a restructuring 21st century economy. The municipal government launched its first skills development initiative in 1995 to develop Shanghai as a "highland of talent" in mainland China. However, effective efforts to implement a concerted strategy did not occur until the municipality launched a detailed "action framework" in 2004. Actions include the attraction of returnee high-skilled Chinese émigrés; specialised training programmes to train high-skilled scientists, managers, engineers, politicians and public servants; and wider programmes to reform the vocational training system and upskill Shanghai's labour force. Many different agencies and institutions are involved in delivering the strategy, which has a clear set of targets, and has led to the development of 49 new pieces of city level legislation.

Different localities have different skills issues, and in some states and regions, bottom-up partnership approaches are being encouraged which involve a broad range of different private and public sector agencies, and focus on particular employment sectors. In 2004, the Governor of Michigan embarked on a state-wide project to improve the efficiency of local workforce development and educational systems in meeting businesses needs. Recognising that local labour markets have their own specific needs and that local entities best understand them, the state turned to local stakeholders to form partnerships to identify skills needs, develop the strategies to address the needs, and carry out proposed activities. With the financial assistance of a charitable foundation, the state offered one-year start-up grants totaling over USD 1 million for the initial development of 13 "regional skills alliances" across the state. All the skills alliances have involved a business-led approach, with strategic aims and objective being developed locally in consultation with local employers.

Upgrading the skills of local workers

While attracting new talent can help to address current and future skills shortages, concerted strategies to upgrade the skills of those already present within a region are particularly important, particularly those that address the low-skilled. The region of Mackay in Australia recognised that some local people were having a problem holding down apprenticeships, and that this was leading to skills shortages that were holding back growth in key manufacturing sectors of the economy. In response, manufacturing companies in Mackay formed an industry cluster named "Mackay Area Industry Network" (MAIN) with the purpose of both helping local people and addressing skills-shortages quickly and effectively. The result was the MAIN CARE programme – a programme designed to recruit, select and manage apprentices in the workplace, which has had some success in improving retention rates within local apprenticeship programmes.

Sometimes a community-based approach is necessary to improve skills levels, particularly in areas where both the supply and demand for skills has fallen to a very low level. The Mississippi Band of Choctaw Indians (MBCI) provides a case study of a successful community-based strategy which has addressed not only high rates of unemployment and poverty, but also a lack of employment opportunities in an indigenous tribal community. The Choctaw's have approached skill-development through a method of self-reliance and self-determination as well as collaborative partnerships with government agencies. The focus for workforce development has been on the hospitality industry, as well as technology intensive manufacturing. The results have been remarkable, with poverty and unemployment rates dropping significantly since the early 1970's from highs of 80% to a recent full employment status at 2% in 2007.

Better managing migration

At the same time, we cannot ignore the fact that people are increasingly mobile and that migration will play an increasing role in local skills strategies. Two case studies in OECD countries illustrate joined-up local approaches to better integrating newcomers into the work-force so that their skills are not wasted.

In the mid-1990s the city of Malmö experienced both economic structural change and significant levels of immigration, to a large extent of refugees. During the second half of the 1990s a new vision was developed for the city, to transform it into a centre for service, trade and finance related industries.

Improving the skills levels of the local population and attracting new talent have been central pillars of the new strategy. In particular, a number of initiatives have been developed to capitalise on the skills brought by new immigrants. These include new university courses to help highly-skilled immigrants adapt to the Malmö labour market, and a "portfolio-approach" to help make the competences brought by immigrants more visible.

Immigrants in New York City are integral players in the local economy, representing 43% of the city's existing labour force. Recent immigrants to the city have lower levels of educational attainment overall than native-born residents, which presents a barrier to labour market entry and advancement. The final chapter in the book explores how the City University of New York and its partners (including employers, public agencies and unions), are attempting to upgrade unemployed or low-wage immigrant workers' skills through several career pathways models in the health, hospitality and retail sectors.

Overall conclusions

Overall, it becomes apparent, through reviewing local practices in OECD and non-OECD countries, that skills strategies need to concentrate on five strategic emerging issues:

- **Access to relevant information and data.** Local actors need to understand and correctly define the local "skills ecology" to develop the appropriate tools required for evidence-based skills strategies. The Shanghai case study illustrates, for example, the value of collecting annual data on skills demand and skills supply to ensure that training is being well targeted to local business needs. In other localities struggling with a lack of disaggregated data, partnerships with regional and national actors are essential in mapping local supply and demand, and understanding how it fits within the wider economic fabric.
- **Balanced and long term strategies.** The review of local practice shows that, when developing strategies to improve the skills base, localities should strike the right balance between attracting talent, integrating disadvantaged groups into the workforce development system and upgrading the skills of the low qualified. While some localities (such as Shanghai and the regions of Michigan) achieve a broadly balanced approach, in many cases it is clear that only certain aspects of the local skills ecology are receiving adequate attention. There are many factors, including short-termism and a lack of resources, which prevent communities from dealing with more intractable skills problems, such as a low-skilled workforce, or pockets of local people without basic skills. Developing a strong skills strategy may therefore

require providing incentives for local actors to work towards longer-term objectives and invest in sustainable productivity growth.

- **Better mapping skills provision, for example through "careers clusters" and "careers ladders".** Education and training is often delivered in a piece meal fashion at the local level, with few connections between courses, and a lack of reference to employer needs. Joining up disparate education and training systems locally is crucial to helping people to build on their learning over time whilst in and outside of employment. In New York, career ladders have proved a very good way of linking up education and training provision into a coherent system in certain sectors, so that people can see how a basic course in retail can ultimately lead to a management position in a local department store. Such schemes link basic skills training with higher-level training, while also offering better careers advice for adults, an element which is lacking in many localities in OECD countries.
- **Building strong relationships with employers.** In order to produce real change in local labour markets, skills strategies need to address problems of both skills supply and skills demand. This requires close working between public sector actors and employers. While the private sector can be an invaluable partner in highlighting more *immediate* skills demands, governmental actors can play a crucial role in encouraging employers' to think about longer-term skills needs, and improve the way that they utilise skills in the workplace. This will be crucial to improving the quality of employment locally and avoiding problems of low-skill equilibrium. Public sector actors should also have a primary responsibility for ensuring the inclusion of disadvantaged groups. While all of the case studies featured in this book show the value of bringing on board the private sector, the Mackay case draws into question the idea that employers are best-placed to deal with more disadvantaged groups in our local communities.
- **Look to the future and anticipate change.** The success of local skills strategies depends on the ability of local actors to foresee future growth and skills demands. Skills strategies need to be subject to regular review and adjustment as economies and industries evolve. In particular localities need to develop "flexible specialisation", building on specific strengths and local comparative advantage but adapting these to new forms of market demand as they emerge. The Choctaw tribe in the United States demonstrate the benefits of being flexible in the delivery of local employment and training policy in order to be able to respond quickly to new economic opportunity. The development of generic skills will also be key to equipping the labour force with the ability to absorb unpredictable local shocks.

PART I

International Overview

PART I

Chapter 1

Local Strategies for Developing Workforce Skills

by

Francesca Froy

In today's knowledge-based economy, human resources and skills are crucial to long-term growth, prosperity and social inclusion at the local level. A review of practice in OECD countries shows that local stakeholders realise that it is no longer enough just to invest in the formal education and training system, and are turning towards a more diverse range of strategies to increase the supply of skills in their locality. This chapter reviews such strategies in many different parts of the world including Australia, Canada, China, France, Germany, Malaysia, Sweden, the United Kingdom and the United States. The focus is in particular on actions to better attract and retain talent, integrate disadvantaged groups into the labour force, and upskill current workers. The chapter concludes by identifying the obstacles to a truly joined-up approach to skills at the local level, and ways to overcome these.

A promotional slogan of the State of Maryland's Workforce Investment Board (GWIB) is "Workforce Development is Economic Development". The sentiment behind this – that in today's knowledge-based economy, economic development should focus as much on human resources and skills as on infrastructure and inward investment – is increasingly apparent across all OECD countries. On the other side of the world in Australia, a primary goal of a regional development board in Griffith, New South Wales is "building workforce skills and education", followed by "taking a proactive regional approach to meeting infrastructure needs" and "implementing regional sustainability/growth management" (Collins, 2008).

The increasing priority given to human resource development is understandable given that skills are more and more in demand within the knowledge-based economy. It is estimated that by 2010 almost half of the net additional jobs created in the European Union will require people with tertiary-level qualifications; just under 40% will require upper secondary level and only 15% basic schooling (Tessaring and Wannan, 2004). The drive towards higher-level skills is driven, at least in part, by new technologies and globalisation. In more advanced economies, lower-skilled jobs are either being automated or off-shored to where they can be delivered more cheaply by lower-waged workers. In order to remain competitive, localities and regions in OECD countries need to add value to their products and services, producing more specialised goods, designed to meet the diversified demand which characterises today's markets. Higher-skilled people are crucial to this process.

It is generic skills – the ability to create, communicate, and innovate and problem solve that are most in demand. The financial journalist Diane Coyle (2001) has pointed to the fact that the drive towards higher-skills is collapsing the boundaries between services and manufacturing. While the services sector has long valued communication skills and the ability to adapt to customer needs, in manufacturing also, the comparative advantage of advanced economies is increasingly found in good design, creativity and the ability to customise products to reflect consumer preference. At the same time, new technologies such as the Internet encourage greater circulation of information, increasing the need for higher-skilled people to analyse and synergise this information and transform it into valuable knowledge. Softer and more advanced skills are therefore becoming a requirement across the economic spectrum.

The drive for increased skills is unlikely to be reduced by the recent economic downturn. Low-skilled people seem to have been disproportionately affected by the crisis, as employers are quick to shed workers for whom there are low turnover costs. As such positions are shed this will have an impact on future skills demand, as production procedures are redefined and restructuring process. Even before the economic downturn, low-skilled people faired particularly badly in the labour market. On average in OECD countries, 85% of people who had achieved a tertiary education qualification were in employment in 2006. By contrast, only 58% of people without even an upper secondary qualification had jobs (OECD, 2008a). In addition, incomes for low-skilled individuals are dramatically lower than for better qualified people. A study in the United States (Eberts, 2004), showed that the median weekly earnings of college-educated workers were 73% higher than those of high school-educated workers, and the gap is even larger for those who dropped out of high school.

Raising skills levels within the local population is therefore a key goal for local policy makers across OECD countries. However this process is not simple, complicated by the fast pace of technological development, and the demographic changes which today affect many localities and regions. Many OECD countries are experiencing a loss of skills through an ageing population. The ratio of older inactive persons per worker is expected to almost double from around 38% in the OECD area in 2000 to just over 70% in 2050. This is not only a problem affecting OECD Countries: the BRICS (Brazil, Russia, India and China) will also undergo significant population ageing over the next two decades, reflecting both lower fertility rates and improved longevity (OECD, 2007a). In countries such as the United States the impact of demographic change has been worsened by the retirement of the post war "baby boom" generation: in 2006 it was predicted that America's 500 biggest companies would lose half of their senior managers in the next five years.[1] Unless an effort is made to ensure that older workers train up people before they retire, they will take their skills and experience with them.

A further issue leading to the increasing complexity of managing human resources locally is the rising degree of human mobility. Legal international immigration has more than tripled in OECD countries over the twenty years leading up to 2004 and continued to rise by 10-11% in 2005 (OECD, 2007b).[2] In addition, the decline in inter-regional migration observed in many countries since the 1970s seems to have halted in most cases, with gross flows increasing in some countries (OECD, 2005b). When people move this has an important impact, not only on the localities that they leave behind (which may suffer due to a "brain drain" or loss of skills) but also on the localities in which they arrive, which have to consider ways of adapting the skills brought by newcomers to the local labour market. At the same time, the people who do not move, particularly those at the lower end of the skills ladder, may find themselves in competition for jobs with newly arrived populations that are willing to accept poorer employment conditions as they make sacrifices on the road to becoming integrated in a new country. While employers may look to new arrivals as a useful means of tackling skills shortages, local residents in direct competition for low-skilled jobs may not be so positive about these new influxes.

In some localities employers are themselves pushing for the better harnessing of local talent and utilisation of skills. In the best cases they are working together to offer customised training at the local level relevant for their industries. However, in many OECD countries, employers take a back seat. While globally the most productive jobs are increasingly those that are the most knowledge intensive, employers can also achieve competitive advantage by keeping skills levels, and therefore salaries, at a minimum. The phenomena known as the "low-skilled equilibrium" – where a low intensity of skills supply is met by a low intensity of skills demand (Finegold and Soskice, 1988) – can affect not only localities but whole countries, leading to low productivity and low incomes.

Why tackle skills at the local level?

Skills are inherently a local issue. Skills levels vary considerably across different localities and regions. The OECD's *Regions at a Glance* (OECD, 2005a) identified that, in nearly all OECD countries, the highly educated population is more concentrated than the labour force. In 2001, for example, 38% of those with a tertiary education qualification were concentrated in 10% of the regions which the OECD countries studied. Concentration was found to be particularly high in Canada and Australia but also in Mexico, Korea, Portugal, Sweden and the United States. Only in Belgium and the Slovak Republic were tertiary qualifications evenly distributed between regions.

The labour market analyst Anne Green (see Green *et al.*, 2003) proposes a useful typology to understand the complex relationship between skills and supply which exists in different regions. According to this typology, regions can broadly fall into four different categories: regions experiencing a low-skills equilibrium; regions experiencing skills gaps and shortages; regions experiencing a skills surplus; and, lastly, regions experiencing a high-skills equilibrium (see Figure 1.1 below).

In the context of demographic change and mobility many localities find themselves experiencing skills gaps and shortages. A 2004 Employers Skills Survey in Greater Manchester, for example, identified approximately 7 500 skill-shortage vacancies, primarily in aviation, education, engineering, food and drink, healthcare, manufacturing and retail sectors (Simmonds and Westwood, submitted). The forecast skills profile of all employment sectors to 2015 showed that while the demand for lower-level qualifications (National Vocational

Figure 1.1. **Skills typology (adapted from Green *et al.*, 2003)**

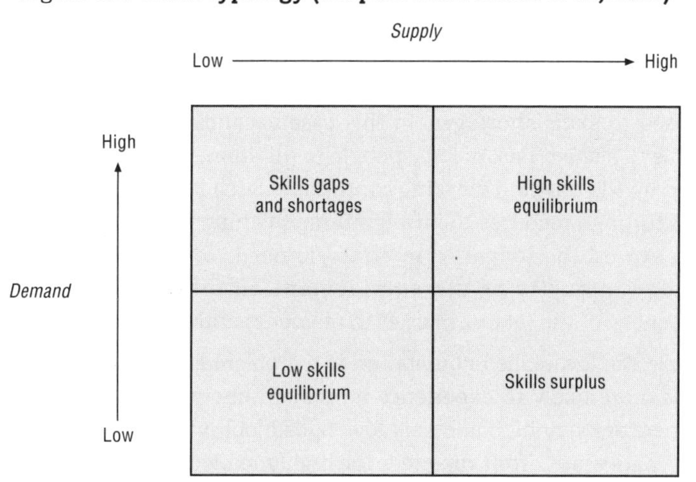

Qualification of NVQ Level 2 or below) is reducing, the number of residents in the workforce with a medium-level qualification (NVQ Level 3) and those with a higher-level qualification (NVQ Level 4) will need to increase by 83 000 and 280 000, respectively, to meet employment demand. These figures may need to be tempered in the context of the recent economic downturn.

Not all localities experience skills shortages however. As identified above, in some regions a low supply of skills is matched by a low demand for skills amongst local employers (the "low-skills equilibrium"). Just as the supply of skills varies, so does the demand. Not all businesses and not all localities progress as fast as others in terms of adopting new technologies and adapting to changing markets. Coyle (2001) identifies a lag time of roughly 50 years between the development of new technologies and the ability of societies and economies to fully take advantage of the potential they offer to improve productivity. The adoption of new technologies requires an adaptation of work organisation within companies, in addition to changes in local governance structures which may be easier to achieve in some localities than others. In the meantime skills utilisation may be sub-optimal and the demand for skills will remain patchy.

The low-skills equilibrium is a particular problem affecting rural areas where a low demand for skills is matched by a relatively weak education and training structure, particularly where there is no local university or higher training institution. Such areas can become dependent on a relatively weak endogenous skill base that "suffers from a lack of outside enrichment [and] where educational attainment and economic performance become entrenched, reinforced by a cycle of low aspirations" (Hildreth, 2006). In such areas, unless simultaneous attempts are made to improve the demand for skills, investing in new supply risks producing a skills surplus (the bottom right hand corner of Figure 1.1), with local people leaving the area at a young age to seek better quality employment opportunities elsewhere. In such situations, local policy makers often become diverted towards "fire-fighting" to fill *labour* shortages, as opposed to skills shortages. In this case vacancies are remaining unfilled either due to a sheer lack of local people to fill them, or because people are not attracted by the pay and working conditions. Such labour shortages are often resolved through recourse to immigration, meaning that policy makers do not have an eye on the longer-term strategic need to improve the quality and knowledge intensity of the employment on offer and to increase the attractiveness of the labour market to residents and newcomers alike.

While the low-skilled equilibrium is a problem experienced by rural areas, cities are more likely to experience a problem known as "skills polarisation", where there are very high and very low-skilled jobs, with a lack of employment between. Cities are often magnets for highly skilled people. On average, the OECD has found that about 49% of the population with a tertiary-level qualification live in urban regions, 33% in intermediate regions and 19% in rural ones. An " Urban Audit" carried out by the European Union in 258 cities also found that city residents were more likely to have tertiary education (European Commission, 2005), reflecting in part the demand for highly qualified people to work in the high value-added industries, public bodies and professional clusters which exist in cities. In recent years almost all of the job growth in London, for example, has been in high-skilled occupations, with a significant decline in the number of low-skilled jobs in the city in the 1980s.

However, cities can also be the site of severe skills "poverty", particularly as they often play host to disadvantaged groups and pockets of deprivation. Many Londoners, for example, have problems with basic skills: nearly one in two London adult residents has problems with numeracy. This has led to a high level of competition for low-skilled jobs and a greater level of "labour market congestion" for this skill level than in any other part of the UK (Simmonds and Westwood, submitted). This combines with other issues, such as the general over-representation of disadvantaged groups in the labour market, and difficulties in sustaining low-paid employment in the context of living costs, to produce a significant effect on employment outcomes. London has the poorest employment rate in the whole of the UK. The European Urban Audit found that this was a problem affecting other European cities. Three out of four cities studied had a lower employment rate than their country as a whole, and in 67% of the cities the unemployment rate was higher than the national rate. Low skills are often concentrated in groups of people, and in neighbourhoods which are particularly isolated from the labour market. Such concentrations introduce additional barriers to accessing education and training; including a low level of access to services, transport, information and low motivation through a lack of positive role models.

Three aspects of developing a balanced local skills strategy

So how are localities responding to these diverse skills issues? A review of local practice in OECD countries shows that local stakeholders now realise that it is no longer enough just to invest in the formal education and training system, and are turning towards a more diverse range of strategies to increase the supply of skills in their locality. Increasingly, strategies centre on three particular themes which are reviewed in more detail below: attracting and retaining talent, integrating disadvantaged groups into the workforce development system and upgrading the skills of the low qualified (see Figure 1.2 and Table 1.1 below).

Figure 1.2. **Developing balanced local skills strategies**

Attracting and integrating new talent can be important for localities that are experiencing skills shortages in very specific areas and/or demographic change. Equally important is ensuring that local employment demand is attractive and of a quality appropriate to retain local people. Many local areas have seen a low level of interest in certain jobs (particularly vocational jobs) which can be challenged through concerted careers advice to schools, and a better marketing of the opportunities and rewards available in these sectors. At the same time it is necessary that other disadvantaged groups are effectively integrated into the labour market. This may include second and third generation immigrations, who in some cases continue to have poor labour market outcomes.[3] Disadvantaged populations may take longer to be trained and integrated to meet local skills needs, but bringing them into the workforce development system will be vital in order to avoid the development of a two-speed economy involving the "skills rich" and the "skills poor". Similarly, if localities focus only on up-skilling the unemployed, and do not work with employers to address skills levels within the workforce itself, they may miss problems of low-skilled equilibrium and fail to work towards the more long term goal of raising local skills demand and hence local productivity.

Table 1.1. **Achieving strategic objectives within local skills strategies: tools and instruments**

Strategic objective	Tool
Attracting talent	Investing in local quality of life, architecture, cultural development and effective city planning.
	Promotion of cosmopolitanism and diversity.
	Developing universities and training institutions. Encouraging university graduates to stay in the area (careers advice, etc.) and developing post-graduate courses.
	Marketing localities, regions, local sectors, and clusters to attract new labour.
	Incentives for returning migrants *e.g.* recognition of qualifications overseas, grants to set up new businesses.
Integrating disadvantaged groups	Outreach training centres/IT kiosks, better marketing of education and training, early years of education.
	Alternative forms of learning *e.g.* practice firms, work experience, mentoring, training through culture, sport and music schemes.
	Activities targeted towards improving retention during training courses, apprenticeships and employment.
	Developing careers clusters and providing adult careers advice. Developing better ladders between basic skills courses and higher-level training.
	Support for immigrants, ethnic minorities, indigenous populations (*e.g.* anti-discrimination, recognition of qualifications, skills audits and portfolio approaches, languages).
	Development of basic training for those adults with very low skills.
Up-skilling those in employment	Customised training.
	Developing career clusters and career ladders.
	Employers co-managing training centres, training provided on the premises of major industries.
	Business partnerships focusing on sharing of innovation.
	Setting up centres of excellence for particular sectors.
	Career planning and mentoring for new starts.
	Setting up partnerships to share innovation and promote technology transfer, and management training on different aspects of work organisation.

In the following section we will look at the types of intervention being taken forward in each of these three areas in both OECD and non-OECD countries, before assessing how they can be combined into a balanced local skills strategy.

Attracting new talent

Today, policy makers, businesses, chambers of commerce and other local stakeholders are openly turning to migration as a means of solving skills and labour shortages and supporting economic development. As the theorist Ewers says, "when specific skills are lacking, the easiest way to improve the knowledge base is to import one" (Ewers, 2007).

In Canada, for example, mayors from Nova Scotia, New Brunswick, Prince Edward Island, Newfoundland and Labrador participated in a conference in 2005 to find new ways of making their region more attractive to immigrants. They felt that immigrants were essential to local economies undergoing ageing and negative demographic change. In Europe, likewise, cities have started to assess whether they are sufficiently open to new arrivals and therefore as attractive as possible to new labour. The Open Cities initiative, coordinated by the British Council, and involving the cities of Madrid, Bilbao, Cardiff, Belfast and Dublin, is helping cities to identify factors which can help to incentivise immigration, ranging from economic factors, regulatory conditions, cultural provision and attitudes, local amenities, connectivity and accessibility, and risk factors (*e.g.* the general perceptions of the stability of the local and political environment).

Ewers (2007) describes the process of developing a city which is attractive to immigration as the process of "becoming sticky to flows of skilled labour". Some cities concentrate on becoming more attractive through improvements to infrastructure and architecture. The city of Malmö, for example, has succeeded in attracting a significant foreign population through implementing a large number of infrastructural changes during 1995-2005 (see Bevelander and Broomé, Chapter 7). Among these were a new bridge to connect the city with Copenhagen in Denmark, an underground transport system, new up-market residential developments in the harbour, the development of a new university and new dockland developments including the Turning Torso (a 190-meter high apartment building which has become the new landmark of the city). Malmö's architectural transformation into a brighter and more creative city has won international awards, and the population has increased by 15% during the last 15 years, with the foreign born population almost doubling from about 36 000 individuals in 1990 to 70 000 individuals in 2006.

Other towns and cities have resorted to surveys to find out what they can do to make themselves more attractive to new skilled workers. In St. Louis, United States, a survey of 200 individuals was undertaken to identify why people moved into the region. The survey revealed that quality of life and access to cultural institutions were key factors in hosting and retaining talent. Elsewhere in the United States, Milwaukee has also analysed the reasons behind 21-39 year old talent choosing the city as a place to live, ranking their performance on a number of the "metro metrics" against the US average. While the most important metrics were the breadth of alternative employment opportunities, other important factors included: availability of continuing education, opportunities to network, access to parks, green spaces and recreation, and a good cultural scene.

One aspect which appears to be particularly important in determining the attractiveness of a place is the extent to which an area appears to be cosmopolitan and open to newcomers. Many immigrants appear to settle in cities, for example, because they already have a diverse population, whereas rural towns and small towns are often felt to be more homogeneous and less open to change. Both St. Louis and Milwaukee have had problems in the past with a negative image in relation to discrimination and homogeneity, and part of their strategy to attract new talent has thus been based on a re-branding of their image so that they appear more cosmopolitan.[4] In 2001, following a suggestion from a local employer, the Metropolitan Milwaukee Association of Commerce embarked on a strategy of "broadening the breadth of the region's talent mix"[5] through an emphasis on "diversity, exclusivity and flexibility".[6] In Malmö, likewise, it was not only a change of image which has occurred in the city but also a change of identity. An attempt has been made to positively highlight the multicultural character of the population with a new city slogan "Diversity, Meetings and Possibilities" to mark this shift.

It is perhaps not surprising that diversity and openness should become more important given the rise in international migration. However, the theorist Richard Florida (Florida, 2002) has highlighted that these factors are now attractive to a broader group of internal migrants, that he terms the "creative class". In today's knowledge based economy, having a local labour force that exhibits strong generic skills (the ability to analyse, create and innovate) may be as important to localities and regions as a concentration of sector-specific skills. Florida defines the "creative class" as a class of workers who generally work in knowledge intensive sectors and are able to problem-solve and innovate across a broad range of disciplines – their designs and ideas are widely transferable and useful on a broad scale. Lin (2007) similarly argues that "differences in the ability of regions to attract new work may reflect different stocks of the particular types of human capital required to create or adapt to new knowledge". Such creative and independent minded people appear to look for a strong degree of tolerance and an open attitude to diversity when making location decisions.

Schemes to attract immigrants to tackle specific skills shortages

Not all localities have great success in attracting new people and indeed it is often those rural areas that are experiencing high levels of ageing and emigration which find it the most difficult to attract newcomers. In recognition of this, both Australia and Canada have recently put in place "regionalisation" programmes to encourage immigrants to move to smaller towns and rural areas outside major cities while at the same time ensuring that immigrants have the skills to meet local needs. Most immigrants to Australia, for example, settle in the metropolitan areas of Australia's east coast.[7] In order to diversify settlement throughout the continent, the Commonwealth government has introduced a range of new immigration pathways for skilled workers to settle in regional and rural Australia.

The local area of Griffith in New South Wales has enthusiastically taken up this opportunity (Collins, submitted). Like many similar towns and cities, Griffith has suffered from a shortage of skilled personnel, particularly senior managers, medical, legal and finance professionals, skilled trade persons and semi-skilled workers. At the same time, Griffith has a manufacturing-based economy which is rather different from the wider economy in Australia, so the region appreciated the opportunity to select immigrants that match their particular demand base. The regional development board has capitalised on the new regionalisation programmes to select new immigrants on the basis of these needs, while also embarking on a bold and proactive programme to maximise the attractiveness of the region (participating in international "Australia Needs Skills" expos while also re-badging the town as "Cosmopolitan Country") and ensuring the retention of immigrants once they arrive (*e.g.* through provision of good multicultural services). Preliminary findings suggest that, while numbers are still small, more that 80% of skilled immigrants are working in the region in jobs related to their skills; there is a low migrant unemployment rate (4%); and immigrants earn an average of 66 000 AUD, considerably higher than the Australian average.

In Canada, several provinces are also working to better match immigration policy to their skills needs, by introducing accords and "provincial nominee agreements" which allow some control over selection procedures. The strongest agreement is the Québec Accord which provides the province with a significant determining role in immigration selection. To reflect the continued importance of manufacturing and technical trades in the region, the selection process has recently given more priority to immigrants with vocational training (people with academic training are given higher priority elsewhere in Canada). The Accord is also complemented by a series of agreements with regional Conferences of Elected Members (CRE) in Québec to finance regionalisation programmes to help smaller towns and rural areas attract immigrants. Currently 83% of immigrants affirm their wish to install themselves in the immediate surrounding area of Montréal, perhaps because of the relative homogeneity of smaller towns and rural areas, and their difficulty in accommodating migrants who are not French speaking (Arcand, submitted). However, research in Canada has shown that immigrants are economically better off if they settle in such communities than in larger urban areas.[8] The regional agreements take the form of commitments to fund local NGOs to develop initiatives to better welcome immigrants into their local area through support for civic and intercultural relations, accompaniment of new arrivals, and welcome for refugees (see Box 1.1 below).

In order to better fit the skills of immigrants to local labour market needs, some localities are engaging in more specific activities to train and recruit people to meet local skills shortages even before they arrive, by developing

Box 1.1. **Regionalisation programme in Québec**

Québec has recently embarked on a programme to regionalise immigration to smaller towns and rural areas in the province. These areas are experiencing a series of problems due to emigration, the ageing of the population and an absence of infrastructure to respond to the changing needs of the knowledge economy. They also appear to have a weaker skills base – Statistics Canada (2008) conclude that while 20% of habitants of metropolitan regions (over 500 000 people) have a university diploma, this falls to 15% in medium sized regions (100 000-499 999) and 10% in smaller regions.

On the basis of a plan of action 2004-2007 "Share Values, Common Interests", the Ministry of Immigration and Cultural Communities (MICC) has set out a strategic aim to favour regionalisation of immigration. In particular, the Ministry has developed a series of 12 agreements with regional Conferences of Elected Members (CRE), to finance regionalisation programmes, of which 8 are still in operation. These agreements take the form of commitments to fund local non-governmental organisations (NGOs) to develop initiatives to better welcome immigrants into their local area. Funding falls under three different categories: support for civic and intercultural relations, accompaniment of new arrivals, and welcome for refugees. Regional representatives of the Ministry also come to Montreal once a month to meet new arrivals and communicate the economic, cultural and social benefits of moving to their regions – some succeed in convincing a percentage of people who come to these meetings but the numbers are still small (3-7 people per month maximum). Unlike in Australia, there is no obligation within the Québec regionalisation system for immigrants to settle or stay in a particular area.

The extent to which local regions profit from these schemes appears to depend on the socio-cultural milieu and the extent of economic growth occurring in the region. A study of two localities, La Mauricie and the Centre of Québec (Arcand, submitted) shows that the latter region was able to be more proactive in creating programmes to welcome new immigrants due to an entrepreneurial spirit and the opportunities created by a growing manufacturing economy. Many local partners signed a specific agreement to ensure full participation of immigrants in the local economy in 2008, and the region has also developed bilateral agreements with Wroclaw in Poland, for example. La Maurice on the other hand has been slower to react and galvanise local stakeholders, in part due to a decline in their principle industry (forestry) and a problem of low productivity in the local economy.

Source: Arcand, submitted.

training courses in countries of origin. Italy has been a front runner in developing such schemes, although initiatives remain relatively small scale at present. Since the end of the 1990s the Lombardy and Veneto regions for example have identifying the needs of local entrepreneurs and designed specific training programmes, often in conjunction with chambers of commerce and professional associations. Each project involves training selected candidates in local areas in their countries of origin. Those immigrants who successfully complete the training are given priority within the annual quota system.[9] These schemes have recently led to changes in national immigration legislation and a national funding system to encourage similar activities in other regions (see Hofer, Chapter 2). In order to avoid the criticism of "brain drain" the national government is also stipulating that such projects involve support for sending regions, through, for example, increasing the quality of education in sending regions; supporting the return of recruited personnel after a certain amount of time and allocating development funds.

One group that regions may particularly target when attracting talent from overseas is returning émigrés. Some estimates (see OECD 2008b) have found that as many as 20 to 50% of immigrants either return or move to a third country in the first five years after they leave their home country. Localities are beginning to capitalise on this as a source of talent for their regions. In Northern Ireland, for example, the Department of Employment and Labour has recently launched a new campaign called "C'Mon Over", which includes both visiting universities in neighbouring Scotland and setting up a page on Facebook, the social networking site. In Shanghai, China, the attraction of overseas Chinese graduates in key fields has also been one of the central pillars of an integrated skills strategy to move the city towards becoming China's "highland of talent" (see Zhang, Chapter 3).

While some localities are looking to international immigration as a means of tackling local skills shortages, initiatives to better manage this process for the benefits of local areas and migrants alike are clearly relatively small scale and piecemeal at present. They have the potential to be a promising development if they can bring about better planning of immigration to meet local skills needs. However, often localities have a limited understanding of the current skills needed in the economy, and such information quickly goes out of date. In addition, immigration represents a particularly blunt tool to address local needs. While it may be possible to attract people with specific skills to the labour market (through for example the Australian regionalisation programme, or the Italian mechanisms for recruitment overseas), retention problems remain high, as people are likely to move elsewhere, particularly to larger cities, when their visa requirements are up. At the same time, those people who stay will thereafter bring their families and have offspring, bringing a whole different set of skills to the labour market. In the long term, therefore, immigration remains a relatively difficult process to manage.

In addition, it is essential that support for immigration is accompanied by strong systems to integrate newcomers. In general in OECD countries many immigrants remain unemployed or overqualified for the work that they do. Adapting skills to new labour markets is a resource intensive process (see OECD 2006a), and governments need to ensure that localities experiencing immigration (particularly those for whom this is a relatively new phenomena) have adequate funding and guidance on this task. Finally, it is important to recognise that not all regions that are attempting to attract migrants are doing so to meet skills shortages. Regions of low-skilled equilibrium, for example, are more likely to be attracting people to meet manual labour shortages that are caused when local people are no longer willing to carry out local jobs due to poor pay and conditions. It is important to distinguish between these different reasons for turning to immigration. While attracting higher-skilled people may be a useful way of meeting skills gaps and providing an innovative and diverse workforce for the future, attracting lower-skilled migrants to fill labour shortages is likely to maintain the economy at a lower level of productivity. At the same time, it may lead to both social exclusion and frustration for immigrants themselves, resulting in high-turnover and undermining the longer-term sustainability of the economy.

Retention of talent

Of course, in a time of rising mobility, it is not just important to attract talent from elsewhere but also to retain skilled people that are already present in a region. Many localities, particularly rural ones, have put in place mechanisms to improve the attractiveness of local jobs to local people. Attempts to retain young people in South East Lincolnshire in the United Kingdom, for example, have focused on improving the image of traditional industries – notably horticulture and associated food industries. Initiatives here include building business-education links between major employers, colleges and schools and showcasing the need for scientific and technical skills within the industry. (Green, submitted). Emphasis is also placed on highlighting the range of opportunities and skill needs (*i.e.* sales and marketing skills, business administration, etc.) in order to illustrate that not all jobs within the food industry are in large "pack-houses".[10] Further, in some rural areas, the focus has been on creating better quality jobs and up-skilling opportunities in growing sectors such as personal service based industries (see Box 1.2 below).

Schemes to encourage graduates to stay in a region can be particularly useful given the skills they possess and their potential to make long term contributions to the local economy. In Manchester, one element of their "City Strategy" (see Box 1.3 below) has been to improve the retention of graduates of

Box 1.2. **Creating attractive jobs and training opportunities in rural France**

Assisted living facilities for the elderly are sparse in rural France; this is particularly true in the 6 000 local authorities with between 700 and 3 000 inhabitants. For people who have spent their entire life in the countryside, it can be traumatic to be re-located elsewhere in their old age. To deal with this, the Bordeaux-based architect and urban planner Philippe Loubens created the Villa Family concept that allows the elderly to continue living in their own village close to relatives and friends, carrying on their lives in a family-setting. This new living concept has triggered a demand for skilled labour and created new jobs in rural areas. The first Villa Family house was opened in 1990 in the *Département* of Creuse, which has the highest number of elderly people in France.

To begin with, the implementation of the original Villa Family concept proved to be difficult, because public-private partnerships have been slow to be accepted in France (particularly as regards social care), and the training of the hosts have not been budgeted for. Given that many mayors in the east of France still embraced the overall idea, two young French entrepreneurs decided to develop the concept further. The company *Âges et Vie* asked local authorities to donate a plot of land for a house for a symbolic price of EUR1. *Âges et Vie* sought out a private investor who was willing to finance the construction of the house. The investor collects rent but is not involved in the management of the operation, which is the responsibility of *Âges et Vie*. When an *Âges et Vie* house is created, a special housing association is set up, comprised of the mayor, the local general practitioner, the elderly and/or their families. The association acts as the employer of the "hosts" who offer care for the people in the house. Hosts are usually women, who either graduated in the field of social work or have professional experience in gerontology or as a nursing auxiliary.

Up-skilling for the hosts is financed through the housing association. Specific training programmes (*e.g.* on pain management) tend to be subsidised by the regional agency. The host job is high in demand as it allows women to combine a highly responsible job with taking care of their children. Also, the monthly salary of around EUR 1 700 gross is attractive (25% above the average salary). The rent is set in line with that of social housing in France. In total, the costs are significantly lower than that of a conventional senior citizen's home. Currently there are 8 *Âges et Vie* houses within a radius of 100 km around the City of Besançan and about 15-20 Villa Family houses in the East of France.

Source: Elke Löffler, submitted.

Manchester's universities. This includes developing enhanced work experience schemes for graduates as a mechanism for increasing the number of graduates in local jobs.

Integrating hard-to-reach groups into training and employment

While some people may be becoming increasingly mobile, others remain behind but are for a variety of reasons excluded from their local workforce development system. Low-skilled people are generally less likely to access training as adults, and this situation is often exacerbated for individuals who lack contact with local labour markets through long-term, and sometimes multi-generational, unemployment. As unemployed people with low-skills tend to be concentrated in particular neighbourhoods in cities, a spatial-based approach to tackling these issues has been adopted in many localities. A central element of the United Kingdom's "Cities Strategies" initiative, for example, is to target workless residents in certain deprived neighbourhoods, to improve engagement with and access to training and skills provision. In Manchester, the new City Strategy is targeting 93 neighbourhoods in the city where economic activity is lowest (see Box 1.3 below), aiming to increase engagement with workless residents, improving access to training and work.

A central element in Manchester's city strategy is to change the "motivations and behaviours" of lower-skilled residents. This aim is not unique to Manchester – a number of the local skill strategies reviewed (see for example Eberts and

Box 1.3. **Residents not in employment – a latent skills resource**

In Manchester, economically inactive people represent a large pool of local people whose skills are not being harnessed to meet the needs of a growing regional economy. The city of Manchester is a key economic driver for the North West of England but in order to maintain its growing economy a larger pool of skilled labour will be required, especially as the population has only recently stabilised after a period of slow decline. The level of economic inactivity in the city remains high – with 430 000 working age residents unemployed and economically inactive in 2007 this represents a large untapped resource. However, skill levels among these groups are particularly low – 53% of the working age population have low qualifications (compared to 49% for England) while 35% have no qualifications (compared to 29% for England). It is also estimated that in some of the most deprived neighbourhoods over 40% of residents lack basic literacy and numeracy skills. The local city strategy has therefore focused on improving skills and employability levels in these neighbourhoods.

Hollenbeck, Chapter 4, and Green, 2008) seek to respond to a "stagnation of participation" in education and training amongst the lower-skilled. Part of the problem appears to be that disadvantaged groups have become disillusioned with a schooling system which they perceive to have failed them, meaning that a new approach to training and education is needed. Localities are increasingly experimenting with new types of learning opportunities, which can be accessed by students from home and from a variety of different colleges and outreach settings. Music, sport and cultural activities are seen as a useful way of creating learning opportunities without being seen as being specifically "training-based". In addition, "practice firms" and work experience placements can be a good opportunity to learn new skills outside of a traditional educational environment.

It is not just encouraging people to take up training which is important, but also ensuring that they stay in this training. Low retention rates are a particular problem in Germany, for example, with a growing number of youths without or with low school qualifications failing to complete vocational training courses and acquire recognised qualifications. A recent scheme in North Rhine-Westphalia, Germany has been working to offer this target group a more flexible vocational training scheme developed in collaboration with local colleges (Brink, submitted). Approximately 800 youths are involved in the pilot. Under the scheme, all youths who withdraw from their training are enabled to re-enter the learning process within a period of up to five years and to acquire a recognised certificate for the competencies gained successfully up to that point. The "3rd Way in Vocational Training Initiative" has worked with local colleges to adapt their traditional vocational training courses into a series of flexible modules. The initiative has identified that it is necessary to work continuously in very small groups in order to achieve noticeable learning progress and successes. Integration in higher performing groups within vocational colleges usually ends in failure after a short while. Work experience in companies has proven to be particularly successful – the youths very often experience acceptance of their role and knowledge, which strengthens and motivates them.

Martinez (Chapter 5) similarly describes the value of a local initiative, this time run by the private sector, which has improved retention within apprenticeship schemes in the Mackay region of Australia. A group of companies – the "Mackay Industry Network" (MAIN) – set up a project known as the CARE programme which acts as a private sector "apprentice master" that sources apprentices for local businesses, organises their induction process and provides ongoing support for the apprentices during their placement. The retention rate within the local apprenticeship programme is now at 90-95%; although the initiative has had problems improving outcomes for certain groups, such as the local Indigenous population.

Up-skilling those already in employment

Of course, it is not just unemployed people who suffer exclusion in a knowledge based economy but also the "working poor". Indeed, if localities ignore the working population in their skills strategies, they will be missing a large proportion of the local population. In Northern Ireland, for example, educational outcomes for the young population are above average. However, an analysis of local skills levels amongst the working population reveals that they are poor, with a high proportion having low or no qualifications (DELNI, 2004).

Some localities have responded to this problem by providing incentives and subsidies for employers to develop customised training in conjunction with local colleges. In Texas, in the United States, the governor has introduced a "skills development fund" which is used by local community colleges to work with businesses to provide training adapted to business needs in flexible modules that workers can easily participate in. This has been instrumental in the economic development strategy of the Lower Rio Grande Valley, which has succeeded in transforming its local industrial base into a "rapid response manufacturing centre". Mechanisms to rapidly upskill the local workforce were essential to the economic transformation of the region (see Troppe *et al.*, submitted).

Elsewhere, the public sector has "seed funded" initiatives where private sector companies work better together, pooling training provision so that both large and small companies alike can offer training to the lower-skilled (see Box 1.4 below, which outlines the Penang Skills Development Centre initiative).[11]

Analysis has shown (*e.g.* OECD 2006b) that employers are particularly unlikely to invest in the training of low-skilled staff – particularly as lower-skilled people are increasingly employed on a temporary basis, with it being unusual now for such workers to gain a "career for life". Public sector impetus may be necessary in order to make training for such workers happen. In some localities, particularly in the United States, public institutions have been working together to re-create traditional internal career ladders externally. For example, in New York, customised training courses have been linked together to form "career pathways initiatives" for the lower-skilled, often joint funded by the private and public sectors to promote career progression for low paid workers (see Grossman, Chapter 8).

Such an approach is also reflected at the federal level in the United States as part of the Career clusters initiative, which has been adopted by many states and regions, and customised to their local labour market needs. A career cluster is a grouping of occupations and broad industries based on commonalities. At the foundation, learners are exposed to an entire industry and how different careers interact and rely on one another. Within each career cluster, there are anywhere between two to seven career pathways from secondary school to two- and four-year colleges, graduate school, and the

Box 1.4. **Penang Skills Development Centre**

In Penang, Malaysia, a private-run training initiative has proven crucial to maintaining the state as the electrical and electronics hub of Malaysia, earning Penang the title of the "Silicon Valley of the East". In the 1980s, there was the realisation that in order for Penang to progress up the manufacturing value chain and continue to attract foreign direct investment it needed to ensure the supply of appropriately trained and skilled human resources. The state government, through its investment and trade promotion arm, the Penang Development Corporation (PDC), initiated discussions with Hewlett Packard, Motorola and Intel to set-up a skilled manpower training centre in Penang.

The Penang Skills Development Centre (PSDC) was established in May 1989 as a not-for-profit training and development centre. At initial start-up, the PSDC received support from the Penang State government in the form of subsidised rental of premises, and an annual training grant for the centre. As it grew in relevance it attracted the attention of the federal government. Starting in 1993, the PSDC received capital grants to assist with its capacity building expenditure, which included equipment and machinery. The PSDC invites membership from manufacturing and related industries and to-date has a member base of 130 companies. It is managed and led by industry but representatives from six different government agencies and a university also sit as "ex-officio" members of the Board. It offers a wide variety of training for both member companies (from whom it receives fees) and the unemployed (through government grants). In the last 18 years the centre has trained 128 050 participants, largely in the electronics and electrical sector. The PSDC also formalises the technology transfer process between the larger international conglomerates and the smaller local companies by tapping into the expertise of the former to provide recognised training programmes for the latter.

Source: Heem, submitted.

workplace. They enable low-skilled low-income workers to make connections to future goals, providing motivation for working harder and enrolling in rigorous courses. The network of clusters is overseen by the National Association of State Directors of CTE (vocational training) and delivered through a partnership approach involving state, schools, educators, employers, industry groups, and other stakeholders who have worked together to create curriculum guidelines, academic and technical standards, assessments, and professional development materials for the clusters.

Improving skills utilisation

Career pathway models have been criticised by some (*e.g.* Fitzgerald, 2006) for focusing too much on supply rather than the demand for skills. Fitzgerald has pointed out that in order for career ladder programmes to really work, intermediary/middle-order jobs need to be present in the local economy for people to "move through" to higher positions. She identifies that in many local economies, professional or paraprofessional work (with skills, salaries and career trajectories to match) has been broken down to a series of low-wage, high-turnover jobs. As a result, many local economies suffer skills polarisation – a growth in both highly skilled and low-skilled jobs, with few intermediary positions in between. Fitzgerald feels that career ladder programmes must be directed "as much toward encouraging employers to restructure the workplace as towards helping workers obtain needed training".

The latter is perhaps the most challenging area for any locality developing a comprehensive local skills strategy. In regions where demand for skills is low, it may not be enough just to provide training for workers. Public agencies also need to work with employers to improve skills *utilisation*. Some localities are starting to take on this challenge. The Holbeach campus of the University of Lincolnshire in the United Kingdom has been at the forefront of improving productivity in local industries and hence improving the quality of local job opportunities (Green, submitted). South East Lincolnshire shows particular problems associated with the "low-skilled equilibrium". Before the economic downturn, unemployment was not an issue for the region and there was no overall shortage of jobs. However, productivity had been low and falling and academically able young people were leaving the area for careers elsewhere in the United Kingdom. The local economic development and skill strategy identified a preponderance of low-skill, low value employment and a lack of opportunity for progression as a key local economic development issue.

In response, the University of Lincoln set up a specialist campus for the food manufacturing sector, developed from a partnership between Lincolnshire County Council and regional stakeholders. It has become a Centre of Vocational Excellence (CoVE) and has National Skills Academy status for Food and Drink. The campus offers "state of the art" training and educational resources, including part-time and distance learning programmes to students who are working in the food sector. At the same time, strong links have been established with employers, who exchange the latest technological developments and research/innovation through a Food Industry Technical Training Partnership. The exchange of information enabled by the partnership has enabled employers to change their work organisation practices and raise productivity.

One group that has particularly benefitted from the rise in the demand for skilled positions in the region is the local immigrant population. The training alliance identified the local immigrant population as a latent and untapped local skills resource, given that many are working below their skills and qualifications levels in seasonal work within the agricultural sector. Just under a third of all participants in the alliance's courses are immigrants, and in addition in 2005/6 the Holbeach campus delivered twenty-six English as a Second Language (ESOL) courses for fourteen different companies in the food sector. There were 356 enrolments over this period, with a retention rate of 68%.

Two examples of balanced strategies: Shanghai and Michigan

As identified above, an effective local skills strategy would ideally combine such different strategic elements – attracting and retaining skilled people, integrating disadvantaged groups into the labour market, up-skilling workers and stimulating the demand for such workers – into a joined up and balanced approach. While such a complete approach is rare amongst the case studies reviewed, two case studies in particular – from Michigan in the United States and Shanghai in China – provide a valuable demonstration of how such overarching strategies can effectively balance a number of different strategic elements to produce sustainable change (see Eberts and Hollenbeck, Chapter 4 and Zhang, Chapter 3 respectively)

In 2004, the Governor of Michigan embarked on a state-wide project to improve the efficiency of local workforce development and educational systems in meeting businesses needs through developing "regional skills alliances". Each alliance adopted a business-led approach, with strategic aims and objectives being developed locally in consultation with local employers. However, broadly each alliance has developed a balanced set of priorities that include attracting new workers into local industries, upgrading skills within these industries and integrating disadvantaged groups (see Figure 1.3 below).

The Shanghai Highland of Talent Initiative is a particularly strong example of a bottom-up municipal, city wide strategy. Again the strategy includes a balanced approach between attracting talent, integrating disadvantaged groups into training and employment and upgrading the skills of the workforce (see Figure 1.4) although it took some time before all these elements were addressed. As identified above, a key part of the strategy involves attracting returning émigrés from overseas. In addition, the municipal government has rationalised the city's existing piecemeal training system (mainly focused on unemployed people), and now provides training for both unemployed and employed people under a common municipal training system. Despite the broad success of the Shanghai skills strategy, it was criticised in recent years for focusing only on higher-skilled people in the city and failing to act to support the large number of rural migrants (accounting for 42% of Shanghai's total labour resource) who had arrived in the city following China's urbanisation programme. In recognition of this, since 2006 new initiatives were set up to support the better integration of this group of residents, with the municipal government approving a proposal to build a Training Centre for Migrant Workers, with a central campus attached to the Shanghai Industrial Technology College, and branch training centres in each

Figure 1.3. **Balancing different aspects of a skill strategy in Michigan**

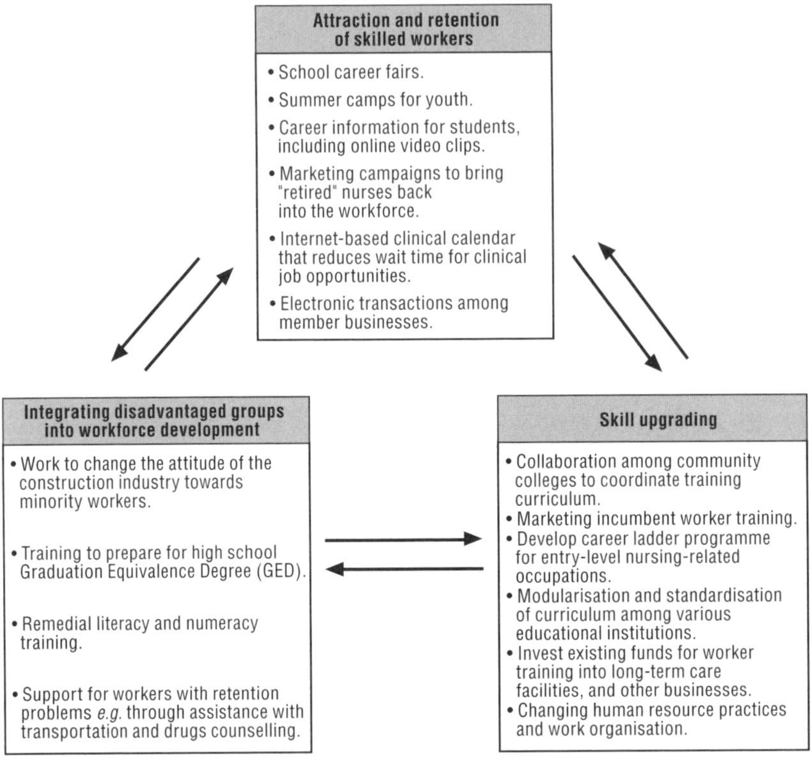

of Shanghai's 19 districts. The outcome of such a balanced and targeted approach has been encouraging. The portion of highly skilled workers as a per cent of Shanghai's total skilled workers increased to 14.98% by 2005, compared with 6.2% in 2002, and 9.4% in 2003.

Obstacles to a balanced approach

While developing an integrated skills strategy has many advantages, incorporating these different policy strands into a coherent overall approach is not an easy task. In order to make the right decisions, and effectively balance interventions, policy makers need to have a detailed understanding of the skills supply and demand in their local labour force – what is known as the local "skills ecology" (European Commission, 2004). Different options need to be analysed and negotiated, taking into account the trade-offs which exist between developing and resourcing different policies with a limited overall budget. Once priorities have been set, local actors need to effectively work in partnership to achieve these goals, given that skills are a transversal issue addressed by policy makers in fields as diverse as education and training,

Figure 1.4. **Balancing different aspects of a skill strategy in Shanghai**

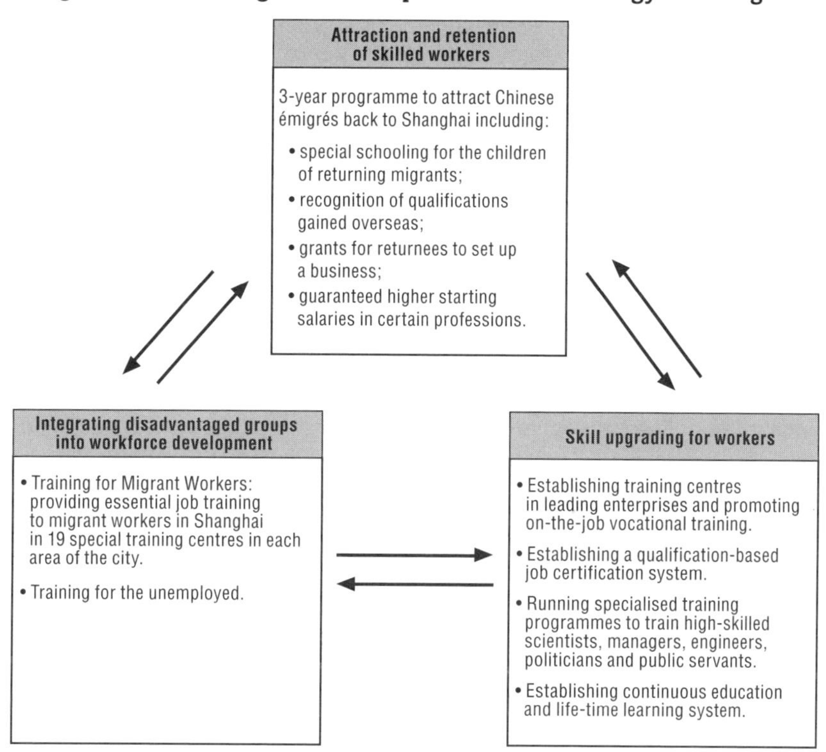

employment, economic development, social development and entrepreneurship. However, in order to work effectively in partnership, local actors need to have sufficient authority within their own policy sector to actively influence the delivery of services. This is not always the case, given that both vocational training and employment policy is managed in a centralised way in many OECD countries. In the following section we look at each of these implementation challenges in turn.

Avoiding short-termism

One reason why it is difficult to achieve balanced skills strategies is that resource investment appears unequal across different activities and policies. Funding issues may explain the reluctance of local actors to get involved with addressing more entrenched issues and problems, particularly where local resources are scarce. In many cases, however, decisions are made without a full understanding of how resourcing needs will pan out over the long-term. Some areas of action, such as the reform of the vocational training system and the upskilling of disadvantaged groups to fill vacancies, are more costly and time consuming in the short-term than others, reducing the attractiveness of these options. In comparison, recruiting well-qualified immigrants to meet local skills shortages may seem less resource-intensive. However, in the longer term integrating immigrants can prove a costly process, in terms of adapting skills learnt abroad, providing adequate language training and ensuring that the children of immigrants access good quality education.

A number of factors prevent such long-term thinking from happening. Public sector budgets and performance management systems which emphasise short-term outputs can create a particularly limited approach to skills issues. For example, the unemployed frequently receive relatively short training courses in many OECD countries, despite the fact that evidence shows that a higher level of investment is often needed to make a real impact on long term sustainable employment (see Box 1.5). However, it is not just the public sector which is at fault. Private sector, "demand-led" partnerships can also be at fault where they respond to shorter term skills gaps without seeing the "bigger picture" of how a local economy fits within broader regional, national and global trends, and how it is likely to evolve in the future. Public sector actors in such partnerships have a responsibility to help employers to plan for the future, whilst also ensuring that they are utilising local skills to the full (OECD, 2008c).

Box 1.5. **Does short-term training make a difference?**

One issue which affects unemployed people in many OECD localities is the lack of longer-term training available which will really improve their employment chances. The Public Employment Service often funds relatively short, low intensive courses which do not produce long term sustainable outcomes.

In the United States, for example, Osterman (2005) has identified a lack of longer-term training available for unemployed and low-skilled people. However, analysing data on the returns from training for dislocated workers, he shows that short-term training leads to small or non-existence gains in employment position and salary level whereas more substantial long term training does seem to improve the earnings of dislocated workers to an important degree. This is reflected in the outcomes for those attending community colleges in the US in the 1980s and late 1990s. For those that have attended a community college for a year or more there is substantial benefit, particularly if they go on to achieve an associate degree (which will increase earnings by 14%) however most people do not manage to stay long enough to reap these benefits and for these people the return is close to zero.

Thinking longer-term approach also means ensuring that local populations have the generic skills to adapt to changes in their local economies. Only providing people with specialised technical skills for one industry may be a risky action, for example, if that particular industry does not survive in the longer term. Local skills strategies may work best therefore through promoting "flexible specialisation" – concentrating on certain sectors, but ensuring that the labour force has a broad range of skills which can be adapted as industries evolve. A review of successful local regions by the European Commission in the context of the Lisbon agenda, for example, has shown that where a broad range of complementary skills and competencies exist in a locality, with a strong generic knowledge element (*e.g.* communication, leadership and entrepreneurial skills), there is greater scope to absorb local shocks (European Commission, 2004).

Joining up fragmented delivery at the local level

A further barrier to the delivery of effective local skills strategies is the fragmented nature of local education and training delivery systems. In many of the case study areas, a variety of different providers (colleges, private training institutions, the public employment service) are delivering courses in "silos" that did not effectively link together. In particular, basic skills and occupational skills are often delivered separately, which means that lower-skilled people are not offered the "ladders" they need to train towards higher-skilled occupations. In the light of this confusion a primary aim of a recent London-wide skills strategy developed by the mayor of London's Skills and Employment Board (LSEB), was a re-work of the employment and skills support available for Londoners, to develop a streamlined supply chain that included "bridges" to help people move into work while also helping existing employees progress and/ or develop new skills.

The breadth of issues being considered within local skills strategies means a broad network of local players need to work together, not just those directly working on education and training issues. The case studies highlight that skills-levels are a highly dependent phenomena, being linked to a variety of other factors such as lifecycle mobility, quality of life, level of cultural integration and openness to diversity, house prices and accessibility.

Despite the potential for short-term thinking identified above, private sector actors are also crucial partners to bring on board when developing skills strategies. This is important at the strategic stage, when employers can be invaluable to identifying skills needs and planning business-friendly interventions – in Michigan the regional skills alliances have strong private sector representation on their boards, for example – and at the delivery stage, when they can help to implement schemes to upskill their own workers. Employers can also be brought together to develop joint-training initiatives, particularly on a sector by sector basis (see for example the cases of Penang mentioned and South East Lincolnshire above).

Creating more flexibility in the delivery of policy

Another crucial factor in the achievement of a joined-up local approach is the availability of flexibility to local actors in the delivery of relevant policies (see OECD, 2009). In order to work effectively in partnership, local actors need to have sufficient authority within their own policy sector to actively influence the delivery of services. Indeed local flexibility in delivery was particularly crucial to the success of a number of the local skill strategies. In Shanghai, the power invested in the municipality to make education and training decisions was one factor which enabled them to take a holistic and balanced approach (see Zhang, Chapter 3). In Mississipi, local tribal control over training and education activities has also played a significant role in allowing the Choctaw tribe to develop a coherent workforce training system that was responsive to change and able to fuel dramatic growth in the local economy (Philips, Chapter 6).

The case of London is illustrative, however, of the problems of developing skills strategies where local actors do not have sufficient power to influence all component parts of the skills development system. London has struggled with these issues for a number of years. A series of cross-London partnerships and strategies have been set up since the 1990s in order to develop a local approach to London's skills needs, including the London Development Partnership, the London Skills Commission (which published a Framework for Regional Employment and Skills Action in 2002) and more recently the Regional Skills Partnership.[12] However, these first partnerships shared similar weaknesses in that the arrangements were politically unaccountable at a regional level; and lacked serious traction on the mainstream skills and employment national budgets (Simmonds and Westwood, submitted).

In 2005 the London mayor, in discussion with government, challenged the lack of power for the capital and demanded greater powers of devolution over the skills and employment infrastructure. Following a review by national government the regional skills partnership was replaced by a new employer led London Skills and Employment Board (LSEB) to be chaired by the mayor. The mayor was also given statutory duties to promote skills in London and to prepare a new statutory skills strategy for London setting priorities and budget direction. While the board now has greater control in the area of adult training, it has been granted limited responsibility for employment services in the capital, despite the fact that these services are also developing nationally along a more flexible, employer-led approach. Arguably, the extent of real devolution of new powers over either skills or employment to the Board (and to the mayor) remains small, reducing the number of elements that can be meaningfully included in the capital's strategic approach.

Deciding on the local "skills ecology" – information and data

Knowledge of local labour markets is also a principle issue for stakeholders seeking to develop balanced strategies to raise skills levels in their locality or region. In order to plan targeted approaches to addressing local skills issues, local actors need to understand the situation in their own particular locality. One problem which was experienced in both Australia and Canada when attracting immigrants through rural migration programmes, for example, was the difficulty in gaining accurate information about local skills needs and in maintaining such information up to date. In Manitoba, Canada, the province has recently downplayed their emphasis on skill requirements for new immigrants to attract new immigrants, partly because the labour market was changing too fast to allow effective forecasting. Knowledge of local labour market demand is also crucial when integrating lower-skilled people into the workforce development system. Rath (2002) has stressed that it is vital that the labour market context, and in particular the local "opportunity structure" is taken into account when developing local initiatives – otherwise individuals risk being trained for jobs which do not exist.

Box 1.6. **Tools for improving the availability of information and data on the supply and demand of skills**

A number of tools and instruments were used in the case studies for improving the availability of skills including:

- Labour market observatories.
- Annual skills development catalogues (listing skills in demand and training available to meet these demands).
- Analysis of job advertisements.
- Skills surveys of the unemployed.
- Surveys as to the level of skills present in the local workforce.
- Sectoral analysis as to the level of concentration of skills in particular sectors.
- Skills forecasting (projecting future cluster development on the basis of current systems and strengths).
- Business representation in partnerships.

A number of the skills strategies included in this publication have given prime importance to the collection of local labour market information (see Box 1.6 above for a list of tools and instruments used). For example, in Michigan, United States, the new "regional skills alliances" have been given access to disaggregated labour market information collected by the state as a basis for identifying key local opportunities and threats (see Eberts and Hollenbeck, Chapter 4). In Shanghai, training has been based on an annually updated talent development catalogue (see Zhang, Chapter 3). The type of sophisticated data required to target skills needs and forecast future industrial change remains a "black box" for many local strategies, however. Most local actors do not have the access to sufficiently detailed information or analytical capacities to make forecasts, or indeed acquire a comprehensive understanding of current demand. Confidentiality clauses can be particularly restrictive in allowing policy makers access to information about local businesses and individual jobseekers, and national information is frequently not disaggregated to a sufficiently low level to inform strategies. In the absence of such data, localities often have to resort to frequent, and costly, local surveys which quickly go out of date.

There is also a trade off, however, between too closely determining the types of skills that are required in the current labour market, and ensuring that people receive training in generic skills that may prove more useful in the longer term. Given the importance of generic skills (such as the ability to problem solve, to analyse, to be creative, to innovate – those competences central to Florida's "creative class" or the "knowledge worker"), localities could do well by ensuring that all local people are not just trained to meet specific current skills gaps but have a more rounded education. In Griffith, for example, local stakeholders expressed some frustration that they could only recruit immigrants with certain listed skills "in demand" in their locality when in fact a broader set of individuals would have contributed to the economy (Collins, submitted).

Making strategies concrete

Another important lesson from the case studies is the importance of making strategies concrete, and based on a clear allocation of tasks between partners, linked to the actual powers of each partner to influence policy delivery locally. In Shanghai, the municipal government launched its first talent development initiative in 1995 to develop Shanghai as a "highland" of talents in mainland China. However, the initial strategy was felt to be too general and vague. The municipal government responded by creating a clear action framework which included clear targets and responsibilities, and made certain elements of the strategy enforceable by law (see Box 1.7 below). It was only then that the strategy really started to make a difference.

Box 1.7. **Putting in place instruments and targets**

Effective efforts to implement a concerted talent and skills upgrading strategy in Shanghai did not occur until the municipality launched a detailed "Action Framework for Implementing Shanghai Talent Strategy" in 2004. The new action framework defined ten priorities to be addressed between 2004 and 2010 which included: *i)* to expand the size of Shanghai's talent pool from 1.49 million people in 2003 (people with a junior college diploma or above, or having a professional qualification of medium level or above) to 2.2 million people in 2010; *ii)* to increase the number of specialised technicians from 1.29 million in 2003 to 1.8 million in 2010; *iii)* to increase the number of high-skilled talent workers from 0.14 million in 2003 to 0.25 million by 2010; *iv)* to upgrade the average education level of new entrants to the labour force to 14 years of education by 2010; *v)* and to increase the number of long-term expatriates working in Shanghai from 70 000 in 2003 to 150 000 by 2010.

In addition, a number of policy incentives and instruments, and new institutional setups were designed and managed in order to implement the strategy, a number of which have now been codified as local regulations. By 2006, Shanghai had issued 49 local regulations regarding the promotion of talent development.

Conclusions and recommendations

In conclusion, the cases of local skills strategies reviewed in this chapter raise the following issues for consideration by policy makers at the national and local levels:

National level recommendations

Encourage regions and localities to develop local skills strategies	There is a strong rationale for developing local responses to skills issues. Both the demand and supply of skills are unevenly spread within OECD countries, with strong local variation. Strategies that may be relevant in some areas (such as addressing the low-skill equilibrium) will not be relevant in others. In addition, local stakeholders are particularly aware of the skills needs of local businesses, and can integrate training activities into broader local development strategies that will attract and retain skilled people and knowledge-intensive employers. Further, local agencies are well placed to develop the flexible approaches which are needed to address the multiple barriers to education and learning which can affect people with low-skills in disadvantaged neighbourhoods.
Provide flexibility at the local level in the management of education and skills policy	Local stakeholders will have a limited ability to tackle local skills issues if they are not given the flexibility to adapt and direct the use of policy locally. The reviewed case studies demonstrate, as with wider LEED research (see *e.g.* OECD, 2009), the importance of awarding local institutions flexibility in adapting their policies and strategies to local needs and local objectives agreed in partnership. It is only when public actors can really influence their own services and delivery arrangements that they can participate effectively in strategy development at the local level. This will also enable them to better discuss and consider the resourcing trade-offs between different types of action (attracting, integrating and up-skilling).

Assist localities in maximising the skills bought through immigration, but with caution	Governments should consider assisting local areas that are losing population, through demographic change and rising mobility, in attracting new talent to fuel economic growth. Regional immigration programmes in Canada and Australia have proved helpful in attracting immigrants to smaller towns and rural areas that may have trouble attracting immigrants but may offer good economic prospects in the longer term. However, it is important that policy makers note the difference between localities attracting talent to meet skills shortages (therefore fuelling local growth) and those attracting migrants to fill labour shortages (therefore potentially undermining necessary restructuring of the local economy).
Ensure availability of information and data	Information and data is a key issue which is holding back local policy makers wishing to take a proactive approach to tackling skills issues at the local level. National governments have a responsibility to ensure that disaggregated data is available for as many dimensions of the skills issue as possible. Capacity building is also necessary at the local level to ensure that local actors both understand current and future trends within their labour markets and can strategically plan the best means of responding.

Local level recommendations

Develop a balanced approach	It is essential that a balanced approach is taken to skills issues, so that actions to attract or retain talent are developed in tandem with actions to build a responsive education and training system, integrate disadvantaged groups into the labour force, while also up-skilling those already in employment. Taking a longer term perspective is often the key to developing such a balanced approach.
Pay close attention to problems of low-skilled equilibrium	OECD research shows the strong variation in the supply and demand for skills in different localities and regions. Where regions have both low supply and low demand for skills, a dual approach is necessary for tackling skills issues, investing not only in the skills of the local labour force but also in the skills utilisation of local employers, in both the public and private sector. Local actors can work on this area in a number of ways, through promoting new means of work organisation, providing management training for SMEs, and promoting innovation and technology transfer.*
Join up delivery	It is essential for both newcomers and disadvantaged populations that local education and training is well connected in coherent systems which offer clear route maps into good quality employment. The careers clusters framework developed in the United States represents a good model for joining up education and training, while also adapting training to the needs of incumbent workers and those with families and other obstacles to training. Further, it is not only education providers that need to link up. Labour market agencies and colleges cannot work alone, but must also bring on board a number of other local actors such as: universities, local development agencies, employers and non-governmental organisations.
Ensure skills needs are better signaled	When clear information is available about skills needs and skill shortages in a given locality, this can speed up the process of training people for local jobs. It is not just important to know about skills shortages and vacancies, but also the skills required more generally by employers, and the degree of skills utilisation in the workforce. Also important are methods of measuring people's skills informally (*i.e.* not just relying on qualifications), which can be especially helpful when seeking to integrate immigrants into the labour market.

* These issues are being explored in more detail in an OECD LEED project on Skills for Competitiveness: Tackling the Low Skilled Equilibrium (2009-12).

Make sure strategies are clear and robust	It is important that strategies are concrete and robust, based on a clear allocation of tasks to partners. Given that government policies are rather centralised in many OECD countries, it is important to only allocate tasks which reflect the actual powers of local agencies to influence the delivery of policy locally. In the absence of effective powers it may be more useful to lobby central and regional government for more appropriate policies, at least in the short-term.
Support the development of generic skills	A longer-term approach is important to ensure that regions are not simply reactive but prepare for the future. Ultimately those localities that host a local workforce that has the generic skills necessary to adapt to change (in both the services and manufacturing sectors) will be the most likely to succeed.

Notes

1. *The Economist*, 7 October 2006, p. 4.
2. Overall, for the seventeen countries with existing comparable data on "permanent-type" legal immigration, inflows increased by about 11% in 2005 relative to 2004. Among the other OECD countries, there was an increase of about 10% between 2004 and 2005, largely due to greater inflows in Spain. At the same time, high temporary movements were observed in countries such as Australia, Canada, and New Zealand.
3. The second generation generally has a higher employment probability than recent immigrants; however, the gap with children of the native-born is still large, particularly in European OECD countries, where the incidence of unemployment is about 1.5 to 2 times higher (OECD, 2007b).
4. Other cities have watched, for example, the dramatic rise to national prominence of Atlanta following the drive by the 1980s mayor, Andrew Jackson, an American civil rights activitist, to encourage international investment. A study by Metro Atlanta Chamber of Commerce showed that the city had increased its share of 25-34 year old university graduates faster than any of the 50 largest metropolitan areas – a rise of 46 %.
5. Wisconsin Economic Summit IV White Paper, presented by Shelley Jurewicz, Executive Director, MMAC's Young Professionals of Milwaukee.
6. A network of employers and employees was set up ("Fuel Milwaukee") which now has an active membership of over 56 employers (including AT&T, Deloitte, Ernst and Young, Manpower, and local hospital and healthcare providers) and over 4 500 individuals (employees and jobseekers). The network has been working with employers to create flexible work environments that can accommodate diversity while also increasing community engagement and leadership amongst employees, planning events to showcase the region, and organising cultural events to promote the local visual and performing arts scene.
7. 2001 census data shows that some 40 % of new immigrants to Australia settle in New South Wales, mostly in Sydney: between 1997 and 2002, 93.5% of NSW immigrants settled in Sydney (DOTARS, 2003).
8. A recent study by Statistics Canada (2008), for example, has show that despite the fact that many immigrants settle in larger cities, it is not necessarily the best economic choice. Immigrants achieve income parity with Canadians much faster in smaller centres, especially when they have a university degree. Incomes were lowest in the largest urban areas and highest in small urban areas. The medium

income of immigrants in large cities was CAD 16 800 while in small towns and rural areas it was CAD 18 800. The larger the area, the larger the gap with the incomes of non-immigrants.

9. Indeed from 2006 onwards, a specific share of annual labour permits (roughly 2 000 in 2006) has been reserved for migrants coming through this route. In addition to professional training (for which a qualification/diploma should always be provided), such courses also involve training in the Italian language.
10. Warehouses for storing goods.
11. For a full review of initiatives being used to address this issue at the local level in Canada, Denmark, Flanders, the United Kingdom and the United States see OECD (2006b).
12. The regional skill partnership and FRESAs are part of nationally rolled out programmes to develop a regional approach to skills.

Bibliography

Arcand, S. (2008, submitted), "Local initiatives for the attraction and retention of talent in the Québec context: the cases of *La Mauricie* and the *Centre-du-Québec*", OECD, Paris.

Brink, B. (2008, submitted), "Third Way in Vocational Training – an innovative concept and practice against exclusion of unskilled young people (a learning model)", OECD, Paris.

Clarke, G. (ed.) (2008), *Towards Open Cities*, British Council, Madrid.

Collins, J. (2008, submitted) "Designing Local Skill Strategies: The Case of Griffith", OECD, Paris.

Coulombe, S., J.F Tremblay, and S. Marchand (2004), *Literacy Scores, Human Capital and Growth across 14 OECD Countries*, Statistics Canada, Ottawa.

Coyle, D. (2001), *Paradoxes of Prosperity: Why the New Capitalism Benefits All*, Texere, New York.

DELNI (2004), "Skills Strategy for Northern Ireland", Department for Employment and Learning, Northern Ireland.

DIMIA (2005b), "Fact Sheet 24: Overview of Skilled Migration", Canberra: Department of Immigration and Multicultural and Indigenous Affairs.

DOTARS (2003), "Regional business development analysis: RBOA Action Plan, Australian Development of Rural and Transport Services".

Eberts, R.W. (2004), *The Role of Job Training in Promoting and Sustaining Decent Jobs: The US Experience and Prospects*, Upjohn Institute for Employment Research, Kalamazoo, Michigan, USA.

European Commission (2004), "Successful Local Milieux and the Lisbon Process", *A Fourth Thematic Report of the European Commission*, IDELE Project, Brussels.

European Commission (2005), *Cities And the Lisbon Agenda: Assessing the Performance of Cities*, Brussels.

Ewers, M.C. (2007), "Migrants, Markets and Multinationals: Competition among World Cities for the Highly Skilled" in *GeoJournal*, Vol. 68, pp. 119-130.

Finegold, D. (1993), "Breaking Out of the Low-skill Equilibrium", *Education Economics*, No. 1, pp. 77-84.

Finegold, D., and D. Soskice (1988), "The Failure of Training in Britain: Analysis and Prescription", *Oxford Review of Economic Policy*, No. 4, pp. 21-53.

Fitzgerald, J. (2006), *Moving up in the New Economy: Career Ladders for US Workers*, The Century Foundation, New York.

Florida, R. (2002), *The Rise of the Creative Class: And How It's Transforming Work, Leisure, Community and Everyday Life,* Basic Books, New York.

Glaeser, E. L. (2005), "Four Challenges for Scotland's Cities" in D. Coyle, W. Alexander, and B. Ashcroft (ed.), *New Wealth for Old Nations: Scotland's Economic Prospects*, Princeton University Press, New Jersey.

Green A. E., C. Hasluck, T. Hogarth and C. Reynolds (2003), "East Midlands FRESA Targets Project – Final Report", Report for East Midlands Development Agency, Institute for Employment Research, University of Warwick, and Pera.

Green, A. (2008, submitted), "Designing Local Skill Strategies: The Case of South East Lincolnshire", OECD, Paris.

Heem, P. H. (2008, submitted), "The Penang Skills Development Centre – a case study", OECD, Paris.

Hildreth, P. A. (2006), *Roles and Economic Potential of English Medium-Sized Cities: A Discussion Paper*.

HM Treasury (2006), "Prosperity for All; Skills in a Global Economy", The Final Report of the *Leitch Review of Skills*.

Lin, J. (2007), "Innovation, Cities and New Work", *Working Paper No. 07-25 Research Department*, Federal Reserve Bank of Philadelphia.

Loeffler, E. (2008, submitted), "Le Villa Family: Providing Employment for Young People and Care for the Elderly in Rural France (a learning model)", OECD, Paris.

London Skills and Employment Board (2007), *London's Future: The Skills and Employment Strategy for London 2008-2013*, Mayor of London, London.

Noguera-Tur, J. (2008, submitted), "Building Local Skills Strategies to Improve Quality of Life and Territorial Competitiveness: The Case of CSI-COM in Gandia, Spain", OECD, Paris.

OECD (2005a), *Regions at a Glance*, OECD Publishing, Paris.

OECD (2005b), *Trends in International Migration*, OECD Publishing, Paris.

OECD (2006a), *From Immigration to Integration: Local Solutions to a Global Challenge*, OECD Publishing, Paris.

OECD (2006b), *Skills Upgrading: New Policy Perspectives*, OECD Publishing, Paris.

OECD (2006c), *International Migration Outlook*, OECD Publishing, Paris.

OECD (2006d), "Level of Education of Immigrants and the Labour Market – Estimating the Prevalence of Over-Education", Working Paper, OECD, Paris.

OECD (2007a), OECD *Employment Outlook*, OECD Publishing, Paris.

OECD (2007b), *International Migration Outlook*, OECD Publishing, Paris.

OECD (2008a), *Education at a Glance*, OECD Publishing, Paris.

OECD (2008b), *International Migration Outlook*, OECD Publishing, Paris.

OECD (2008c), "Skills for Competitiveness: Tackling the Low Skilled Equilibrium, a conceptual framework," OECD Publishing, Paris.

OECD (2009), *Flexible Policy for More and Better Jobs*, OECD Publishing, Paris.

Osterman (2005), *Employment and Training Policies: New Directions for Less Skilled Adults*, MIT Sloan School.

Quinn, L.M. and J. Pawasarat (2002), *Racial Integration in Urban America: A Block Level Analysis of African American and White Housing Patterns*, University of Wisconsin-Milwaukee, December 2002.

Simmie, J. *et al.* (2004), *Realising the Full Economic Potential of London and the Core Cities*, OBU, Oxford.

Simmonds, D. and A. Westwood (2008, submitted), "Designing Local Skill Strategies: the Cases of London and Greater Manchester in the UK", OECD, Paris.

Statistics Canada (2008), *Perspectives on Labour and Income*, January 2008, Vol. 9, No. 1.

Tessaring, M. and J. Wannan (2004), "Vocational Education and Training – Key to the Future", CEDEFOP *Synthesis of the Maastricht Study*, Luxembourg.

Troppe, M., M. Clagett, R.Holm, and T. Barnicle (2008, submitted), "Integrating Employment, Skills, and Economic Development: A Perspective from the United States," OECD, Paris.

Waldinger, R. (ed.) (2001), *Strangers at the Gates: New Immigrants in Urban America*, University of California Press, Berkeley.

Zheren, C. (2000), *Objective, Strategy, Policy: A Strategic Program to Build Shanghai as Talent Highland*.

PART I

Chapter 2

Addressing the Loss of Skills to International Migration

by
Andrea-Rosalinde Hofer

In developing countries the loss of skills through emigration can have significant effects at the local level. It seems that better managing the migration process could be beneficial in promoting economic development and skills development in some regions. This chapter looks at emerging policies and local practice to better manage migration, and assesses the possible impacts that this can have on local development paths. The chapter draws on selected case studies and interviews in sending countries, including Ecuador, El Salvador, Ghana, Nigeria, Nicaragua, Mexico, Romania, and Sierra Leone as well as previous LEED work in Albania and Italy.

Sending regions[1] all over the world are characterised by unfavourable conditions for either personal or professional development. In many cases, outward migration is no longer primarily related to conflict, human rights abuses or natural disaster, as were previous migration waves, but to a deterioration of the economy and a lack of appropriate jobs, especially for medium to highly-skilled workers. The local context, which is used by migrants as a basis for decision-making, is shaped by influencing factors that depend little upon individual behaviour. Both national and local governments play an important and often decisive role in shaping such contexts. They can be conducive to personal and professional development or hostile, depending on a range of correlated factors; the majority of which are locally defined and can thus hardly be generalised. However, sending regions often exhibit high unemployment, poor working conditions, low wages, an important informal economy and limited opportunities for employment progression. Governments in these countries may need to intervene to improve living and working conditions in order to prevent significant numbers of people moving overseas because of easy access to transport networks and the existence of cheaper flights overseas.

There is debate as to whether migration policies and management should be integrated and co-ordinated with policies related to social and economic development. However, for regions experiencing high emigration, better managing the international movement of human capital can be beneficial. Fan and Stark (2007) identify that migration can lead to "a process of acquisition of human capital which, in turn, may well lead to economic betterment for all". It is also clear that returnees, if relevantly skilled and willing to invest upon their return, can become a source for economic take-off (Gosh, 2000).

Managing migration for skills and economic development is not a new phenomenon. Diaspora and hometown associations have long been active in community development back home. While such activities are rarely driven by public policies, governments are increasingly choosing to support them, understanding "transnational communities"[2] to be key drivers for the re-orientation or technological adaptation of local economies on both sides of the sending and receiving relationship. The often cited spill-over between the very different development trajectories of Silicon Valley in California and Hsinchu-Taipei region in Taiwan[3] is not unique, but provides an instructive example of how appropriate public policy intervention can utilise skills migration for knowledge and technology transfer, which, in turn, can stimulate policies to enhance the growth potential of sending economies and a change of direction towards a high-technology development path.

Agreements between local governments and educational institutions in sending countries, and similar institutions in receiving countries are also being put in place to ensure that migration is accompanied by skills attainment and development for both migrants and people back home. Temporary placement or exchange of graduates, researchers and academic personnel is becoming a more widespread practice. In some cases, sector specific programmes exist to train people abroad, often initiated by institutions in receiving regions, with the facilitation of local employer organisations such as chambers of commerce and their national level umbrella organisations. Bilateral agreements and employer recruitment by itself does not necessarily translate into economic development and growth, however. Public policy will need to intervene.

In this chapter we look at different initiatives in sending regions throughout the world to manage migration better, and assess their impact on both general economic outcomes and the specific issue of skills. The chapter draws on selected case studies and interviews in sending countries, including Ecuador, El Salvador, Ghana, Nigeria, Nicaragua, Mexico, Romania, and Sierra Leone as well as previous OECD LEED work in Albania and Italy.

The problems and opportunities posed by migration

In the short-term, and in the absence of appropriate management approaches, labour migration can result in a number of negative consequences for economic development. Stark and Fan (2007) summarise the following three: firstly, migration leads to a reduction in the number of better educated individuals, which limits the economic development trajectories a country or a locality could choose amongst; secondly, the output of an economy will shrink, as the gaps and shortages created by out-migration cannot be addressed in time; and, thirdly, the out-migration of the highly skilled reduces state revenues and return on prior public investment in their education.

In reality, the impacts of out-migration of the workforce, skilled or unskilled, are ambiguous. Governments in sending countries are often confronted with the following two scenarios: on the one hand, international labour migration could cause labour market shortages, severe lack of skills, declining state revenues and reduced returns on prior investment in human resources; and, on the other hand, it could imply a relief for tight labour markets and public budgets. When deciding which of these is the most likely, governments often fail to fully understand the level of interdependency between labour migration and economic development. The impact of migration on economic development may change over time, as economic structures develop and the demand for labour evolves. What seems to be a current surplus of low-skilled labour may turn into a future deficit. Furthermore, applying a merely national perspective in identifying and forecasting skills needs is not sufficient as impacts will vary in different localities. Moreover, in the absence of local data, nationally aggregated data is often based on estimates and does not give a clear picture of what is happening on the ground.

In relation to low-skilled workers, two phenomena can be noted. Firstly, the majority of today's international migrants, accounting for approximately 175 million people, have little education and limited skills (Lowell and Kemper, 2004). And, secondly, immigration policies and practices in OECD countries reflect a declining demand for the low-skilled. This goes along with less interest in most sending countries to retain this part of their workforce. The loss of low-skilled labour to international migration is thus not necessarily of high concern for sending countries, where the supply of unskilled labour often far exceeds current and projected demands. In the case study regions in Ghana, Nigeria and Albania, illiteracy and school drop-out rates are high, or on the rise. Those concerned often have limited possibilities to partake in formal technical and vocational training, and end up in informal training or in jobs with no particular skills requirements.

Governments in all the case study countries are currently more concerned with the likely consequences of high-skilled emigration. Certain sectors of the economy appear to suffer more. Healthcare services, for example, are often geographically limited to the economic centres of a country, and these areas can become hardest hit by the migration of highly skilled professionals abroad. The Nigerian National Policy Committee on Health estimated in 2006 that about 26% of Nigerian doctors are either working abroad or have changed profession for more financially rewarding jobs. High-skilled emigration also has a broader impact on the technology path of an economy: while engineers with many years of work experience are still a minor share of emigrants in Nigeria and Ghana, those who have left have also created significant skills gaps. Universities have insufficient capacities and, in some faculties there are not enough students to quickly close gaps caused by migration.

Out-migration of the skilled workforce is likely to increase regional disparities and negatively affect development trajectories of rural and urban areas in decline. Furthermore, shortages of skilled professionals can affect local development and job creation by reducing capacities within local governments. In Ghana, outside the few core economic centres of the country, most local authorities and local branches of national government agencies are poorly equipped and loss of personnel affects service delivery. This has an impact on policy capacity. As rotation and staff delegation are not yet practiced, limited possibilities exist to establish a decentralised public administration capable of effectively addressing the impacts of international migration.

Time is a relevant factor to be considered by local skill strategies in sending countries: a person's skills may increase considerably over the course of migration, even if new skills are predominantly learnt on an informal basis. While migration can cause severe shortcomings for local development in the short run, it can also be a source of future economic development. Labour migrants, who leave unskilled, will, in most cases, gain the skills needed to start-up a micro enterprise on their return. However, in order to utilise this new resource for income generation, or the creation of jobs, certain framework conditions need to be in place. In many sending regions, the absence of transparent markets with no barriers to entry and exit, and adequate business support infrastructure, poses difficulties for new entrepreneurship and reduces chances of firm survival and growth. Even if business growth rates by returnees and locals are increasing, new economic activity is often very locally focused. Niche markets in general do not exist because of the lack of skills to modernise and diversify, or a lack of access to finance. The local business environment varies between rural and urban areas with the existing business stock and local market saturation being important factors for firm development and growth. Evidence from rural Ghana suggests that although survival and early growth opportunities might be higher for new firms outside key economic centres, especially if these firms are focused on local services and products, the lack of public services and amenities does not attract returnees (Bokuma, submitted).

Local action to interrelate migration impacts with local development will need to be adaptive and flexible over time in order to stimulate and enhance skills-levels and economic activity. With the right policies in place, it may be possible to trigger gradual movement towards a sustainable development path, away from a low-skill equilibrium, where insufficient demand for skills is balanced by emigration of surplus labour.

Local strategies for the management of migration processes

Governments in sending countries have several options to promote economic growth and workforce development in the context of international migration.[4] They can either be *defensive*, that is, through restriction of international mobility and reparation for loss of human resources and capital; or *strategic* by collaborating with host countries and localities to better manage migration, resource diaspora, recruit international labour to address skills shortages and stimulate and retain return migration. Whereas defensive policies are on the decline, national governments and their agencies are increasingly engaging with local governments, the business sector and civil society organisations in strategic partnerships.

The following section reviews selected strategic policies and practices in this field including decentralised co-operation, working with diaspora, mechanisms for managing the recruitment of labour internationally and support for return migration.

Decentralised co-operation and inter-regional agreements

Decentralised co-operation is one vehicle for better managing migration. Decentralised co-operation (which can be roughly defined as partnership-working between cities, towns and regional territories in different countries, as opposed to bilateral co-operation at the national level) has become common practice in EU countries,[5] with the aim to stimulate and strengthen community and local development in sending countries, and facilitate integration of migrants in receiving localities. Decentralised co-operation is also becoming more and more important for recruitment of skilled labour. Local governments and non-governmental organisations (NGOs) are key actors of decentralised co-operation activities, which involve agreements between local governments. In Spain and Italy local governments take on a more active and formal role in initiating and co-ordinating agreements, whereas in France, Germany and Austria NGOs are given greater responsibilities. In all of these countries, the private sector is an important partner.

In Italy, decentralised co-operation has, since the late 1990s, provided regional, provincial and municipal governments with a framework for activities related to co-development and the internationalisation of their local labour markets. Particular attention is paid to localities abroad that host an Italian community or its descendants and send migrants to Italy. As part of the bilateral co-operation agreements, local governments often work with Italian NGOs in the implementation process. For the purpose of the agreement, NGOs are also created in the partner locality. Migrants and migrant associations in Italy can be involved in the preparation, monitoring and evaluation of projects. Involvement in actual project implementation in sending localities also occurs, but less often.

Decentralised co-operation projects in Italy can receive financing from central government and the European Union, but projects are, for the most part, fully financed by regional budgets. Participation in co-ordination activities, reporting and evaluation activities is voluntary. Recently, the Directorate General for Co-operation in the Italian Ministry of Finance assigned a government agency to map and categorise decentralised co-operation activities in order to increase co-ordination and integration in the huge pool of on-going activities, and to propose new themes for centrally funded initiatives.[6]

Local governments in larger cities in Spain, such as Madrid and Barcelona, run their own public competitions to identify local partners within their jurisdiction and in sending localities for small-scale development projects. The majority of projects are destined for countries in Latin America and Sub-Saharan Africa.[7] To address the risk of fragmentation and to increase co-ordination, a territorial co-ordination body, established in addition to an inter-ministerial entity for decentralised co-operation, allows for an exchange of information between all local governments, and for a greater integration of local initiatives into a wider national strategy. Spanish NGOs are increasingly important partners for local governments and many have established co-ordination boards that ensure that NGO initiatives are linked to a wider strategy. At the national level, a regularly convening council aggregates the inputs of local boards and involves private sector and civil society as consultative partners in policy processes.

Universities are becoming more and more involved in decentralised co-operation activities. Apart from direct collaboration between institutions in sending and receiving countries, employer organisations in receiving countries also interact with universities abroad. Whereas the former focuses on exchange programmes for students and researchers, or the advancement of joint research in specific scientific areas; the latter is often used to channel academics and the highly skilled into labour markets abroad.

In Italy, for example, joint university studies and degrees are developed to address shortages in highly skilled labour. Most activities are focused on the health sector, where joint degrees in nursing have been established between higher education institutions in south-eastern Europe and Italian universities. Teachers and technical instructors are trained in Italy or in their country of origin, and students are offered internships in Italy. The recognition by Italian authorities of qualifications gained offers students greater chances on the Italian and international labour markets. In the Albanian capital Tirana, for example, four private universities offer graduate degree studies for nurses. Aldent, Medikadent, Universiteti Kristal, and *Universiteti Zoja e Këshillit të Mirë* have established relationships with health education institutions in Italy and Greece, both major receiving countries, to provide training for subsequently internationally recruited nurses. However, this relationship adds only little to research and technological development in the sending region, but is directed to meet labour demand by recruiting suitably skilled labour.

The case studies show that increased co-ordination and integration of decentralised co-operation activities is needed to avoid duplication and to increase the likelihood of outcomes that are linked with broader local development strategies in beneficiary countries. Co-ordination in decentralised co-operation is not always easy to achieve, particularly if local governments act independently. The case study on Ecuador (Salazar-Medina, submitted) suggests the disquieting possibility that the activities undertaken by local governments in receiving countries might reduce the attention paid by stakeholders in sending countries to the local impacts of emigration. In some Ecuadorian regions the number of government interventions, both by central and local governments, decreased over time during the period of decentralised co-operation, as well as with changing governments.

Collaborating with diaspora

Diaspora can be a major source of innovation and new economic activities for sending regions. Migrant organisations and hometown associations have well established mechanisms for enabling migrants to maintain relationships back home, beyond family bonds, and provide advice on the best ways for migrants to progress in their new host locality. Diaspora organisations also stimulate, to a lesser but growing extent, technological change and skills development back home by transferring skills and remitting both ideas and capital for innovation.

Whereas more traditional activities develop as part of the migration process and the result of social bonds, government action is needed as a catalyst for diaspora to act as a transporter of technology and know-how. Collaboration with diaspora and hometown associations can produce a range of benefits in sending regions, including skills transfer to national or local level organisations in the form of summer schools and distance learning arrangements, remittances to support infrastructure development related to education, as well as assistance for highly skilled migrants who wish to return to seek employment, start-up a business or act as a mentor or business angel for young firms.

Developing stable relationships between governments and diaspora is not easy. Kuznetsov (2006) argues that diaspora networks are more the result of serendipity than of government support. The case studies suggest that establishing relationships locally and steering their input into local development is easier than operating through national channels. Local policy makers are increasingly working with diaspora and hometown associations to better manage migration, yet it is not clear as to whether they have the capacities and the right governance arrangements in place to play a decisive role in this relatively new policy area and to unite relevant non-state actors in pursuing common strategic aims.

Problems include a lack of trust by hometown organisations in the capacity of local governments to implement projects, and accusations of favouritism, bribery and corruption related to open calls for tender and a general lack of transparency. All the same, the hometown organisations lack time, and organisational and managerial capacities which renders involvement in project implementation and result monitoring difficult. The case studies confirm that local governments need to do more than just involve diaspora organisations through remote forms of participation and interaction. Political commitment and a governance framework, characterised by policy integration and co-ordination, transparency, possibilities to participate, and the absence of corruption are all prerequisites for success.

Across receiving regions in the OECD area, local governments and NGOs provide support for the work of diaspora and hometown associations, who often become important partners in combating illegal immigration. Ghanaian immigration to Italy, for example, has been largely illegal, involving either entering the country illegally or overstaying visas (Caiani, submitted). In 2002, diaspora organisations formed COGNAI (Council of Ghana National Associations of Italy), an umbrella organisation for Ghanaian diaspora in Italy. Today, COGNAI is recognised by both Ghanaian migrants and Italian state and non-state institutions as a reliable partner. It links the different local associations with each other and maintains contact with state and non-state institutions back in Ghana. COGNAI is not only considered an active promoter of legal migration, but also stands for effective community development projects in Ghana.

Intermediary organisations

Intermediary organisations can play an important role in overcoming communication difficulties between diaspora organisations and governments back home, and in facilitating diaspora participation in local development. The case studies on Mexico, El Salvador and Ecuador illustrate this point (Flores-Macías, submitted; Rodríguez-Acosta, submitted; Salazar-Medina, submitted).

The *Instituto de los Mexicanos en el Exterior* (IME) is the main agency responsible for the implementation and regular update of the *Programa para las Comunidades Mexicanas en el Exterior*, started by the Mexican government in 1990. The IME was established with a two-fold aim. Firstly, it co-ordinates migration related policies and measures of different ministries and integrates these into a wider strategy, and it provides a platform for dialogue between national and local governments and for consultation with representatives from business and civil society. Secondly, it establishes and maintains communication channels with diaspora and hometown associations, and thus facilitates a greater degree of collaboration and consultation between the different organisations. The IME has helped to gather the hundreds of smaller migrant organisations and groups that were formed by migrants from Zacatecas in the 1960s and provided them with more influence and negotiation power towards the state and local governments. Educational activities, including secondary and tertiary education and professional training, in both the host country and in Mexico, are one of IME's key areas of work.

In El Salvador the government created a new directorate in the Ministry of Foreign Affairs in 2000 that should work as an intermediary organisation and one-stop shop for Salvadorians living abroad (Rodríguez-Acosta, submitted).

The directorate was upgraded in 2004 to the Vice-Ministry of Foreign Affairs for Relations with the Diaspora and now collaborates closely with the state administered fund for social investment and local development, *Inversión Social para el Desarrollo Local* (FISDL) and Salvadoran diplomatic missions abroad. Facilitating the investment of remittances and promoting return migration form an important part of its work. The Vice-Ministry is co-ordinating relationships and activities with national and international actors involved in migration and development issues. Increasing collaboration with diaspora led to the organisation of conferences "Salvadorans in the World" (*Salvadoreños en el Mundo*), in Los Angeles, Washington, DC, and Boston. The Vice-Ministry also maintains an online accessible talent base where highly skilled El Salvadorians abroad can register, and a virtual market place for El Salvadorians companies, who would like to export their products and services with the help of the El Salvadorian community aboard, can find and be found by trade partners. Skills development initiatives are often linked to acute shortages in local social service provision. The massive emigration of highly skilled professionals in the health sector has created gaps in the quantity and quality of healthcare in many rural areas and smaller towns (Rodríguez-Acosta, submitted). The government maintains an Internet platform which allows diaspora and hometown associations to access information on current and planned government action and how to contribute.

In January 2007, the Ecuadorian government decided to join ministerial efforts in a single agency and created the National Secretariat for Migrants (SENAMI), *Segretariá Nacional del Migrante*. In addition to the main office in Quito, local offices were established throughout the country. The head official of SENAMI has the rank of a minister. Within one year SENAMI prepared a National Human Development Plan for Migrants. SENAMI demonstrates innovativeness in its efforts to establish closer contacts to the diaspora: their website contains a link to a short ten minute video on the National Human Development Plan for Migrants on *www.youtube.com* with key statements on what the SENAMI aims to achieve. The video was launched in April 2008 and the number of visitors to the site is increasing. Outreach to diaspora is important for SENAMI, but, as the case study reports, there are internal barriers within the government that need to be addressed for the agency to fulfil its role (Salazar-Medina, submitted). There is overlap in policy areas that goes beyond migration matters, such as social and economic development issues. Responsibilities have not yet been defined. Also, SENAMI's role in decentralised co-operation projects is unclear to both local governments in Ecuador and international partners. This causes overlap and duplication. Salazar-Medina (Salazar-Medina, submitted) suggests that the role of diplomatic missions abroad will need to be strengthened and their relationships with SENAMI expanded in order to allow for a greater policy impact of the agency's work.

The involvement of intermediary organisations in promoting transnational activities of migrants and a more productive utilisation of remittances has increased over the last decades. In some European countries, such as France, Italy, and Spain, national and local governments have earmarked funding for diaspora organisations collaborating with intermediary organisations.

Government-diaspora collaboration around healthcare

Some governments have sought to build synergies with diaspora organisations to implement specific policy priorities. In all case study countries the improvement of healthcare services is an area that benefitted from the active involvement of diaspora in infrastructure and human resource development. Most interesting were the approaches developed in Senegal, Nicaragua and Nepal.

The Senegalese association Njambur Self Help in the Italian city of Bergamo collects money from its members to invest in the public hospital in the town of Louga in Senegal (Sterzi, submitted). The majority of members of Njambur Self Help are originally from Louga. The association has branches in other Italian cities, in France and also maintains a small reference point in Louga. The provincial government of Bergamo signed a twinning agreement with the Region of Louga regarding collaboration in the health sector and was involved in the decision about which hospital should benefit from the investment, and which additional skills development and international exchange activities will be organised. The Italian NGO Nord-Sud in Bergamo was crucial in ensuring financial support by the Province of Bergamo, the Region of Lombardy and the involvement of the health agency Ospedali Riuniti in Bergamo. After the implementation of the main project to renovate the hospital and to organise training activities for doctors, nurses and administrative personnel, Njambur Self Help continues its assistance. The NGO finances the maintenance of the hospital, organises with the help of its local branch in Louga the transfer of medical equipment to Louga and runs regular training activities.

In Nicaragua a number of active medical professional associations have been established with the involvement of diaspora. Yet, fundraising efforts have remained limited, at less than USD 10 000 per year. The American Nicaraguan Foundation, one of the most active associations of upper middle class Nicaraguan emigrants, is responsible for significant investments in healthcare training and service delivery, but the foundation does not maintain relationships with other diaspora organisations. Orozco (submitted) identifies as a cause the absence of an integrated approach on the side of the Nicaraguan government with regard to diaspora involvement in education and skills development.

Collaboration with diaspora an skills

Skills development is not always a shared priority between government and diaspora organisations, in particular when certain geographic areas of a country are concerned. In Nepal, the American Nepal Medical Foundation, established in 1988 by Nepalese expatriates with the aim to form a network of Nepalese medical practitioners abroad, is collaborating with local authorities in rural Nepal to ensure medical coverage of remote areas by financing short-term employment of diaspora to train local medical doctors. The collaboration with local authorities is facilitating the work of the American Nepal Medical Foundation, but the low level of national government acknowledgement and buy-in means that opportunities are missed for wider skills development initiatives and international technological collaboration.

Activities of diaspora to promote a high-skills development path back home are, however, on the rise. Intellectual diaspora organisations are considered by Meyer and Brown (1999) to be formal knowledge networks that link high-skilled expatriates with their home. They distinguish the following types: student/scholarly networks, local associations of skilled expatriates, and intellectual/scientific diaspora networks. Intellectual diaspora organisations seek to collaborate with higher education institutions in their home countries as well as with professional associations. In many cases, contacts and established relationships with central governments of their home countries exist. This kind of diaspora engagement is also promoted by international organisations.[8]

Increased internationalisation of local higher education institutions by attracting teachers, researchers, undergraduate and graduate students from abroad can also counteract migration tendencies and increase local employment opportunities. The Nigerian government recognises the economic development potentials of a greater involvement with the diaspora and has established the Nigerians in Diaspora Organisation (NIDO) office closely linked to Nigerian higher education institutions (Adepoju, submitted). The relationship started to develop through a series of academic conferences in Abuja between Nigerian academics from all over the country and their expatriate colleagues.

Under the auspices of NIDO, a programme known as Linkages with Experts and Academics in the Diaspora (LEAD) was started in 2005 to target highly skilled migrants (Adepoju, submitted). During July 2005 several meetings were held to define the approach of the programme and responsibilities of Nigerian partners in and outside the country; 25th July was declared "Diaspora Day" to commemorate the contributions of expatriate nationals to national development. The LEAD programme seeks to gain high-skilled expatriates to contribute to the development of the Nigerian university system through short-term (3 to 12 months) academic appointments. The focus is on several disciplines, including information and communications technology, science management and business administration, mathematics, medicine and dentistry, and mining. The programme does not only involve higher education institutions, but also private companies, who want to benefit from knowledge transfer activities. The university or firm of assignment provides diaspora teachers with a return economy class air ticket, accommodation for the duration of their stay in Nigeria and a Nigeria-rate professorial salary based on the academic field and the candidate's level of experience.

Private sector collaboration with high-skilled expatriates is also gaining importance (Adepoju, submitted). In 2005, the NIDO branch in the Nigerian State of Osun contacted the state governor with a proposal to establish a Skills Acquisition and Exchange Centre in the city of Osogbo. The Australian corporation ACDC Engineering Pty. Ltd. partnered with Osun State in their collaboration with NIDO. Specialist training courses in digital and technical equipment engineering and small-scale research activities are organised as part of LEAD and scholarships to study in Australia are available for the best performing students. There are also examples of Nigerian firms engaging with NIDO, such as Osogbo Steel Rolling Mills and Machine Tools. The state government also followed the recommendation of the Osun Economic Summit, organised in collaboration with NIDO in 2004, and established a free trade zone to promote graduate entrepreneurship and knowledge exchange with diaspora.

In Sierra Leone, the TR'SURE initiative, TRainSUstainREtain, is co-financed by the Ministry of Education. It is part of Sierra Visions, a local NGO that established a successful platform for skills development activities with highly skilled expatriates. Trainers are recruited from amongst the diaspora through Internet based on-line registration and telephone interviews. Training areas are of key importance to local business development and include information and communication technology, human resource management, finance and accounting, marketing, sales and distribution, customer care, law, and business administration. Selected trainers will be paid their accommodation and support towards travel costs. For continuous service full travel cost coverage is granted. Training sessions last for one week; trainers work with existing material and do not have to possess prior experience in adult education. In general, training participants are recruited through Internet based on-line registration, but tailored training programmes also exist for whole companies.

Promoting entrepreneurship and access to new markets abroad

There is also growing evidence that governments in sending countries seek to utilise the experience and skills of expatriates and diaspora organisations for the promotion of entrepreneurial attitudes and motivations amongst the student population and to foster new entrepreneurial activities on international niche markets.

In Mexico, the co-operation between the *Tecnólogico de Nochistlán* and the *Federación de Migrantes Zacatecanos del Sur de California* is one example of promoting student entrepreneurship and spin-out activities (Flores-Macía, submitted). This co-operation led in 2006 to the opening of an incubator facility where eight computer engineering students started their own company. The incubation phase lasts for two years. Even if this co-operation does not immediately lead to the creation of new jobs it is providing an important means for highly skilled young Mexicans to start a growth potential business, while expatriates are offered a way to invest back home.

"Sierra" Visions has successfully built a network in Sierra Leone that brings together international corporations, such as Celtel and the SBTS Group, with local companies, diaspora organisations and higher education institutions. Sierra Visions facilitates student exchange activities in the capital region, while a recent expansion to other parts of the country will soon allow a wider outreach. So far, only a few international placements have been organised, mainly with South Africa and the United States, and these were restricted to a prior agreed duration, and students agreeing to a subsequent return to Sierra Leone. Both the numbers of applicants and companies is increasing with a match-making rate of almost 80%. Spin-out rates are still lower than technology transfer activities, but future investment into incubation facilities and start-up assistance is planned.

Increasing market shares of Fair-Trade products in receiving regions has opened access to markets overseas and stimulated growth of existing companies as well as business start-ups. International solidarity movements in receiving countries work together with diaspora organisations, which are often the first contact for starting trade activities.

Ghanacoop, a social enterprise located in Modena, Italy and promoting trade with exotic fruits is an example of such an initiative. According to Caiani (Caiani, submitted) developing the Ghanacoop partnership was not an easy process. On the Italian side, major obstacles included the absence of trust and mutual understanding regarding motivations for involvement, the limited use of formal channels to transfer remittances, as well as a low interest of migrants to invest in community development projects. The human factor in making this partnership effective needs to be underlined, as working attitudes and entrepreneurial mindsets where not always compatible between the beneficiaries in Ghana and the Ghanaian or Italian actors in Italy. At the same time, difficulties and barriers in developing Ghanacoop's activities in Ghana were mainly related to overregulation and extended bureaucratic procedures in national administration. Caiani (submitted) reports that except for the Ministry of Agriculture, a greater involvement of diaspora is not facilitated by national government. This is exacerbated by a lack of capacities and capabilities in dealing with international non-state actors in issues related to policy making.

Besides Ghanaian and Italian state and non-state institutions, the business sector is an important partner. Large Italian retailers, such as NordConad, Coop Estense, GS Carrefour, CIR Ristorazione, are now involved in trade activities and training. The University of Modena is a strategic partner for Ghanacoop. The faculty of economics helped Ghanacoop by introducing a label called MIDCO (Migrants Initiatives for the Development of the Country of Origin) that recognises the local development impact generated by diaspora activities. In developing this label Ghanacoop also receives institutional support from the International Organisation for Migration and FairTrade Italy.

Linked to the trade activities, training is organised to improve the quantity and quality of agricultural production and marketing. An important component is the enhancement of computer literacy, which is often limited to the use of simple Internet applications. Besides technical know-how in marketing and certification issues, awareness is being created for solidarity activities that are linked to income generation. Highly skilled migrants were involved; however, their success was limited in comparison to the involvement of low-skilled migrants. Key reasons are the geographic focus on selected areas of Ghana and the predominance of low-skilled migrants involved in the activities. Although the geographic focus guarantees, according to Caiani (Caiani, submitted), both formal and informal relationships with counterpart institutions and beneficiaries, it risks excluding other Ghanaian nationals from a more active participation.

Channelling remittances

An important part of the work of diaspora organisations in contributing to local development is pooling remittances that would otherwise go to families and individuals for community use. Most of the activities are focused on small-scale investment in the construction of schools, community centres and road infrastructure. Co-ordinating these activities and increasing their outcomes could be achieved through integration into wider development strategies. However, this appears to be difficult, as such strategies either do not exist or are unknown to diapsora.

In El Salvador, the introduction of regional strategies for socio-economic development is expected to prompt a more co-ordinated approach that will give diaspora organisations a more formal role in local development processes. Currently, the lion's share of remittances by diaspora and hometown associations destined for community use is channelled into religious and traditional festivities. These do not necessarily have a wider economic impact, unless combined with tourist activities and local product and service provision for migrants. Rodríguez-Acosta (submitted) suggests that more can be done by local governments, local business associations and individual companies to use these occasions for economic activities.

National governments can enhance the local development impact of collective remittances by matching them with government funding. This has been piloted with considerable success in Mexico. Already in the late 1980s the Zacatecas government agreed to financially match collective remittances. In the early 1990s, the partnership between migrants associations and state and local governments was joined by the Federal Ministry for Social Development (SEDESOL). Initial difficulties were caused by the absence of separate budgets for the interventions, which reduced planning security and often left initiatives without financing as the matching government funds had not been secured. In 1999, both state and federal governments introduced an additional item to their budgets to ensure matching funds.

Over the first year all four partners each contributed USD 300 000 and a total budget for community investment of USD 1.2 million. This amount increased over the years and reached in 2005 single contributions of USD 4.5 million and a total investment of USD 18.4 million. From 1999 to 2007, USD 76.8 million has been invested. The partnership's success as multiplier of collective remittances in Zacatecas prompted the federal government to replicate this initiative in other states with high levels of international migration, such as Jalisco, Michoacán, and Guanajuato. Today, participation is possible in all 31 states. In 2006, the federal Congress allocated MXD 119.5 million (USD 10.8 million) for 3 x 1 partnerships all over Mexico. The scheme has also benefitted from private sector support. In 2006, First Data Corp, owner of Western Union, got involved in the 3 x 1 partnership in Zacatecas and contributed USD 1.25 million. First Data Corp is not involved in the decision-making process. The case study (Flores-Macía, submitted) confirms that a further involvement of the private sector is fundamental to further expand venture capital functions of the initiative.

SEDESOL has representatives in the Mexican consulates in Chicago and Los Angeles, which advertise the programme and recruit partners. These efforts led to improved organisational capacity and bargaining power of migrant associations. Over time the 3 x 1 partnership has become an important resource for local community development in Zacatecas, and it enables the more than 300 Zacatecan migrant associations in the US to contribute.

Although far from resolving Zacatecas's development problems, the 3 x 1 partnership constitutes a significant endeavour in ameliorating the skills gaps that have resulted from emigration. By itself, the partnership cannot halt emigration or bring back those who already left Zacatecas. It can, however, contribute to the generation of employment opportunities, the retention of talent, and skills upgrading of the labour force through investment in education, and the start-up of micro- and small enterprises. The partnership emphasises job creation at different scales, from medium sized to micro-sized companies and self-employment. On average, projects that receive funding have created between 10 and 25 direct jobs. Investment in infrastructure development creates additional temporary jobs.

The 3 x 1 partnership has also been successful in tackling issues such as high school dropout rates because of economic hardship. Scholarships for primary and secondary education as well as for vocational training are awarded. The aim is to provide youth with an entrepreneurial skills base to raise their employability and their interest in undertaking entrepreneurial activities. Subsidised vocational training programmes include irrigation-based agriculture, aquaculture, animal husbandry, mining, construction, tourism and hospitality services, marketing, as well as computer assembly and repair. The involvement of the federal government is considered to be a trigger for this. Between 2004 and 2006, USD 52 million were allocated for human resource development. And, although there is no regulation which foresees a certain share of investment into education and training, this area has received increasing attention from migrant associations and government partners.

Clearly, the current dependency of local development interventions upon remittances in Mexico needs to be addressed, as it cannot be considered a guaranteed investment inflow. Flores-Macía (Flores-Macía, submitted) argues that the 3 x 1 partnership framework directly challenges the "entitlement mentality", where individuals feel entitled to government assistance without any involvement or ownership. It needs to be added, however, that certain basic state functions and services will need to be improved if the situation of out-migration is to be reversed into sustainable local development. This appears to be the trend as Mexico is now reporting a growing number of agreements between migrant associations, universities and technical schools, and business associations, outside the core agreement between central and local governments and diaspora organisations. The aim of these new agreements is to match ideas and technical capacity with migrant investments.

Similar to the Mexican experience, the El Salvador government is also stimulating and enhancing skills and wider economic development by offering matching funds (Rodríguez-Acosta, submitted). The state administered fund for social investment and local development, FISDL (founded in 1990), invites El Salvadorian communities abroad to contribute to local development initiatives within the *Programme Unidos por la Solidaridad*. The programme runs yearly competitions for funding of small- to medium sized development projects, which is open to application for hometown associations in co-operation with El Salvadorian local governments, and NGOs, and single or joint applications by El Salvadorian local governments. The total amount of diaspora funds leveraged by this initiative is rather small, but their engagement led to a more strategic relationship between national and local governments and diaspora.

While not directly matching remittances, the Chinese government has introduced a policy which grants migrants investing back home substantial tax breaks and facilitates foreign direct investments. Although evidence on whether and to what extend this policy has caused economic growth and increased employment opportunities is missing (Lucas, 2004), this kind of facilitative government intervention provides migrants with attractive alternatives that can stimulate an increase of remittances as well their more productive utilisation.

Recruiting labour internationally and building inter-regional labour markets

Another area where sending regions are co-operating with receiving countries is in the recruitment of labour. At the level of nations, collaboration between governments of sending and receiving countries is today well established in the form of bilateral agreements. In recent years, collaboration on temporary labour migration and recruitment by receiving countries, localities or intermediary private agencies has become more frequent practice. The requirement is predominantly for highly skilled migrants, but specific local demands in receiving countries, combined with *ad hoc* training measures, are also leading to a greater consideration of the low-skilled as a target group. Besides numerous private intermediary agencies active in the recruitment of international labour – often using local newspapers or the Internet as communication channels – local governments are also becoming more active in recruiting suitable workers for the labour markets under their jurisdiction.

Local co-operation between sending and receiving countries

The private sector in receiving countries is often a promoter of local co-operation in labour recruitment. In El Salvador, the national training agency INSAFOPR conducts training at the request of employers abroad linked to temporary labour migration (Rodríguez-Acosta, submitted). The programme, *Trabajadores Migrantes*, in co-operation with the Salvadoran Ministry of Labour and Social Security and the Ministry of Foreign Affairs, is organised for unemployed workers who are interested in short-term employment abroad. Since 2002, a long-standing collaboration has been established with the Canadian meat processing companies Maple Leaf Olymel and Lake Side Packer. INSAFOPR provides basic and advanced training in meat processing as well as language training. According to INSAFOPR, 708 El Salvadorian workers were employed by these companies by the end of 2006. At present, the two governments are further negotiating temporary migration agreements concerning the agricultural, tourism and construction sectors. Other countries in negotiation with El Salvador for temporary labour agreements are Australia, Mexico and Spain.

In Italy, the national government created in 2002 a new legal framework that allows local governments to facilitate the recruitment of international labour. The national immigration law (189/2002) explicitly favours the entry of labour migrants with prior completed professional training. The 2005 amendment of the Italian national immigration law gives Italian central government agencies, regions, provinces and local training organisations a mandate to prepare specific projects, tailored to the needs of local labour markets, and to organise vocational training abroad. The Italian Ministry of Labour and Social Policies in the framework of an agreement that is generally referred to as "Directorial Decree, 16 May 2005", allocated EUR 5 million in 2005 to Italian regions and provinces for recruitment initiatives. Local governments need to match national funding for projects by 15%, which could be covered by the European Social Fund (ESF).

In most cases training and recruitment is handled by national authorities in partner countries and the selection process is centralised in the country capitals or cities with Italian diplomatic missions (Sterzi, submitted). The development of the legal framework was preceded by activities and initiatives by Italian regional governments who began to get involved in the training and recruitment of international labour in the late 1990s. The regional governments of Lombardy and Friuli-Venezia Giulia have been the most responsive to local business needs.

Courses have a minimum duration of 80 hours and consist of a technical and a general compulsory part. The latter includes language training, work safety, civic education and elements of Italian culture. Training locations are generally in the country of origin and organised in Italian companies, or collaborating local institutions. Trainees are listed in a separate database of the Ministry of Labour and Social Policies and benefit from a special entry quota. They enter Italy with visa for study purposes either with a pre-agreed apprenticeship, internship or labour contract. In the case of a concluded work contract, visas can be adjusted and prolonged up to a maximum of three years. Training for recruitment by Italian offshore companies is subsidised. Project initiatives target citizens of sending countries all over the world, who are at present living in their home country and are employed or intend to be employed by Italian offshore companies.

The regional government of Lombardy commenced in 2000 with the "Word Job" programme to manage migration flows of non-EU citizens, including *ad hoc* training according to local labour market needs (Sterzi, submitted). The project was financed by the regional government, the regional labour agency and the chamber of commerce. It was implemented in partnership with regional employer associations, professional organisations and local police offices. The Italian embassy in Tunisia, the Tunisian Ministry of Labour and the Italian trade office in Tunis conducted the selection process. The project included a selection of 100 Tunisian workers, out of more than 200 applicants, for the construction sector in Lombardy. After a successful completion of the training, 20 workers were recruited by local companies in Lombardy. The regional government then initiated similar projects with Moldova, the Slovak Republic, Bulgaria and Egypt.

In 2006, the region of Friuli-Venezia Giulia started recruitment projects with several south-eastern European countries (Sterzi, submitted). A project in Bosnia and Herzegovina implemented by the provincial training centre in Pordenone, Italy has been recruiting industrial workers in the Bosnian canton of Zenica-Doboj. Italian partners include the Chamber of Commerce, Crafts and Agriculture in Pordenone, industrial associations, individual companies, trade unions and their training institutions, the labour office, Caritas and local NGOs active in migration issues. Project partners on the Bosnian side include the vocational training school of Tesaj, cantonal and local labour offices, the Bosnian cultural centre in Sarajevo and an Italian cultural association. The target group includes Bosnian and Herzegovina citizens in the age group 18-40 years-old, with completed vocational training and, for older applicants, professional experience in metal and mechanic works. Out of 125 applicants, 118 were selected on the basis of submitted curriculum vitas; further testing then included a written exam on technology, technical drawing and general culture, an interview, and a practical examination. A total of 60 trainees were subsequently employed by firms in Pordenone. Unselected applicants have a preferential status in future recruitments within this project.

The initiatives by the regions of Lombardy and Friuli-Venezia Giulia are examples of decentralised co-operation recruitment projects. Approaches of this kind have been criticised for likely causing severe skills shortages in sending localities and thus hampering economic development. Training and employment in Italy are sector restricted to domiciliary assistance and care, social and health assistance, tourism industry, metal and mechanic industries, construction and building, agriculture, and transportation. The selection of economic sectors suggests that recruitment is focused on short-term employment responding to structural needs of the receiving local economy and provides, in general, little room for skills upgrading. Although training in starting-up and running a business is offered, most of the initiatives target future dependent workers.

International integration of niche labour markets

Decentralised co-operation activities can also stimulate the creation of international inter-regional niche labour markets. Between the regional governments of Veneto and Timiș in Romania an agreement on the offshore settlement of Italian companies and the creation of joint ventures has been in place since the late 1990s (Cartwright and Pop, submitted). In 2006, 3 500 Italian companies were located in the region of Timiş with around 20 000 Italian employees, most of them from the region of Veneto. Initially having the aim of providing better healthcare services for Italian nationals in Timiş, the regional governments of Veneto and Timiş signed an agreement in June 2006 to develop telemedicine services that would allow closer co-operation in diagnosis and training with co-financing from the European Space Agency, Gruppo Veneto Banca, and Banca Italo Romena, its Romanian subsidiary. The initiative "Near to Needs" connects the health agency in Treviso (Veneto) via satellite with the Judetean Clinical de Urgenta, the regional hospital in Timişoara. This allows for real-time consultation – currently piloted for neurosurgical and cardiology cases – videoconferencing and an e-learning service to train medical doctors and nurses. To establish and ensure the maintenance of the technical system and to develop the skills development component, the Region of Veneto delegated one of its experts on a long-term basis to the *Judetean Clinical de Urgenta*.

This initiative is a form of international integration of niche labour markets, which, if appropriately managed, can facilitate balancing of surpluses and deficits on labour markets. So far, the initiative has allowed medical staff to increase their knowledge and technical skills in a niche area and thus be more competitive on the international labour market. Telemedicine is becoming an important solution for the provision of high-quality healthcare services (particularly in rural and remote areas), and will facilitate the international migration of trained healthcare personnel, if their skills are not absorbed locally. According to the *Judetean Clinical de Urgenta* around 100 nurses left the hospital in 2006, most of them for Italy. This has not yet become a public concern, as the general belief is that these nurses will return, even better skilled, and their departure offers employment opportunities for others (Cartwright and Pop, submitted).

International labour recruitment in sending countries

The possibility of finding a job abroad with a good earnings potential, and the fact that many migrants provide financial support for the family left behind, has reduced the need for some people to become actively integrated in the local labour market in sending economies. Hence, certain professions, which require manual labour and low levels of skills, while offering low remuneration and job satisfaction, are less in demand by the local labour force. Many sending countries have thus become receiving countries, and national governments are signing bilateral agreements to import labour. Local governments in sending countries are less involved, but this might change as private sector demands and requests for international labour are on the rise. To date, informal labour seems to satisfy large parts of the demand, but in the long run this might become insufficient as the example below from Neamţ, Romania suggests.

In order to tackle the loss of skills produced by emigration, local firms in Neamţ have resorted to importing labour from abroad (Ioanita, 2008). Recruitment is not restricted to neighbouring countries, but reaches out to major sending countries in the rest of the world. Local textile companies firms in Neamţ, most of them in joint venture with, or producing for, larger international or global companies, started to hire foreign workers in 2002. To date, 800 workers, mainly women from rural China, are hired on one-to-two-year contracts. The recruitment was carried out by a Chinese recruiter, who also acts as a contractor and employer for the hired workers. This relationship makes it very difficult for the Chinese workers to change employment in Romania. Participating companies in Neamţ, Suceava and Bacău organised a one-week training programme to familiarise the workers with machinery and requirements of production processes. The companies provide basic accommodation. No reliable data exists on remuneration, but according to estimates the monthly wage for a worker ranges between EUR 150-180, which is below the national average wage of approximately EUR 280.

Importing foreign labour is a new experience for Romania. The National Strategy for Migration, adopted in 2004 and amended several times since then, provides the legal framework for meeting labour shortages by international labour. Import of labour has so far been restricted and the administrative procedures remain burdensome (Ioanita, 2008). This might be caused by an inexperienced bureaucracy, but political pressure, underemployment and the likelihood of increased unemployment once emigration flows drop, are factors not to be neglected.

Supporting return migration

The strategic response which may have the most direct impact on local development is encouraging return migration. Yet, not many national and local governments in sending countries are advancing into this direction. Making return economically successful for the migrant, the wider society and the state requires certain framework conditions to be in place. Skilled returnees generally demonstrate risk-taking behaviour. In order to act as representatives for economic take-off, according to Gosh (2000), the following conditions need to be met: relevance of skills and knowledge acquired abroad for the local economy, and willingness and possibilities to apply skills upon return. It is important to remember that the factors affecting migration decisions can be very broad, including for example, the existence of local democracy and opportunities for participation in policy processes. The absence of personal safety and a guarantee for human rights are often stated as factors that increase emigration tendencies among the highly skilled, for example (Lindsay/Findlay, 2002). Greater opportunities to participate in policy processes could thus be an incentive to return, especially as such possibilities are limited in host countries, or accessible only after time and to those that have successfully integrated.

Enhancing voluntary return or circular migration is not yet a common policy practice in the case study countries. Initiatives to promote return migration follow mostly a top-down approach, leaving thus only little room for local governments to become involved. However, some sending localities have increased their efforts to establish relationships with receiving countries related to temporary migration agreements and the creation of regional labour markets, which could facilitate a greater interest amongst migrants in circular migration. Central government agencies in some of the case study countries produce studies and statistical data on return migrants. Yet, these are often not fully developed and, in general, do not reveal representative data or tendencies. Nor are these studies used for policy development.

In Dropull i Poshtem, a commune with around 20 000 inhabitants close to the Greek border in the South of Albania, the mayor maintains regular contact with the diaspora organisations in northern Greece (OECD 2004a). These contacts, although informal and very much linked to the individual, facilitate investment activities by migrants and create opportunities for return, as demonstrated by increased business start-up rates. However, the lack of national government support makes replication of such initiatives elsewhere in the country difficult. At the regional level, the government of Tirana is working on the establishment of a database of skills amongst expatriates from municipalities and communes under the region's jurisdiction. Questionnaires have been sent to all 18 local governments to gather information about migrants' demographic characteristics and skills attainment upon departure, and, if accessible, also during emigration. The aim of the survey is to integrate the information into regional strategic planning, so as to tailor initiatives. A full inventory of skills might be difficult to create, as international co-operation with labour market institutions to this end has not yet been established.

The Ecuadorian government recently launched an Internet portal that provides useful information for returnees. As well as information on the administrative procedures required by those returning to their home country, recent policy initiatives to improve living conditions are also represented, such as the government's initiative to fight corruption and to increase transparency in state institutions. Returnees interested in starting-up a business will also find information about the El Cucayo initiative, an easy-to-access credit scheme for returnees. In addition to financing, the initiative runs a mentoring scheme that provides returnees with valuable information on doing business in Ecuador. Mentors are managers of existing companies or retired businessmen. Returnees can also become mentors. The combination of mentoring and financing helps to address the problems of limited and insufficient start-up financing and a lack of awareness amongst returnees of local market behaviour.

Conclusions and recommendations

In this chapter we looked at different strategic options to source the impacts of international labour migration for skills and wider economic development. Most of these have been developed within the framework of inter-regional agreements between sending and receiving countries or governments working with diaspora organisations. While both of these governance frameworks seem to be managing the same process, they do not necessarily address the same issues. Inter-regional agreements tend to focus on addressing illegal migration and matching the international demand for skills with local supply, *id est*, matters of institutional co-operation, whereas diaspora organisations focus their activities on social and infrastructural development for communities and co-national individuals in their home country. There is however a certain degree of interdependency between diaspora organisations and inter-regional agreements: the existence of an inter-regional agreement clearly facilitates the policy contribution of diaspora. The case study analysis revealed that bilateral agreements at the level of nations are facilitative, but as diaspora organisations are based on local connections, the more localised the relationship, the more can be expected from diaspora in terms of local development contribution. Highly skilled expatriates are increasingly considered by governments as a resource for innovation and growth, and institutionalised relationships with intellectual diaspora is understood to have the potential to instigate economic development through innovation and changing trade patterns. Yet, these cannot be achieved by current practice alone.

Although all of the following instruments have been reported to contribute to a better management of migration, only some seem to trigger a path towards greater skills development for the sending economy.

- Recruitment activities by receiving regions which invest in education and training in sending regions.
- Decentralised co-operation which supports community development, entrepreneurship and skills development in localities overseas, with consequent positive effects for receiving regions in terms of international trade and better managed immigration.
- Diaspora and hometown associations, which channel resources into the development of new local community services, and hence opportunities for employment, skills development and entrepreneurship activities. This may involve matching personal remittances with government funds to support community economic development.
- Intellectual diaspora organisations that remit ideas, transfer skills and invest in innovation and knowledge transfer.

- Support for wider forms of knowledge transfer, including promoting consultancy by highly skilled expatriates to sectoral and employers organisations back home, and providing incentives for members of diaspora organisations to return for periods of volunteering and the provision of technical support to local development activities.
- Linkages between higher education institutions in sending and receiving regions to support knowledge transfer and shared university courses, facilitating return migration and transportability of qualifications.
- Mechanisms to support the integration of regional niche labour markets in sending and receiving countries.

The case studies indicate that while these policy approaches offer a promising line of action to manage migration locally they have not yet had a major impact on local development, and in particular skills development within sending regions. The case studies suggest that this is because of a lack of capacity and governance as well as a focus on skills supply side interventions which means that private sector development and initiatives to stimulate a greater local demand for skills is not addressed. These two issues are discussed below.

Fostering private sector development

For many sending economies, low-skill equilibria[9] and low value added goods dominate trade patterns. Private sector development is often suppressed by a wide spread informal economy. Restructuring of economic sectors and the re-allocation of resources – both key to structural change – are on-going processes, but often produce few outcomes. Skills development strategies, if they are to instigate change towards a high-skill equilibrium – in which high-skilled people are locally absorbed by jobs that demand these skills – will need to be accompanied by broader business sector development, including entrepreneurship and SME policies that increase demand for new skills and their local absorption. This will involve a future oriented priority setting in public funding. Business support services need a strong reference to criteria such as potential to increase the local utilisation of technology, the potential for value added, export orientation and, most importantly, global market potential. In the long run, modernisation and a greater involvement of high-technology foreign investment can trigger a gradual increase in demand for high level generic skills and a flexible labour force. Public policy will need to facilitate this.

Better harnessing diaspora activities for skills

Despite the importance of skills development for economic growth in today's knowledge economy, up until now there has been relatively little focus on skills development efforts within diaspora activities. Diaspora organisations have begun to experiment with networking activities between highly skilled expatriate nationals and academics back home, which might be developed further into systematic skills transfer activities. However, more broadly, while diaspora and hometown associations are often involved in social service provisioning, small-scale community and local development initiatives, their involvement in skills development efforts remains marginal. Remittances can play a role in up-scaling these efforts.

In order to redirect the utilisation of remittances towards skills development initiatives, more needs to be done to establish the nexus between economic development and skills as a priority for both policy and local action. Regarding monetary remittances this will require a different understanding, that is, a form of foreign direct investment rather than a means to alleviating poverty and closing budgetary deficits. Diaspora-led foreign investment can support skills development by increasing demand for skilled labour. In addition foreign firms or joint ventures can stimulate competition with domestic firms. The latter is likely to increase the skill demand of local firms as these, in order to catch-up, will try to modernise and secure greater market shares for their goods and services, and will thus have a greater demand for skilled labour. Diaspora-led foreign investment may destroy jobs by out-competing domestic firms, but it can still break up an existing low-skill equilibrium and lead to greater interest in, and demand for, skills development by individual workers, who are likely to receive greater returns on education and skills attainments from both foreign and domestic firms.

Increasing local knowledge and data

In order to provide more coherent policies in this area, governments will require more evidence collection and improved evaluation practices across different levels of governance. If inter-regional agreements and diaspora organisations are to contribute to skills and economic development, they will require regular information on development indicators, in particular on the kinds of skills needed. A pre-requisite for integrating the initiatives of inter-regional co-operation, hometown associations and diaspora into a local skills development strategy, will be an up-to-date evidence base on the needs of local businesses, forecasts of development and growth trajectories of local industries, and the skills offer and demand sides of the local labour market.

Improving governance and local capacity

A broad range of factors influence people's decisions to migrate or to return to a region, and hence policy responses to the loss of skills need to be embedded in wider strategic approaches to promote the economic and social development of economies. Yet, much of the above policy approaches are still isolated and rather *ad-hoc* in their application, and are not integrated in wider strategies – either because these are inexistent or because co-operation between national and local governments and non-state actors is inexistent or weak. The existence of a local strategy helps to co-ordinate different initiatives, contributes to the integration of different policies and increases the degree of stakeholder co-ordination.

The analysis shows that in all of the case study areas, barriers to such a broad-based and coherent strategic approach exist at the level of both central and local governments. In receiving regions, the private business sector, although not always in possession of a formal mandate, currently assumes a relatively important role in strategic planning and in pushing for skills development through better managing immigration at the local level. However, left alone such initiatives may not do a great deal to promote local development in sending regions and can on the contrary exacerbate the loss of skills. At the same time, migrant organisations may find that their actions to promote community development back home have little impact if they are not joined up with wider public policies and initiatives. And finally, while the role of local government in receiving countries to promote local development in sending countries is growing (particularly through concern over illegal immigration, and the promotion of decentralised co-operation), such institutions may not be sufficiently aware of needs in sending regions, meaning that the full engagement of institutions in sending countries is vital if interregional agreements are to succeed. There is a strong role for the local government in sending countries to get involved in this policy area, to integrate private and voluntary sector actions and international interventions into broad local strategies. While national governments can step in, and take over the role of local governments, this could reduce interest by diaspora to invest back home in their specific localities.

A better co-ordination of the local actors involved and a further integration of their activities is also needed across levels of government to create synergies and to avoid overlap, duplication, a waste of resources as well as false promises that might reduce legitimacy. Inter-regional agreements can in fact negatively impact the integration of promoted activities with existing policies if co-ordination between central and local governments is weak. Limited policy integration causes a lack of synergy between interventions and in some cases duplication. The non-involvement of local governments may limit spill-over of migration management initiatives into social and economic development, reducing in turn the success of attempts to upskill, retain and attract labour force. Limited capacities for evidence-based policy making also translates into generic instruments that might not necessarily address particular needs. Moreover, the absence, or very limited existence, of evaluation practices further impedes improvements of policy processes.

It is interesting to ask why, until now, local governments have not fully taken up their potential role in this area. This may be either because they have not been given an explicit mandate to develop policy in relation to migration management, or because they lack financial and human capacity to act, or both. The degree of local governance and stakeholder involvement in migration management and skills development varies country by country, however local governments in sending countries seem to be mainly involved in implementing activities rather than developing policies and strategies.

The involvement of local governments in initiatives relating to the management of migration is currently much lower in sending regions than in receiving countries, despite the fact that they are often obliged to address matters of local concern by law. Table 2.1 identifies the role of local governments,

Table 2.1. **Local migration management in case study countries**

Local migration management instrument	Diaspora	Receiving countries				Sending countries			
		Central Gov	Local Gov	Private sector	NGO	Central Gov	Local Gov	Private sector[1]	NGO
Decentralised co-operation	CON IMP	LEG FIN IMP	LEG FIN CON IMP	CON IMP	CON IMP	LEG IMP	CON IMP	IMP	IMP
International niche labour markets	CON IMP	CON IMP	LEG FIN IMP	FIN CON IMP		CON IMP	LEG FIN CON IMP	CON IMP	
International labour recruitment		LEG FIN	LEG FIN CON IMP	CON IMP		LEG	CON IMP		
Sourcing diaspora for local development	FIN CON IMP		LEG FIN	CON IMP	CON IMP	LEG FIN IMP	FIN CON IMP		CON IMP
Knowledge transfer through expatriates	FIN CON IMP	FIN				FIN CON	LEG FIN	CON IMP	CON IMP

Legend: Gov = government; CSO = civil society organisation; LEG = sets legislative framework; CON = is being consulted; FIN = is a major source of financing; IMP = is involved in implementation.

1. For the purpose of simplification, the private sector in sending countries excludes offshore companies from receiving countries.

amongst other stakeholders, in each of the policy fields reviewed above (decentralised co-operation, the creation of international niche labour markets, international labour recruitment and diaspora-led co-development). It shows that local governments in sending countries are most likely to be consulted on initiatives and involved in implementation. They are more rarely involved in the design and financing, particularly in the fields of decentralised co-operation and international labour recruitment.

Capacities are a key issue in making local migration management effective. To play a greater role local governments require organisational capacities that are not always existent in sending regions, particularly in local economies that have lost skilled public officials to both internal and external emigration. Effective local involvement depends to a large extent on the existence of effective local governance frameworks and strong institutional capacities. Decentralisation has occurred in many countries, with local governments and other stakeholders getting more involved in policy processes. However, local governments and organisations from the private business sector or civil society often lack sufficient competencies and capacities, as well as technical skills to be fully influential in these processes. Besides more competencies and capacity building, national and regional governments will need to increase co-ordination and integration efforts in order to make local action an integral part of wider policies.

Notes

1. Regions that experience high rates of emigration.
2. Portes (1996) defined a transnational community as a community spanning borders that offers as its key assets shared information and contacts.
3. For a further discussion on the role of increasing interdependencies for regional economies, see Saxenian and Hsu (2001).
4. For an overview of policy responses with regard to labour emigration, see Lowell and Findlay (2002).
5. New EU member countries are, as yet, more sending than receiving countries.
6. IPI (2006).
7. Fauser (2007) provides an overview of decentralised co-operation projects of the municipal governments of Madrid and Barcelona.
8. The United Nations Development Programme (UNDP) runs in a number of sending countries "Transfer of Knowledge through Expatriate Nationals" programmes (TOKTEN). The objective is to involve nationals residing abroad in the provision of short-term services for economic and social development in countries of their origin. Qualified emigrants volunteer their services without enforced required government service, or commitment to permanent return.
9. In a low-skill equilibrium a low-skilled labour force is absorbed by the local demand for low-skill labour (see the Glossary to this publication). People with a higher level of educational and skills attainment can choose between a low-skill job and emigration.

Bibliography

Adepoju, A. (2008, submitted), "Skills Development and International Migration in Nigeria", OECD, Paris.

Bokuma, A. (2008, submitted), "Decentralisation, Skills and Migration. A Case Study on Ghana", OECD, Paris.

Caiani, G. (2008, submitted), "Ghanacoop: From a Bilateral Agreement to a Social Contract", OECD, Paris.

Cartwright, A. and Pop, D. (2008, submitted), "Mutual Interests and Dual Developments in Italy and Romania", OECD, Paris.

Fan, S.C. and O. Stark (2007), "The Brain Drain, 'Educated Unemployment', Human Capital, and Economic Betterment", *Economics of Transition*, Vol. 15, No. 4, pp. 629-660.

Fauser, M. (2007), "The Local Politics of Transnational Cooperation on Development(s) and Migration in Spanish Cities", paper presented at the conference on *Transnationalisation and Development(s): Towards a North-South Perspective*, Center for Interdisciplinary Research, Bielefeld, Germany, 31 May-1 June, 2007, in: COMCAD Arbeitspapiere – Working Papers, No. 24.

Flores-Macías G.A. (2008, submitted), "Migrant-Government Partnership in Zacatecas, Mexico", OECD, Paris.

Funkhouser, E. (2008), "Role of Remittances and Hometown Associations in Local Labour Markets in Nicaragua", OECD, Paris.

Gosh, B. (ed.) (2000), *Return Migration: Journey of Hope or Despair*, IOM, Geneva.

Ionita, S. (2008, submitted), "Dealing with Labor Market Rigidities in Neamţ County: A Case Study", OECD, Paris.

IPI (2006), *Raccolta e Catalogazione delle Iniziative Progettuali di Cooperazione Decentrata*, Rome, Italy.

Kuznetsov, Y. (2006), *Diaspora Networks and the International Migration of Skills. How Countries can Draw on their Talent Abroad*, World Bank.

Lindsay L., B. and Findlay, A.M. (2002), "Migration of Highly Skilled Persons from Developing Countries: Impacts and Policy Responses", synthesis report, IOM, Geneva.

Lowell Lindsay, B. and Y.B. Kemper (2004), "Transatlantic Roundtable on Low-skilled Migration in the Twenty-first Century: Prospect and Policies", in *International Migration*, Vol. 42, No. 1, pp. 117-140.

Lucas, R.E.B. (2004), "International Migration Regimes and Economic Development", *executive summary prepared for the Expert Group on Development Issues in the Swedish Ministry of Foreign Affairs*.

Meyer, J.-B. and M. Brown (1999), "Scientific Diasporas: A New Approach to the Brain Drain", paper prepared for the *World Conference on Science*, 26 June-1 July, 1999, Budapest, Hungary, *www.unesco.org/most/meyer.htm*, accessed 14 February 2008.

OECD (2004a), "Return Migration and Local Development in Albania", internal document, *Local Approaches to Integrate Returning Migrants into Local Labour Markets in Albania*, OECD Trento Centre.

OECD (2004b), *Migration for Employment: Bilateral Agreements at a Crossroads*, OECD, Paris.

Orozco, M. (2008, submitted), "The Nicaraguan Diaspora: Trends and Opportunities for Diaspora Engagement in Skills Transfers and Development", OECD, Paris.

Portes, Alejandro (1996), "Global Villagers: The Rise of Transnational Communities", *American Prospect*, March-April.

Rodríguez-Acosta, C.A. (2008, submitted), "International Migration and Local Skills Strategies: The Case of El Salvador", OECD, Paris.

Salazar-Medina, R. (2008, submitted), "Migration Patterns and Human Resources in Ecuador: Analysis of the National and Local Context in the Provinces of Pichincha, Tungurahua, Chimborazo and Canar", OECD, Paris.

Saxenian, A. and Hsu, J. (2001), "The Silicon Valley-Hsinchu Connection: Technical Communities and Industrial Upgrading", *Industrial and Corporate Change*, Vol. 10, No. 4.

Schwab, K., M.E. Porter and J.D. Sachs, (2001), *The Global Competitiveness Report 2001-2002*, Oxford University Press, Oxford, New York.

Stark, O. and Fan S.C. (2007), "Losses and Gains to Developing Countries from the Migration of Educated Workers: An Overview of Recent Research, and New Reflections", *Analytical report prepared for the MIREM Project Migration de Retour Au Maghreb*, Robert Schuman Centre for Advanced Studies.

Sterzi, A. (2008, submitted), "Decentralised Co-operation in Italy", OECD, Paris.

Taylor, J. Edward (1999), "The New Economics of Labour Migration and the Role of Remittances in the Migration Process", *International Migration*, Vol. 37, No. 1, pp. 63-88.

PART II

Case Studies

PART II

Chapter 3

The Shanghai "Highland of Talent" Strategy

by

Rufei Zhang

Having invested heavily throughout the 1990s in physical infrastructure, the Shanghai Municipal Government (SMG) began a parallel investment in 2003 to strengthen human capital in the metropolis and move Shanghai towards becoming a global city. The SMG announced an integrated strategy of competitiveness building human capital development via four key themes: attracting Chinese overseas graduates, vocational training of on-the-job workers, training for local workers without jobs, and training of migrant workers. This strategy has had considerable success, largely through taking a balanced approach (attracting talent, up-skilling the labour force and integrating the hard to reach) while also setting clear targets and achievable goals for local stakeholders.

Introduction

Shanghai is the core metropolis in a large, rapidly urbanising and industrialising corridor stretching from Ningbo through Hangzhou, in Zhejiang, to Shanghai, and then northwest through Suzhou, Wuxi, and Changzhou to Nanjing, in Jiangsu Province. Recently completed bridges mean that the megalopolis now includes a corridor of smaller cities along the north shore of the Yangtze River. The megalopolis, which is 250 km long but less than 50 km wide, constitutes China's largest megalopolis, with a population of 76 million. The megalopolis covers 1% of China's land area but, in 2004, held 6% of China's total population, contributed 18.7% of China's total GDP, 32% of China's import and export trade, and attracted 48% of the total foreign direct investment in China.[1]

Shanghai is clearly the principal hub of the Yangtze Delta Megalopolis. It accounts for 22% of its population and produces 23% of its GDP. Despite Shanghai's prominence, the Yangtze Delta Megalopolis is a complex network of metropolises, large cities, intermediate cities, small cities and towns, many of which have experienced economic growth rates higher than Shanghai's over the past decade. There has been considerable direct foreign investment into these smaller cities in the manufacturing, tourism, retail, transport and infrastructure sectors.

The city is located on the eastern fringe of the Yangtze River Delta, along the centre of China's coastline, covering a land area of 6 340 km^2 comprising 18 districts and 1 county (Figure 3.1). By 2005, the city had a total population of 18 million (13.6 million registered residents, and 4.4 million migrants).[2] Just over half of its population is concentrated in the core city, the urban area of 660 km^2 within the outer ring road.

There are considerable social, economic and demographic differences among Shanghai's nineteen districts and one county, particularly between the nine suburban districts and county, and the nine urban districts. Although there is no official difference between urban and suburban districts in Shanghai from an administrative perspective, Shanghai's urban districts usually refer to the nine traditional districts within (or having most of their areas within) the outer ring road: Huangpu, Luwan, Jin'an, Xuhui, Changning, Hongkou, Putuo, Zhabei, and Yangpu. Suburban districts refer to the eight districts of Baoshan, Minhang, Jiading, Jinshan, Songjiang, Fengxian, Qingpu, and Nanhui (the last six districts were upgraded from counties after 2000). Pudong New Area was designated in 1990 as a special development zone of

Figure 3.1. **Map of Shanghai**

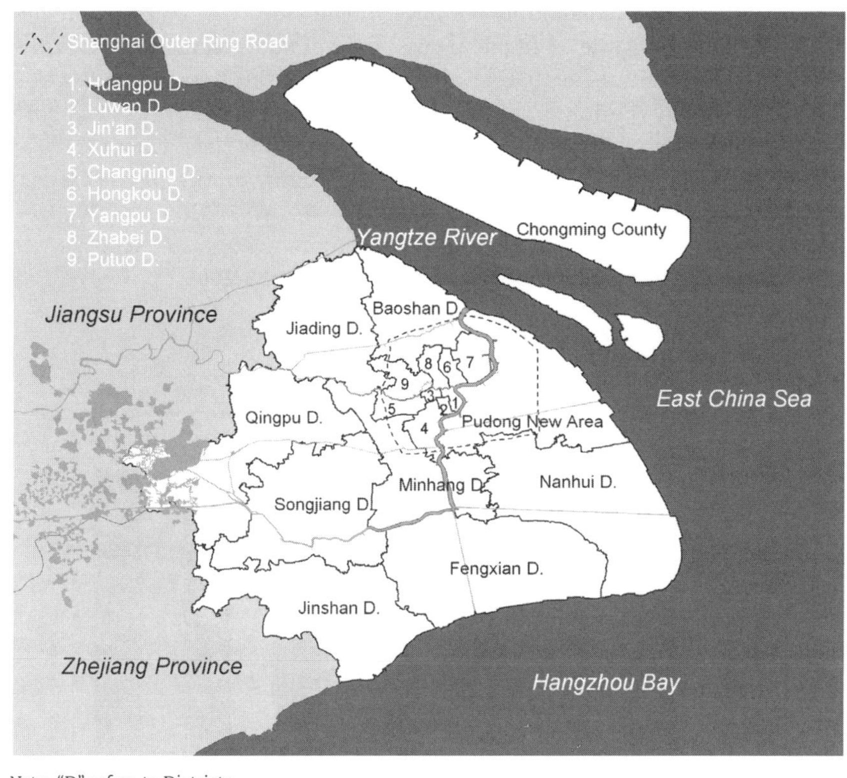

Note: "D" refers to Districts.
Source: Chreod.

Table 3.1. **China's top five cities of talent, 2000**

	Number of people with education attainment of junior college and above per every 1 million of local population	Ranking
Beijing	1 684	1
Shanghai	1 094	2
Guangzhou	931	3
Tianjin	901	4
Chongqing	280	5

Source: China National Census 2000, and Sun Luyi, "Talent Strategy and International Metropolis", page 23.

350 km^2 along the east side of Huangpu River; it was upgraded to a district in 2000 and its territory expanded to 523 km^2.

As China's most populous city and the country's preeminent economic centre, Shanghai has the second largest talent pool among all China's cities, only outranked by Beijing which is the country's capital city (Table 3.1). Over the last decade, Shanghai Municipal Government (SMG) has allocated higher priority to developing the city's talent pool, and has successfully expanded the pool from 0.89 million in 1998 to 1.67 million by 2005 (see Figure 3.2 and Box 3.1: Shanghai's definition of talent). Being China's largest industrial base and service centre, Shanghai also retains a substantially sized labour force of skilled workers (1.5 million in 2003), making Shanghai one of the largest labour markets of skilled workers in China.

Figure 3.2. **Shanghai's talent pool, 1998-2005**

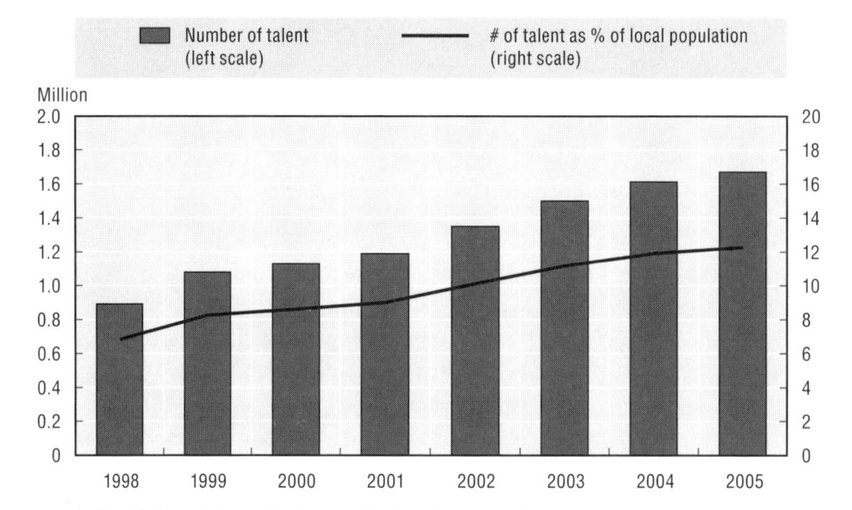

Source: i) *Shanghai Statistic, Yearbook 2006*, ii) Shanghai Municipal Personnel Bureau: *Annual Report of Shanghai's Human Resources*, 2005, iii) Sun Luyi, "Talent Strategy and International Metropolis", page 23.

Economy growth and transition

Gross domestic product (GDP) in Shanghai in 2005 was CNY 915 billion, accounting for 5.0% of China's total GDP. Shanghai's per capita GDP (including migrants) was CNY 50 856 in 2005, around 3.6 times the national average.[3] This corresponds to a purchasing power parity figure which places Shanghai at the higher end of middle income countries according to this key indicator of living standards and productivity. Since 1990, Shanghai has experienced growth in real GDP of over 11% per year (Figures 3.4 and 3.5), placing Shanghai among the most rapidly expanding regions in China and within the global economy. Increases in living standards, as measured by per capita GDP, were also substantial at over 9% per year.

The cumulative effects of a large number of interrelated factors explain the strong growth and comparatively high living standards in Shanghai. The metropolis has a high rate of urbanisation (at least 90%) and high densities of population and production.

Shanghai has comparatively large (and expanding) tertiary sectors. It is now the major financial and commercial centre in mainland China. The transformation of Shanghai's economic structure over the past decade or so has been dramatic. The tertiary sector accounted for only 26% of Shanghai's GDP in 1985, when the secondary sector was dominant with a 69.8% share of GDP. Two decades later, in 2005, the secondary and tertiary shares of Shanghai's GDP are roughly equivalent (49% secondary, 50% tertiary), and the long-term trend for the tertiary sector share is clearly upward.

Services now dominate the metropolitan core, whereas the secondary sector remains the most important source of production and jobs in the rest of the region. This reflects the relocation and direction of secondary activity from the urban core to the Pudong New Area, the suburbs and counties over a very short 10-year period. Accordingly, an important factor in Shanghai's growth performance is the emergence of a strong quaternary sector that provides high wages, generates high productivity, uses more advanced technology, and supports significant trade with other regions of China and overseas: this includes banking, insurance, real estate, scientific research and advanced technical services.

The dramatic economic growth of Shanghai over the last 15 years has been grounded on a national development strategy, introduced by the Government of China in 1990, of having Shanghai drive the country's economic growth through the development of the Pudong New Area. Decades of underinvestment had constrained the growth of the east side of the Huangpu River, which bisects Shanghai. Recognising the potential for controlled policy experimentation in an area contiguous with the country's largest metropolis, the government designated Pudong as a "New Area" for testing a range of financial and economic reforms; a similar model of policy experimentation had been followed a decade earlier in Shenzhen, adjacent to Hongkong.

Attracted by favourable policies under the Pudong development initiative, which dominated the country's economic policy throughout the 1990s, significant investment from various sources, particularly foreign investment, poured into Shanghai. The city's economy took off quickly and grew at over 15% annually in the first half of 1990s.

However, the sustainability of this growth was constrained by an outdated manufacturing sector, and a relatively undeveloped tertiary sector of producer and consumer services. Historically a key industrial base of China, Shanghai had accumulated a large number of state-owned industrial enterprises (SOE) during more than four decades of state-dominated socialism. Producing outdated products using obsolete technology, and overloaded with redundant employees, Shanghai's industrial SOEs faced intense market competition during the 1990s from foreign joint-ventures and private companies. Widespread stagnation of Shanghai's industrial SOEs became apparent in 1994, and Shanghai lost its economic momentum. While substantial efforts and financial inputs were allocated from both the central and municipal governments to re-vitalise the rapidly deteriorating industrial SOEs in Shanghai, these efforts were largely unsuccessful. Shanghai's economy experienced a sharp downward trend from 1994 to 1998 (Figure 3.3). This forced the SMG to launch a risky and high cost initiative in 1998 to fully restructure the city's industrial sector.

Under this industrial restructuring initiative, Shanghai closed all the industrial SOEs in its traditional industrial sectors characterised by outdated products with no markets, high pollution, and inefficient resource consumption (energy, water, land). From 1998 to 2002, over 1.27 million employees were laid-off due to SOE re-structuring in Shanghai, of which 30% (380 000) were from the traditional textile industry. Shanghai shifted its economic development priorities to the tertiary and higher value-added manufacturing sectors. Industrial restructuring in Shanghai was rapid and thorough: it is generally viewed as a successful model by other cities in China. A combination of government policy incentives to attract foreign and private investment in Shanghai's industry sector, a pool of skilled workers, and the city's advantageous location for accessing large markets in the Yangtze Delta region and inland China, led to significant foreign and private industrial investment. Industrial enterprises in the form of joint-ventures, wholly foreign owned firms, and domestic private companies soon replaced the SOEs in Shanghai's industry sector. By the late 1990s, the city's

Figure 3.3. **Shanghai gross domestic product (GDP), 1985-2005**

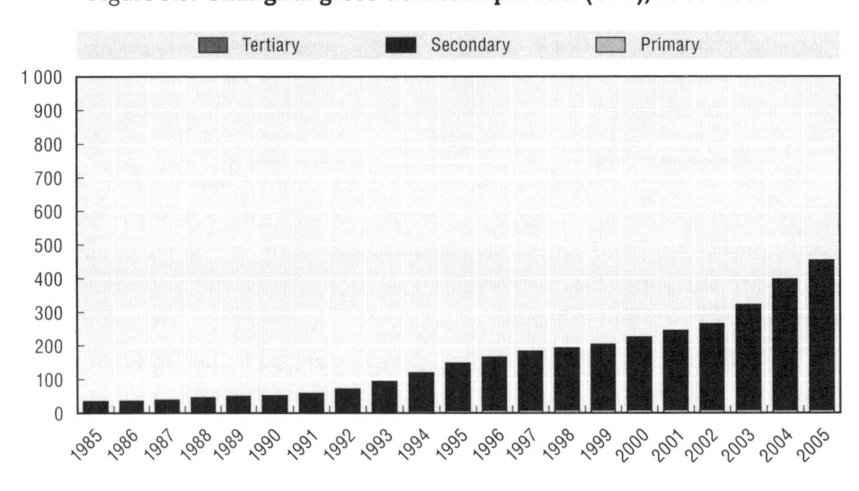

Source: Shanghai Statistical Yearbook 2006.

Figure 3.4. **GDP annual growth rate in Shanghai and China, 1985-2005**

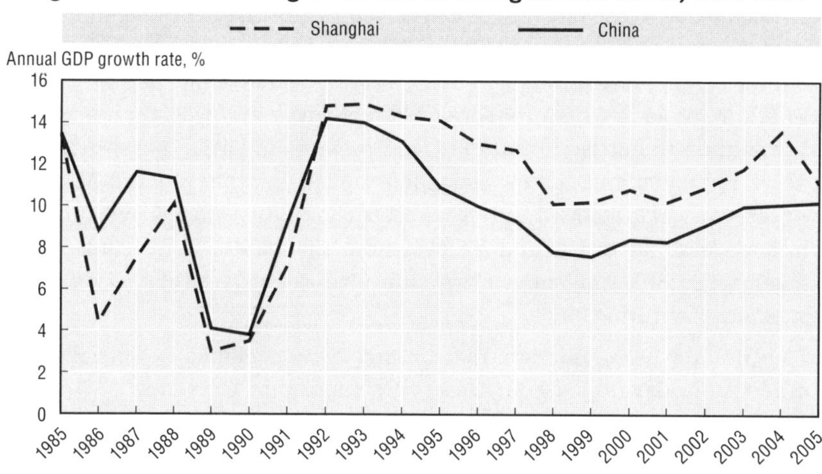

Source: Shanghai Statistical Yearbook 2006, China Statistical Yearbook 2006.

Figure 3.5. **Per capita GDP, Shanghai and China, 1985-2005**

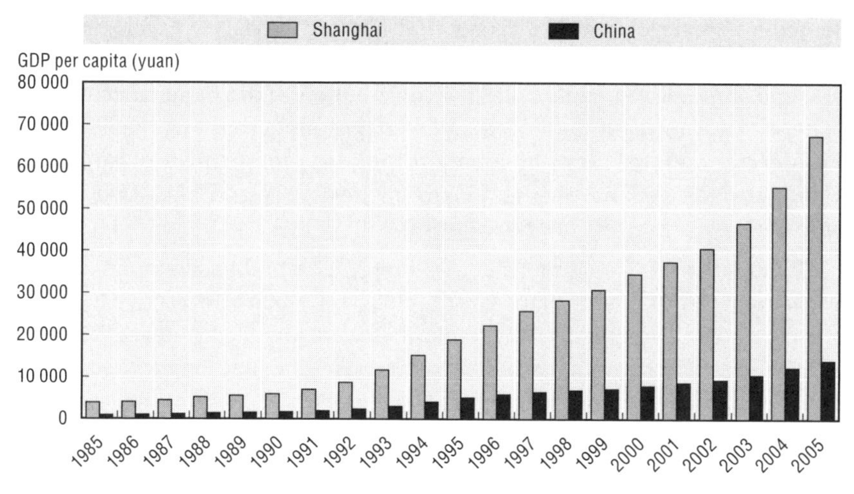

Source: Shanghai Statistical Yearbook 2006, China Statistical Yearbook 2006.

economy was restructured into export-oriented manufacturing and a rapidly growing tertiary sector.

Development strategy towards a global metropolis

Rapid economic growth, particularly after industrial restructuring in the late 1990s, has led to significant increases in business costs. The cost of land in Shanghai is rising due to limited land supply, and limited land that the city can allocate to industrial development. Labour costs in Shanghai have also risen quickly due to the increase of wages tied to growing living expenditures. Rising business costs, particularly of land and labour, have dramatically eroded the comparative advantages that Shanghai had in competing with other cities and regions in China for foreign direct investment (FDI) and private industrial investment. Significant FDI and private industrial investment has bypassed Shanghai and gone to neighbouring cities in Jiangsu and Zhejiang Provinces. With far lower land and labour costs, the cities of Suzhou and Kunshan – which are less than one-hour drive away from Shanghai – have become major destinations for foreign and private industrial investment, particularly for export-oriented manufacturing.

By the late 1990s, Shanghai's economy had developed to a level close to moderately developed countries with per capita GDP over USD 3 000. International experience suggests that economic growth in many developing countries and cities slows or even stagnates after reaching per capita GDP level of USD 3 000, largely due to the absence of new driving forces to sustain the dynamics of urban economies.

Recognising the constraining impacts of rising input costs and the need to activate new driving forces for a stagnating economy, in the late 1990s SMG adopted a new development strategy that had, as its vision, developing the city into an international metropolis and a global centre of commerce, finance, trade and shipping. Given its potential contribution to the national economy, the central government embraced and strongly supported Shanghai's long-term development strategy by incorporating this municipal development strategy into the national Five Year Plans for 1990-1995, and 1996-2000 as one of the nation's key development priorities.

To support the global metropolis strategy, comprehensive programmes and sectoral development plans – with clear, time-bound objectives – were prepared and implemented. Highest priorities were attached to developing the service sector and seven pillar industries in Shanghai. For the service sector, Shanghai has focused on developing subsectors of *i)* information service, *ii)* financial services and banking, *iii)* logistics services, *iv)* culture and creative sector, *v)* producer services of legal, accounting, and advertising services, and *vi)* retail/commercial business. For the industrial sector, Shanghai focused on higher-tech and higher value-added manufacturing in: *i)* information technology, *ii)* equipment manufacturing; *iii)* automobile manufacturing; *iv)* high-end steel products; *v)* petrochemistry; *vi)* bio-pharmaceuticals; *vii)* and ship manufacturing. Shanghai's municipal government has recognised that upgrading the competitiveness of Shanghai is the key for becoming a global city: improving competitiveness is a key theme embodied in Shanghai's new development strategy, in supplementary sectoral strategies (focusing on sectors of service, finance, trade, and shipping) and policy frameworks.

However, SMG also recognises that all of these competitiveness building initiatives and sectoral strategies will flounder unless a focal issue is squarely addressed: the serious shortage of skilled human resources in Shanghai.

Skills strategies in Shanghai

While almost all the municipalities in China have by now prepared a skills strategy, Shanghai was the first to identify the need for comprehensive and sustained programmes of skills upgrading during the second half of the 1990s as it confronted several serious impediments to the development of human capital:[4]

- In 1998, although Shanghai had second largest talent pool in China (only outranked by Beijing) of 0.89 million people,[5] this pool was facing a serious ageing crisis. The city was to lose 90% of its top level leading scientists, 70% of its enterprise executives and managerial resources, and 40-60% of its high level specialised talents in two years (by 2000) due to retirement.[6]
- The city had experienced a severe brain drain as local talent migrated to developed countries during the 1980s and 1990s. From 1978 to 1996, the Shanghai Science Academy (the predominant pool of scientists and researchers in Shanghai) lost 58.8% of its young scientists and researchers to other countries.
- With over 85% of its talent highly concentrated in the fields of civil engineering, education, medicine, and scientific research, Shanghai had very limited talent resources in the industrial and service sectors (finance, banking, logistics, international trade and business). This significantly constrained the development of the service sector and higher-value added manufacturing – the two key driving sectors for Shanghai's economic growth in the long run.

Shanghai was losing its competitiveness in: *i)* competing with neighbouring cities and provinces for foreign direct investment and private investment in industry; *ii)* competing with other R&D and innovation centres (Beijing, Shenzhen) in the high-tech sector in terms of R&D capability and high-tech products manufacturing (information and computer technology and bio pharmacy, in particular). Adding to the competition with domestic competitors was the looming competition from multinationals after China joined the WTO.

SMG launched its first talent development initiative in 1995 to develop Shanghai as a "highland" of talent in mainland China. The priorities were to attract and develop specialised talent and professionals in the service sectors of finance, insurance, foreign trade/business, accounting, and international law, all of which were urgently needed to serve the rapidly expanding demands of Shanghai's service sector and the boom of foreign investment in Shanghai. The Talent Highland Initiative included efforts to attract talented people to upgrade Shanghai's R&D and innovation capacity.

Box 3.1. **Shanghai's definitions of talent**

Codified in 1982, China's current official definition of "talent" for statistical purposes is based on levels of educational attainment and professional qualification. According to this definition, talent refers to people with educational attainment of "specialised secondary school" level or above (中专及以上文凭), or having a professional qualification of primary level or above (初级及以上职称). Over the last few years, the rationale of this national statistical definition of talent has been widely questioned, particularly its low benchmarks.

While this national definition of talent is still widely applied in China's statistical practice, many of China's larger cities, such as Shanghai and Beijing, began to use new talent definitions since 2000 with a higher standard to facilitate the development and implementation of their local talent strategies and policies. In Shanghai (as in Beijing and China's other major cities), the definition of talent refers to people with junior college diploma or above (中级及以上职称), or having a professional qualification of medium level or above (中级及以上职称). Using this definition, Shanghai has a talent pool of 1.67 million in 2005.

In SMG's literature of talent strategy and human resource management, talent is classified into three categories: *i)* talent of the party and government (including leaders and officials in the party and the government of various level in Shanghai); *ii)* professional and technical talent (including scientists, academics and technicians); and *iii)* talent of managers and executives. The framework of SMG's talent development strategy and implementation programme reflects this talent classification.

It should be noticed that parallel to SMG's new talent definition (with junior college diploma or medium-level professional qualification), a broad definition of talent is also used in SMG's practice of talent statistics and human resource planning. The size of Shanghai's talent pool under this broad term definition of talent is 2.67 million in 2005, including:

1. Party and government talent of all the formal staffs in the party organisations and public servants in the government at various levels in Shanghai.
2. Managerial talent of all the employees in managerial/administrative positions in enterprises.
3. Technical talent of all the employees on technical positions or employees doing non-technical jobs but holding professional qualifications (of any level).

However, the objective of sharpening Shanghai's competitiveness was not achieved as anticipated, since the 1995 Talent Highland Initiative was too general and vague, and lacked clear and focused directives that could guide feasible action programmes. The 1995 initiative also concentrated on the attraction and retention of high level talent and failed to adequately address the need to upgrade the skills of the existing workforce. This partially led to a severe shortage of the skilled workers who were increasingly demanded by Shanghai's modern manufacturing sectors. The restructuring and downsizing of the city's deteriorating industrial SOEs in late 1990s also distracted SMG's efforts in implementing the Talent Highland Initiative. Although the initiative had been included in Shanghai's Five-Year Plans and SMG's annual workplans since the mid 1990s, effective efforts to implement a concerted talent and skills upgrading strategy did not occur until SMG promulgated a detailed "Action Framework for Implementing Shanghai Talent Strategy" in 2004.

In 2004, the Shanghai Talent Strategy was revamped with a greater focus on the needs of Shanghai as an international metropolis and a global centre of finance, trade and shipping by 2015. The strategy was structured in a more comprehensive and consolidated way with the scope of talent development activities expanded to cover not only high-level talent, but also the skills upgrading of Shanghai's existing labour force.

The Action Framework of the Shanghai Talent Strategy defined ten priorities to be addressed between 2004 and 2010. With the approval of this action framework by the Municipal People's Congress, and committed inputs from the municipal government, the implementation of the Action Framework over the last few years has been progressing well, and outcomes are encouraging. The ten-priority programme of talent and skills development includes:

- Talent development programme for the party and government leaders.
- Programme for developing top-level leading talents (scientists, academics, and researchers).
- Talent development programme for professional managers and executives.
- Skills upgrading programme for public servants.
- Talent development programme for 21st century engineers.
- Programme for developing highly skilled workers.
- Programme for attraction of overseas talents.
- Education and training development programme.
- Talent development programme for Shangai Expo.
- Regional talent development co-operation programme.

Shanghai's talent strategy action framework set out clear time-bound goals (by 2010) for the overall talent strategy and each of the ten component programmes. It also defined the institutional settings, responsibilities, policy measures and evaluation mechanisms to support the programme's implementation. The targets of the action framework are: *i)* to expand the size of

Shanghai's talent pool from 1.49 million people in 2003 (people with a junior college diploma or above, or having a professional qualification of medium level or above) to 2.2 million people in 2010; *ii)* to increase the number of specialised technicians from 1.29 million in 2003 to 1.8 million in 2010; *iii)* to increase the number of high-skilled talent workers from 0.14 million in 2003 to 0.25 million by 2010; *iv)* to upgrade the average education level of new entrants to the labour force to 14 years of education by 2010; *v)* and to increase the number of long-term expatriates working in Shanghai from 70 000 in 2003 to 150 000 by 2010.[7]

To facilitate the timely fine-tuning and adjustment of the talent and skill development programmes in responding to the changing market, SMG has released a talent development catalogue annually since 2004 (the SMG's talent development catalogue was only updated every 3-5 years before 2004). Based on actual market information, the SMG's talent development catalogue provides key information on demand/availability of talents and human resources in various sectors, and market outlooks for sectors in which trained and skilled workers will likely be under- or over-supplied (see Box 3.2 below). The catalogue also defines the prioritised sectors or fields that those implementing the government funded talent/skills upgrading programmes should address in their annual workplans.

At the same time, policy incentives and instruments, and new institutional setups were developed and issued to support the programme implementation, and to scale up the outcomes and effectiveness of the talent/skills development programme. Effective policy instruments applied by SMG included:

- Tax incentives.
- Financial assistance (including subsidies, grants, low-cost loans).
- Social security benefits (providing local residency certificates (called *Hukou*), pension and health insurance benefits).
- Family benefits (schooling for children, jobs for spouse, and housing assistance).
- Career development (high positions in government or public academic institutions, enterprises owned by the government, and high wages).

Once the policy incentives and instruments are tested and judged to be feasible, effective and sustainable, SMG recommends that the Municipal People's Congress codifies them as local regulations. By 2006, Shanghai had issued 49 local regulations regarding the promotion of talent development, the largest number of local regulations for promoting talent/skills development in China.[8]

SMG anticipated that, upon completion of the Action Framework and its ten point talent development programme by 2010, Shanghai would have addressed the shortage of talent in key sectors, and that the city's goal of being a national pole for talent (called "Talent Highland" by SMG) would be fulfilled.

Box 3.2. **SMG's talent development catalogue**

As one of the activities identified in SMG's municipal talent strategy, Shanghai Municipal Personnel Bureau develops and issues a *Catalogue of Talent Development* (人才开发目录). The catalogue is updated and issued on an annual basis with the first edition issued in 2001. The highlight of the catalogue is the listing of talent types that are most needed or likely will be needed in a short term of 1-3 years in Shanghai. The preparation and updating of the catalogue is grounded on comprehensive information relating to Shanghai's labour market, and the inventory and registration database of the cities talent. The prioritisation of the catalogue list reflects the priorities identified in the city's mid and long term development plan (SMG's rolling Five-Year Plan), and the municipal annual work plan. It also reflects the need and changing trend of talent demand/supply on the city's labour market. As the leading organisation of the task, Shanghai Municipal Personnel Bureau conducts wide consultations with other stakeholders, including related government agencies, leaders of Shanghai's major industries, major academic institutions of HR, leading HR companies and job agencies in Shanghai. For example, in preparing and updating the catalogue of 2005 and 2006, twelve major municipal bureaus and commissions were involved and worked jointly on the task.

SMG's annual *Catalogue of Talent Development* serves as a barometer for guiding the implementation of all the talent and skills programmes under SMG's Talent Strategy. Each of these programmes is fine-tuned every year to conform with the priorities of the catalogue. The catalogue is also embraced by colleges, training institutions and vocational training schools (of both public funded and private) who take the catalogue as an important guide in designing and updating their training courses and curriculums. Shanghai Municipal Personnel Bureau and Municipal Labour and Social Security Bureau are the two key actors for developing and implementing SMG's talent and skill initiatives. They collect and maintain comprehensive information to support their work on talent policy development and talent/skills programme design. Major information that the two bureaus managed include:

1. Labour market information: sourced from *i)* the Municipal Labour and Social Security manages a web-based public platform for job application/ recruitment. In 2004, over 70 000 enterprises released their recruitment needs for total jobs of 1.003 million, and over 1.03 million applicants applied on the this job recruitment system; *ii)* job application/recruitment records from the Municipal Job Recommendation Centre and its branches that SMG established in each district; and *iii)* data and records from the official job-matching fairs organised by the Municipal Labour Bureau. In 2005, the Bureau organised 880 job-matching fairs in Shanghai. Over 48 000 enterprises participated in these job fairs with a total requirement for more than 500 000 jobs; *iv)* labour market tracking information collected and managed by a local non-public HR Agency Association (the association shares their data with the Bureaus).

Box 3.2. **SMG's talent development catalogue** *(cont.)*

2. Population census information: China conducts a full-scale national census of population every ten years, and a sample survey of population every two years (1-5% sampling). The census and sample surveys of population provide basic data of demographic and educational attainment, jobs and other essential information. At the municipal level this census is managed by the Shanghai Municipal Statistic Bureau.
3. Statistical data: the annual statistical data managed by the Municipal Statistic Bureau provides information of education (scale of enrolment in colleges and schools of various level), and other social and economic activities in the city.
4. Inventory and registration data of professional qualification and skill qualification: managed by the Municipal Personnel Bureau (responsible for professional qualification) and the Municipal Labour Bureau (responsible for worker skill qualification).
5. Information from specific surveys conducted by the two bureaus.

Attraction and retention of talent

The shortage of high-level talent in the specialised fields of management, economics, finance, information technology and new material research became a bottleneck to SMG's efforts to build up the city's competitiveness, and to develop the city into a global centre of commerce, finance, trade and shipping. The process of scaling up Shanghai's modern manufacturing sector was constrained. Parallel to reforming the city's education system to develop local talent in the key sectors, the attraction of overseas Chinese graduates and talent in the key fields was viewed as an efficient and quick way to tackle Shanghai's talent shortage in the short term.

In 2003 Shanghai launched a three-year programme to target young professionals who migrated to, and were educated in, advanced economies during the 1980s and 1990s. SMG expected to attract 10 000 talented overseas Chinese to Shanghai within three years. It sent talent recruiting delegations to countries where young Chinese talent concentrated, including the United States, Canada, UK, Germany, France, Japan, and Australia. The recruiting delegations were headed by high level SMG officials, and consisted of managers of top financial firms, VC firms and large manufacturing enterprises. Resident missions were set up in the key cities of these countries for the continuous promotion of highly paid and highly sought after positions in Shanghai to overseas Chinese talent, and to help connect the overseas talent with SMG and firms in Shanghai.

When the first phase of this overseas Chinese Talent Attraction Programme ended in late 2005, Shanghai had: successfully attracted 10 203 overseas émigrés; recruited high level talent for 4 045 positions; and assisted other returnees to set up private firms. This attraction programme was closely tied to SMG's talent development catalogue. Of the total number of more than 10 000 Chinese émigrés returned under this programme, over 60% are specialised in the fields of management, economics, finance and banking, information technology and new material technology, and 12% are specialised in law, media, and culture.

Following the success of the first phase of this attraction programme (2003 to 2005), the implementation of the second phase (2006-2008) of the programme was launched in 2006 with the goal of attracting another 10 000 talents over a three year period. The newly launched second phase expanded the scope to cover not only young overseas Chinese émigrés, but also foreign professionals, and high-skilled people in Hong Kong and Taiwan. In 2006, the programme helped to attract another 9 492 skilled people to Shanghai, including overseas Chinese (accounting for 50.5%), foreign expatriates (46.4%) and professionals from Hong Kong and Taiwan (3.1%).

Design of the Overseas Talent Attraction Programme

SMG set up a high profile programme office chaired by senior officials from the municipal government; it also established resident missions in major developed countries. The key responsibilities of this programme office and its resident missions are: *i)* promoting the programme to overseas Chinese talent; *ii)* collecting and consolidating the recruiting requirements of firms and institutions in Shanghai, and introducing these vacant positions to the communities of overseas Chinese talent; *iii)* collecting information on overseas Chinese talent and recommending candidates to firms and institutions in Shanghai; *iv)* conducting market research, monitoring and evaluating the performance of returning talent; *v)* providing advisory services and support to overseas talent regarding SMG's policies, business establishment, and adjustment assistance.[9]

The funding of the Programme is fully covered by SMG's municipal fiscal budget. SMG asks all government organisations, public universities and research institutes, public hospitals, top firms owned by SMG and state-owned banking and financial firms and institutions in Shanghai, to provide top level positions for attracting overseas talent, with the level and number of positions clearly defined by SMG for each type of institution and government owned enterprise.

Complementary to the high pay and high level positions for overseas talent, a package of policy incentives was provided by SMG:

- Local residency certificate (Shanghai *Hukou*), for returnees (and their children and spouse). For those with foreign citizenship, provision of a special residency certificate equivalent to a Shanghai *Hukou*, with full access to all the public and social security services.

- Special schooling programmes for the children of returnees to help them adjust to new living and school environments. The children of returnees have full access to the SMG's schooling and education systems, from primary school to universities.
- Returnees can apply for professional qualification certificates under Shanghai's professional qualification/certification scheme.
- Grant funding schemes at both municipal and sub municipal levels, with government fiscal input to support returnees in starting their careers, setting up private firms, and short-term lecturing in Shanghai.
- Exemption from individual income tax for returnees working in the prioritised sectors.
- Higher salary level than local employees for returnees who obtain positions in Shanghai's government institutions, public institutions and enterprises owned by SMG.

Grant funding scheme for attraction of overseas talent

As part of its Programme for the Attraction of Overseas Chinese Talent, SMG initiated a special grant funding scheme in 2005 at both the municipal and sub-municipal levels to provide funding assistance to returnees. While the high-level and high-paying positions provided to returnees by SMG can attract and retain part of the returning overseas talent pool, the scheme called Pujiang Programme,[10] can be of much more benefit to high-skilled émigrés who are considering returning to Shanghai.

Designed to support returnees to Shanghai to start their private firms and conduct research, the Pujiang Programme is managed jointly by the Shanghai Municipal Personnel Bureau and the Municipal Science Commission with an annual total grant of CNY 40 million allocated from SMG's fiscal budget. Overseas Chinese who return to Shanghai to continue their research, set up their own firms, or lecture are eligible for grant assistance from the funding scheme. Varying by sector and by activity, and in line with the priorities of SMG's talent strategy, the grant funding under this scheme ranges from CNY 50 000 to CNY 500 000 per person or per application.

Complementary to the Pujiang Funding Programme at municipal level and modelled on the same design, each of the 19 sub-municipal governments in Shanghai set up similar grant funding schemes at the district level. The size of the district grant funding scheme varies from CNY 5 million to CNY 10 million per year with input from the sub-municipal government annually.

Shanghai's programme for the attraction of overseas talent has proven to be well designed and effectively implemented. By the end of 2005, Shanghai had attracted over 63 000 overseas skilled migrants. Over 3 200 firms have been established by returnees with a total investment of USD 450 million (registered capital). The number of skilled returnees attracted to Shanghai accounts for over 33% of the total number of returning overseas talent in the whole country. In comparison, during the period of 1978-1999, a total number of 16 000 overseas talents returned to Shanghai which accounted for 16% of the total number of skilled people from overseas returning to China during the same period.

Surveys show that about 80% of skilled Chinese emigrants consider Shanghai as their first choice of destination for their career development when they return to China.[11]

Upgrading the skills of the current labour force

As China's predominant industrial base, Shanghai has one of the top largest pools of skilled workers in the country. During four decades of China's planned economy, a large number of polytechnics were established under Shanghai's state owned enterprises (SOEs) on various industrial subsectors to educate and train skilled workers needed by the SOEs. Vocational training and on-the-job training were also provided by SOEs to their employees at their polytechnics.

The large scale re-structuring and downsizing of Shanghai's industrial SOEs in the late 1990s led to a huge number of workers being made redundant. Over 1.27 million skilled workers were laid off between 1998 and 2002. Following the large-scale restructuring, Shanghai's polytechnic system, which was structured under individual SOEs, also shrank dramatically. The teaching capacity and curriculums of SOE polytechnics were typically established in line with the outdated technology and products of the parent SOEs. When Shanghai fully restructured its industry sector towards modern manufacturing in upper value chains by 2002, the city faced a big challenge: the increasing shortage of qualified workers with the skills needed by newly established manufacturing enterprises (typically manufacturers with foreign investment) or restructured large enterprises who were adopting new technology.

In addition to the shrinking number of skilled workers resulting from SOE downsizing, early retirement and the collapse of polytechnics, the quality of the worker pool was also poor. In 2003 when the shortage of skilled workers in Shanghai peaked, over 60% of the workforce had only low or very rudimentary skills. Workers with a high level of skills accounted for only 6% of Shanghai's skilled labour force. The low skills of Shanghai's labour force, in particular the scarcity of highly skilled workers, became a critical constraint for SMG to upgrade its industrial sector toward higher value-added manufacturing. In 2003, only 10-20% of the market demands for highly skilled workers could be met in Shanghai.[12] While efforts to scale up the new manufacturing industries in Shanghai were constrained by the lack of sufficiently skilled workers, what worried SMG more was the increasing number of unemployed workers resulting from SOE layoffs, the new generation of school leavers, and growing numbers of rural surplus labourers moving into the city. Although SMG had provided piecemeal job training to different jobless groups since the mid 1990s, this was typically structured to address unemployment pressures. The training initiatives were fragmented and did not contribute much towards upgrading the skills of Shanghai's labour force.

Challenged by the severe shortage of skilled workers and the pressures of increasing unemployment, SMG launched a comprehensive programme in 2003 to upgrade the skills of Shanghai's labour force. This skills upgrading programme consolidated the piecemeal job training initiatives into a systematic programme with clear objectives over the short and long term. The skills upgrading programme expanded training activities to cover all segments of Shanghai's labour force. A highlight of this programme was to fully reform the polytechnic and vocational training system in Shanghai towards market-oriented practice, and align the training programmes with the city's economic development strategy, focusing on modern manufacturing and service sectors.

Eight training programmes tailored for different labour force segments were designed and implemented under SMG's skills upgrading initiative launched in 2003:

- Skills building and upgrading: focusing on the training and skills upgrading of existing workers, new generation of school/college leavers, and jobless labour force.
- Developing highly skilled workers: expanding Shanghai's resource pool of highly skilled workers through the focused training and skills upgrading of workers such as numerical control machine operators, highly skilled nurses etc. The objective of this programme is to increase the proportion of highly skilled workers as a percentage of Shanghai's total number of skilled workers from 6% in 2003 to 15% by 2005, and 25% by 2010 to meet the market demands for highly skilled workers in Shanghai.
- Training of agriculture workers: providing training and knowledge transfer to agricultural workers in modern farming technology, processing and marketing of agricultural products.
- Training to migrant workers: providing essential job training to migrant workers in Shanghai. The majority of migrant workers do not have any skills for urban jobs.

- Establishing a continuous education and life-time learning system: A long term effort to establish life-time learning and continuous education services for residents in Shanghai.
- Establishing training centres in leading enterprises and promoting on-the-job vocational training: establishing specialised skills training centres within the enterprises of industry leaders in major industrial sub-sectors, and promoting vocational training to workers.
- Establishing a qualification-based job certification system.

Substantial efforts and fiscal inputs were made by SMG in implementing these skills upgrading and training programmes. By 2006, three years after the programmes started, achievements were observed, particularly in the components of *i)* training and skills upgrading of existing workers and the jobless labour force; *ii)* expanding the resource pool of highly-skilled workers; and *iii)* encouraging enterprises to provide vocational training to their on-job workers. The shortage of skilled workers has become a nationwide bottleneck constraining the country's industrial upgrading process. Today almost all of China's cities are struggling to tackle the shortage of skilled workers within their local markets. Shanghai is one of the very few cities in China (if not the only city) not to be heavily affected, because SMG addressed the issue one step earlier than other Chinese cities.

In 2006, SMG conducted a review and assessment of the design and implementation of its skills upgrading initiatives. Based on the results from the review and the analysis of the changes and trends of market demands, and in line with national skills building initiatives newly launched by the central government, SMG revised its municipal skills upgrading initiative in 2006. The overlapping of training activities and overlapping of implementation responsibility allocation were removed, and the training components were more consolidated and focused on five key tasks:

- Developing highly skilled workers: effectively implemented from 2003-2005 with solid and encouraging outcomes. SMG considers this component as high priority, needing continuous efforts and inputs given its significance in supporting SMG's economic development strategy in service and modern manufacturing sectors.
- Training programme for rural surplus labour: a new training initiative launched by the central government in 2004 under the national urbanisation strategy, focused on providing training to rural residents to build their basic skills for urban jobs. Training under this programme is fully funded by government (cost sharing between central and local government with major contribution from central government).
- Training for agriculture workers.

- Vocational training for on-the-job and workless labour forces.
- Training for migrant workers, where only limited achievement occurred during 2003-2005.

Design of the skills upgrading programme

The skills upgrading programme touches on many sectors and government agencies. Implementation responsibility and funding arrangements for each of the training components have been clearly defined by SMG and allocated to specific agencies for implementation through discussions with relevant agencies and lower-level government. The Municipal Labour Bureau (responsible for highly skilled worker training, vocational training, migrant worker training) and Municipal Agriculture Commission (responsible for rural surplus labour training, agriculture workers training) are the leading agencies for implementing SMG's comprehensive skills upgrading programme.

Implementation frameworks for each of the five training components (seven components before consolidation in 2006) were designed in detail, tested and further developed during implementation. Supporting instruments, policy regulations and institutional settings, funding arrangements and financial assistance were prepared and issued in Shanghai to facilitate the implementation of these training components. Given the size of the city, with a total population of 17.8 million (including 4.38 million migrants) and a labour force pool of 8.63 million people, the complexity and scale of the resources mobilised in implementing a programme of skills upgrading for the whole labour force in Shanghai is enormous. Among the five training components that are under implementation, the component of vocational training for on-the-job and workless labour forces is an example of how the training programmes in Shanghai are designed and implemented.

The training programme for groups of on-the-job workers and the workless was derived from the training assistance given to laid-off SOE employees launched in 1998 by SMG. As part of the SOEs' downsizing and re-structuring programmes, SMG provided necessary training to those laid-off by SOEs to help them build up essential skills needed for the new jobs recommended to them by SMG. Since most of the workers laid-off by SOEs had low levels of education, SMG provided training courses for jobs with low skill requirements, such as taxi driver, cook, typist, gardener, home maid service, restaurant service, etc. An implementation agency, the Shanghai Municipal Skills Training and Support Centre, was set up by SMG in 1998 under the Municipal Labour Bureau to organise and manage the training courses for redundant SOE workers. Designed as "set-meal" courses, those laid-off by SOEs picked the training courses relative to the jobs they wished to pursue. SMG provided full funding for the job training of these workers with an accumulated input of over CNY 100 million during the period of 1994-1998. Over one million redundant SOE workers were trained under this programme.

Recognising the effectiveness and contribution of the job training programme for redundant SOE workers, SMG decided to expand the job training programme to cover other labour force segments in 2002, when the industrial SOE downsizing task was completed in Shanghai.

Still managed by the Municipal Skills Training and Support Centre, SMG's skills training programme was further developed and gradually expanded to serve more segments of Shanghai's labour force: *i)* jobless groups (1998); *ii)* on-the-job workers (covered in 2002); *iii)* rural surplus labourers (2003); and *iv)* new graduates from schools and colleges (2004). SMG's skills training programme experienced a transition from a specialist training programme tailored for a specific group of the labour force (redundant SOE workers), to a comprehensive skills upgrading and training initiative covering literally all the urban labour force groups (except migrant workers). The training courses and curriculums provided by the programme were also expanded from low-skilled job training *e.g.* taxi driving, cooking, gardening, and road cleaning to higher-skilled jobs ranging from high-skilled manufacturing to financial services. Each year SMG releases a catalogue of training courses that are eligible for support from the municipal skills training initiative. The catalogue mirrors the priorities of skills and jobs defined in the municipal talent strategy. The most recent catalogue issued in 2007 has 138 types of skills training courses.

As the executive agency of SMG's skills training programme, the Municipal Skills Training and Support Centre does not provide or organise training courses itself (although it did organise "set-meal" job training courses for redundant SOE workers in its early stages). Rather, it authorises training service providers for the programme. Training service providers, including colleges, universities, private or foreign training institutes in Shanghai, can receive endorsement from the centre if they pass the training capability assessment. The list of qualified training service providers and a training course catalogue is published on the centre's website. So far, 650 training service providers have been qualified for the skills training programme. Applicants (with Shanghai *Hukou*) can choose their training course and training service provider from the list. Applicants are supposed to pay the training cost themselves in the first instance. When the course has been completed, and if the applicant successfully passes the final exams, they can get their training costs refunded from the Municipal Skills Training and Support Centre. Depending on the type of applicant, the skills training programme refunds 50-100% of training costs: 100% is refunded for jobless and rural surplus labour, 50-70% for on-the-job workers, 50% for new graduates from schools and colleges. There is no limit to the amount of training for each applicant except for the limitation of one training course per year per applicant. From 2003 to 2005, over one million workers were trained by the municipal skills training initiative, accounting for 74% of Shanghai's total number of skilled workers. In 2005, 290 000 people were trained through this programme, of which 183 000 participated in training for medium and high skills, and 127 000 were jobless or rural surplus labour.

The funding of the municipal skills training programme is provided by the municipal government, sourced from its fiscal budget.

SMG further developed the skills training initiative in 2006 with an innovative plan to establish a special account of skills training for each individual worker. Similar to a bank savings card, SMG made a personal card available to each worker with a fund of CNY 2 000 (EUR 197) on each card. The deposit on the card can only be used for the payment of training costs (technically not "real money") and cannot be cashed. The objective of this personal training account is to encourage people to plan and participate in training and to upgrade their skills, through simplifying the procedures of training payment reimbursement and pre-payment made by the trainees. The first batch of personal training accounts was created for 300 000 jobless people and rural surplus labourers in 2006 (150 000 urban jobless workers, 150 000 rural surplus labourers). It is scheduled to gradually establish individual training accounts for other eligible groups of the labour force in Shanghai.

Funding for individual training accounts comes from the municipal unemployment security fund. The "fund" in the individual training account is valid for the life-time of the holder. The average cost of training is about CNY 500 (EUR 49) per person per course in Shanghai. This means the training account can support the holder for training over four years on average. Additional funds will be transferred into the account from the municipal unemployment fund if the fund in the account is used up. The idea of creating individual training budget accounts for each worker received very positive feedback from Shanghai local residents, and received praise from the Ministry of Labour.

Integrating hard-to-reach groups into the skills development system

Of the city's total population of 17.8 million (2006), 4.38 million are migrants (long term migrants over six months), accounting for 25% of Shanghai's total population. In a rapidly aging city (age 60+ accounts for over 20% of Shanghai's local population), migrants, typically young singles or young families from rural inland areas of the country, make up a significant portion of Shanghai's labour resource pool. Of the city's 8.63 million labour force, 3.7 million are migrant workers, accounting for 42% of Shanghai's total labour resource.

Compared with the local labour force, migrant workers in Shanghai generally have a much lower level of education: only 76.3% have passed through primary school.[13] The low education level of migrant workers has led to their high concentration in low-skilled and low-paying jobs: civil construction, restaurant services, street cleaning, landscape maintenance, low-skilled manufacturing of clothing, toys, etc.

As in all other cities in China, the municipal social services in Shanghai (programmes of pension administration, healthcare, housing, unemployment, and public schooling) are limited only to local residents with a Shanghai urban *Hukou*. Without a Shanghai *Hukou*, low-skilled migrant workers are not eligible for any of SMG's subsidised skills training schemes. The reasons for blocking migrants out of the municipal subsidised training programme and other urban social services are: *i)* the limited fiscal resources that China's municipalities can allocate to scale up these schemes to cover the large migrant populations, and *ii)* the high mobility of the migrants moving between cities and regions over time, which creates concerns within the city government regarding the long-term return or benefits from their investment in upgrading the skills of migrant workers.

Shanghai's local skills strategy cannot be a complete strategy and will not achieve full success if the strategy ignores the group of migrant workers in Shanghai, which accounts for almost half of Shanghai's total labour resources. Some emerging factors recently changed SMG's perception towards integrating services and training for migrants into the city's social and talent development schemes:

- While the first generation of migrant workers from a rural area typically will return to their rural home when they age, the second generation of migrants who are born into migrant families and grow up in the city, are less likely to move back to their rural home with their parents. Born with a non-Shanghai *Hukou*, the children of migrant families number over 370 000 in Shanghai; they are not eligible for any of the public schools in Shanghai funded by SMG. As a result of this, hundreds of sub-standard small scale primary schools for migrant children (typically renting warehouses or other abandoned buildings in the suburbs) emerged in Shanghai's suburbs where migrant families concentrated. In the peak year of 2001, there were 519 sub-standard schools for migrant children in Shanghai suburbs.[14] The education quality in these informal primary schools for migrant children is far below national requirements and standards for primary education.

  The national urbanisation initiative launched by the central government requests local governments to gradually phase out the *Hukou* system which strictly separates the access to public services for local and non-local residents. Although the deadline for removal of the *Hukou* system is not defined, SMG understands that it is only a matter of time. The migrant population, particularly the young generation of migrants, will eventually be entitled to the same full residency status as local residents. In 2004, recognising the consequences of having a large proportion of the city's future population with sub-standard primary education, SMG eventually issued a regulation requiring all the sub-municipal governments in Shanghai, (responsible for providing public schooling services), to completely remove the public schooling barrier and provide full access to the public education system for migrant children, as is the case for local children with Shanghai *Hukou*.

- A sizeable pool of low cost workers is critical to many sectors of Shanghai's economy, particularly the construction sector, commercial services (restaurants and hotels), and to the large amount of export-oriented labour intensive industries in Shanghai's suburban districts. To increase the commitment of migrant workers to their jobs in Shanghai, in 2002 SMG established a social security scheme for migrant workers under the existing municipal social security system, providing basic security benefits of insurance against injury at work, healthcare, and pensions.

Training and skills upgrading for migrant workers in Shanghai

The need for training and skills upgrading for migrants was addressed in Shanghai's training and skills upgrading initiatives issued in 2003 and 2006, with a specific component of migrant worker training defined. While the other training and skills upgrading components earmarked for local workers with Shanghai *Hukou* are pooled at the municipal level and implemented through executive agencies at the municipal level, the implementation responsibilities for the training of migrant workers are decentralised to district governments. With no codified funding assistance from the municipal government towards migrant worker training, it is fully subject to the capacity and decision of each district government to design the training the district wants to provide to migrant workers.

In the suburban districts where the predominant portion of Shanghai's manufacturing enterprises are located, such as Jiading, Baoshan, Minhang, and Songjiang, the district governments have a much better understanding of the need for migrant worker training than in urban districts. These suburban districts have a large number of migrant workers attracted by jobs in manufacturing factories. Recognising the importance of low-cost migrant workers to a local economy predominated by manufacturing industries, these suburban district governments have designed and implemented various training schemes tailored for migrant workers to upgrade their skills. Initiated by district government, these training courses and curriculum are typically prepared jointly by the district government, enterprises recruiting migrant workers, and training schools in the district. Training is designed in line with the specific needs of the enterprises. Funding is shared by the enterprises and the trainee. Both district and town governments provide *ad hoc* subsidies to these training programmes. During the period 2001-2004, 264 000 migrant workers were trained in these suburban districts.[15]

With the enterprise and individual migrant worker mainly covering training costs (*ad hoc* and very limited financial input from the government), the scale and level of training for migrant workers is too small in Shanghai, given the size of the migrant labour force and enterprise needs in these suburban districts and especially compared with the achievement of vocational training and skills upgrading programmes for local workers with Shanghai *Hukou*.

In Shanghai's central urban districts, migrant workers typically take low-skilled and low-paying jobs in landscaping maintenance, street cleaning, home maid service, caring for the aged, etc. The urban district governments organise training for migrant workers focused on transferring the essential know-how of these jobs. Compared to training for migrant workers in the manufacturing sector, which has a much higher skills requirement, the average cost for migrant training in the urban districts, for low-skilled jobs, is much lower. The cost of migrant training for urban service jobs is shared by the urban district government and the trainee. The estimated number of migrant trainees in Shanghai's urban districts is around 350 000 per year.[16]

Training and skills upgrading activities for migrant workers in Shanghai scaled up dramatically in 2006. What triggered this change is a top-down national training scheme for migrant workers. In 2004, China's central government launched a nation-wide training scheme for rural surplus labourers under a strategic initiative to accelerate the country's urbanisation process. The objective of this national training programme for rural surplus labour, the China Sunshine Project, is to provide government subsidised training to the increasing number of surplus workers in China's rural areas, assisting them to acquire essential skills for urban jobs when they migrate to cities. Training under the Sunshine Project is fully funded by government grants. The central government contributes the major proportion of the grant and local government is required to contribute some counterpart funds.

The Sunshine Project is scheduled to: *i)* train 5 million rural surplus labourers during 2004-2005, with priority allocated to the country's poorest regions and major out-flowing regions of migrant workers; *ii)* train 30 million rural surplus labourers during 2006-2010, with training assistance expanded to cover the whole country. This means the destination cities of migrant workers, such as Shanghai and Beijing will also receive some grant assistance from the Sunshine Project to subsidise training for migrant workers. In 2004 and 2005, the central government provided grants of CNY 250 million and CNY 400 million to this national Sunshine Project.[17]

Through the national Sunshine Project, SMG raised CNY 45 million in 2006 (including grants from central government, and requested counterpart funds from municipal government). The funds of CNY 45 million were allocated to 19 districts in Shanghai, and earmarked for providing government subsidised training to the migrant workers in Shanghai. With the solid grant assistance from the central and municipal governments, training and skills upgrading for migrant workers in Shanghai scaled up dramatically, particularly in Shanghai's suburban industrial districts where migrant workers are concentrated. SMG recently approved a proposal to build a Training Centre for Migrant Workers, with a central campus attached to the Shanghai Industrial Technology College, and branch training centres of each of Shanghai's 19 districts. Migrant workers in Shanghai, a sizeable hard-to-reach group of Shanghai's labour force, are therefore gradually beginning to integrate into the city's skills upgrading system.

Implementation and allocation of tasks to different stakeholders

As in many other countries, the design and implementation of Shanghai's talent and skill upgrading strategies touches on many stakeholders. In principle, the talent and skills upgrading initiatives in Shanghai are structured into two packages: 1) "Shanghai Talent Highland Strategy" focusing on sectors of high level human resources (party and government leaders, academics and scientists, managers and executives, overseas talents); and 2) "Shanghai Skills Upgrading Initiative" which focuses on skills upgrading and vocational training to the labour force in Shanghai.

In line with the unique political and governance systems in China, the China's Communist Party Commission of Shanghai, which is the real leading organisation at China's local government level, takes the lead for the preparation of "Shanghai Talent Highland Strategy". The personnel department of Shanghai's Party Commission, on behalf of the Party Commission, is the key agency for organising the design of the overall Shanghai's Talent Strategy and the implementation framework. The implementation responsibilities of each programme defined in the strategy and framework are allocated to relevant agencies (commissions or bureaus) of Shanghai Municipal Government depending on the nature and scope of each programme.[18] The Shanghai Municipal Personnel Bureau is the key executive agency for the implementation of most programmes under Shanghai's Talent Highland Strategy. Typically, a programme office is established and stationed in the programme executive bureau or commission for the purposes of programme implementation and management. For example, as the designated executive agency for the "Programme for attraction of overseas talent", the Personnel Department of Shanghai's Party Commission and Shanghai Municipal Personnel Bureau jointly set up and chaired a Programme Office stationed in the Municipal Personnel Bureau. Staffing of this programme office includes the full-time representatives from other municipal agencies that are involved in the programme (Municipal Science and Technology Commission, Municipal Education Commission, etc).

Shanghai Municipal Government takes the full lead in designing and implementing "Shanghai Skills Upgrading Initiative". An institutional arrangement of joint meetings was established to jointly prepare the initiative, design skill upgrading programmes, and coordinate the implementation of the initiatives.[19] The joint meeting is chaired by the top leader of SMG with members consisting of representatives from *i)* the relating government agencies (municipal education commission, labour and social security bureau, personal bureau, fiancé bureau, planning commission, construction commission, commerce commission, agriculture commission; *ii)* leading enterprises of the key industries in Shanghai, and business chambers; and *iii)* training providers. A general office supporting the joint meetings was also set up and stationed in the Municipal Education Commission to manage the implementation of the Skills Upgrading Initiative. The implementation responsibility of each programme defined in the Skills Initiative was commissioned to the relating government agencies. The Municipal Labour and Social Security Bureau is the leading and executing agency for implementing most programmes under this initiative. A programme implementation unit, typically a programme office, is established within the agencies to manage and execute the programme the agencies are responsible for. For example, the Municipal Labour and Social Security Bureau established a programme implementation unit under the bureau, "Municipal Skills Training and Support Centre", for the "Programme of skills building and upgrading" for jobless groups, new graduates, and existing workers. The following figure shows the implementation responsibility allocation of various programmes under Shanghai's talent and skills upgrading initiatives.

Budget

Under the fiscal arrangement between the Central Government and Shanghai Municipal Government, SMG has the prime responsibility for HR/ education expenditures. Except for the fiscal transfers from Central Government for part of the budget of universities/colleges at national level in Shanghai, and occasionally some *ad hoc* grants earmarked for migrant worker training, the entire HR and education budget is fully covered by SMG's fiscal resources. SMG, as for other local governments in China, has full responsibility for providing public education and training services within its territory, including planning, implementing, and financing the Municipal Talent Strategy and Skill Upgrading Initiatives.

SMG's fiscal input in Shanghai's HR activities can be typically grouped into three types: education budget, skill upgrading and vocational training budget, and budget for attraction and retention of talent.

1. **SMG's education budget:** A rapid increase of the education budget, from CNY 21.3 billion in 2001 to CNY 40.4 billion in 2005, reflects SMG's increasing priorities in education and HR development. Typically, the government

Figure 3.6. **Implementation arrangements for the Shanghai talent and skills upgrading initiatives**

		"Shanghai Talent Highland Strategy"								"Shanghai Skills Upgrading Initiative"						
	Key programme under the "Shanghai Talent Highland Strategy" and "Shanghai Skills Upgrading Initiative"	Talent Development Programme for the Party and Government Leaders	Programme for Developing Top-Level Leading Talents (Academics and Scientists)	Talent Development Programme for Professional Managers and Executives	Skills Upgrading Programme for Public Servants	Talent Development Programme for 21st Century Engineers	Programme for Developing Highly Skilled Workers	Programme for Attraction of Overseas Talents	Talent Development Programme for Shanghai Expo 2010	Skills Building and Upgrading for Jobless Groups, New Graduates, and Existing Workers	Programme of Developing Highly Skilled Workers	Training of Agriculture Worker	Training to Migrant Workers	Establishing Continuous Education and Life-time Learning System	Establishing Training Centres in Leading Enterprise and Promoting On-the-job Vocational Training	Establishing a Qualification-Based Job Certification System
	Personal Department of Shanghai Communist Party Commission	■	■					■								
Shanghai Municipal Government	Municipal Personnel Bureau	o	o	■	■	■	o	■	o					o		■
Shanghai Municipal Government	Municipal Science and Technology Commission		■			✓		o						o		
Shanghai Municipal Government	Municipal Education Bureau		o			o		o		o				■		
Shanghai Municipal Government	Municipal Labour and Social Security Bureau				✓		■	✓		■	■	✓	■		■	o
Shanghai Municipal Government	Municipal Agr. Commission											■	✓			
Shanghai Municipal Government	Municipal Adm. Commission of State-owned Assets			o			✓	✓								
Shanghai Municipal Government	Shanghai EXPO Bureau								■							
Shanghai Municipal Government	Municipal Public Security Bureau							✓								
Shanghai Municipal Government	Municipal Foreign Affair Office							✓								
	District Government							✓				o	o			
	Colleges and Training Agencies			✓	✓	✓	✓			✓	✓	✓	✓	✓	✓	
	Enterprises, Industry leaders, Business chambers			✓						✓	✓		✓		o	
	Labour Union						o			✓			✓			

■ Leading and executing agency of programme implementation
o Key supporting agency to programme implementation
✓ Partially involved in programme implementation

Source: Chreod.

resources (including both central and municipal government's inputs) accounts for 65-70% of Shanghai's annual education budget. In the year of 2005, government resources accounted for 66% of Shanghai's total education budget, of which 24% was central government's contribution, and 42% was SMG's contribution.

However, in a global context, SMG's fiscal input in education has been still relatively low in terms of education budget as % of GDP. In 2005, Shanghai's education budget accounted for 3.04% of the city's GDP, comparing with a global average of 5.5% in 1999 (6+ % for advanced countries, and 4+ % for developing countries). Although higher than China's national average, SMG's education budget as % of GDP is considerably lower than Beijing's.

2. **Skill upgrading and vocational training budget:** At municipal level, SMG's budgets for skill upgrading and vocational training come from two primary funding sources: tax revenue, from the Municipal Education Surcharge, and the Municipal Unemployment Fund. SMG has committed 30% of total tax revenues from the education surcharge to finance polytechnic education targeted to skills upgrading and training of Shanghai's labour force. Parallel to the budget input from the municipal level, all the district governments are required to arrange earmarked funds from their annual district government budget for vocational training and skill upgrading activities implemented at district levels. Complementary to these codified public resources from municipal and district governments budgets for skill upgrading and vocational training activities, additional funds from both municipal and district government are arranged for some specific skills upgrading or vocational training programmes on a programme basis (*ad hoc*).
3. **Budget for attraction of talent:** SMG allocated an annual budget of CNY 40 million from its fiscal resources to finance the Programme of Attraction Overseas Talent. Complementary to this municipal budget, each of the 19 sub-municipal governments in Shanghai has a similar budget arrangement to finance the Overseas Talent Attraction Programme at the district level (which is modeled on the design of the municipal programme). The size of the district budget varies from CNY 5 million to CNY 10 million per year with input from the sub-municipal government annually.

The aggregated size of Shanghai's public budget for talent strategy and skill upgrading initiatives in Shanghai is not publicly available. Given the institutional complexity of programme implementation (implementation allocated to various agencies of municipal and district governments) and substantial diversity of funding sources (codified budgets, additional *ad hoc* programme budget from public finance of both municipal and district government), it is difficult to gauge SMG's total budget on talent and skills upgrading.

Conclusions

The Municipal Talent Development Strategy and Skills Upgrading Initiative have been central to SMG in developing, managing and upgrading the city's human resources in line with the city's dynamic economic growth over the last decade. Strategic planning approaches are widely applied in SMG's practice of designing and implementing these skills strategies and initiatives. SMG's talent strategies and skills programmes are grounded in a clear vision of becoming a competitive global city. SMG's talent strategies and skill upgrading initiatives, HR policies and policy instruments that facilitate the strategies' implementation are reviewed and updated on a regular basis to account for changes, trends, challenges and opportunities emerging from the rapid growth of the metropolis and Yangtze Delta region, and from changes in global markets. These municipal strategies are explicitly addressed and disseminated to the various stakeholders involved in the city's HR development: municipal government organisations, lower-level governments, industries, education and training service providers, and individuals.

The outcome from these policies and instruments are encouraging. The number of highly skilled workers as a percentage of Shanghai's total skill workers increased to 14.98% by 2005, compared with 6.2% in 2002, and 9.4% in 2003. However, compared to the rapid increase of market demand for high-skilled workers in the city's labour market, the supply gap is still large: less than 30% of the market demand for high-skilled workers can be met in Shanghai's labour market in 2005. At the same, in the Yangtze Delta Region, only 10% of market demand for high-skilled workers could be met. SMG expects to increase this portion to 25% by 2010.

Innovation is a noteworthy feature of SMG's talent strategy and skills upgrading initiative. Many innovative mechanisms including institutional arrangements, financial instruments, and operational tools were explored, developed, and widely applied after pilot testing. Examples include: *i)* reform to public vocational training delivered directly by the municipal government, replacing it with a new approach of tendering the training provision to qualified training schools (including introduction of a qualification scheme of training service providers), supported by state financial subsidies to individuals who need training; *ii)* establishment of a special account for skills training for each worker to encourage individuals to upgrade their skills; *iii)* the grant-based "Pujiang Programme" for attracting overseas talent, and incentives designed under this programme, including the provision of "Shanghai Residence Certification" to returnees. Many of these innovations in Shanghai were unprecedented in China, and were later introduced to other cities in China.[20]

While many challenges could constrain the effectiveness and efficiency of SMG's efforts to develop the city's talent pool and upgrade the skills of its labour force, the institutional factor is one of the critical issues that SMG has confronted in its HR development activities. Due to the unique political and governance structure in China, particularly at local government levels, the design and implementation of SMG's talent/skills strategies and programme is fragmented across a large number of government organisations at both municipal and sub-municipal levels. With the implementation and co-financing responsibilities dispersed across agencies at various levels (in many cases one programme is allocated to two or more agencies for joint implementation), common understanding, joint-efforts, and cross-institutional coordination and collaboration are critical to ensure the productive and effective outcomes of SMG's skills strategy as a whole. Although SMG has allocated considerable attention to this issue, improvements in inter-agency communication, coordination, and performance measurement and monitoring are still required.

Note: All sources are in Chinese.

Notes

1. *China Statistical Yearbook 2004.*
2. *Shanghai Statistical Yearbook 2006.*
3. *Shanghai Statistical Yearbook 2006, China Statistical Yearbook 2006.*
4. The municipal talent strategy was first initiated in 1994 by Shanghai Municipal Government, which was a precedent among all the local governments in China. In late 2003, the Central Government adopted the talent strategy as a national policy with high priority (2003-12-20, 中共中央国务院召开全国人才工作会议). Under this directive from the central government, talent strategies were soon prepared and implemented by all local governments throughout the country.
5. Sun Luyi, "Talent Strategy and International Metropoli", page 23.
6. Cai Zheren: "Objective, Strategy, Policy: A Strategic Program to Build Shanghai as Talent Highland", p. 22.
7. Communist Party Commission of Shanghai: "Action Framework for Implementation of Shanghai Talent Strategy", 2004-11-11.
8. Shanghai Personnel Bureau: "Study of Establishing Local Regulation for Talent Strategy in Shanghai", 2006, page 10.
9. Huang Weimao, "China Scholars Abroad", 2005-8-23.
10. Pujiang is the name of a major river in Shanghai, considered as a "mother river" of the city.
11. "News Evening" (新闻晚报), 2005-1-11.
12. Wang Sirui, China Business News (第一财经), 27 June, 2005. By 2005, about 30% of the market demands for highly skilled workers could be met in Shanghai.
13. Wang Liming, Vol. 7, 2005 "Tansuo Yu Zhengming" (探索与争鸣).
14. Jiefang Daily, 10 September 2001, Shanghai.
15. China Ministry of Education, 1 August 2005.
16. China Ministry of Education, 1 August, 2005.
17. Xinhua News, 28 June 2005.
18. Communist Party Commission of Shanghai: "Action Framework for Implementation of Shanghai Talent Strategy", issued on 11 November 2004 (上海市实施人才强市战略行动纲要).
19. Shanghai Municipal Government: "Directive for Promoting Vocational Training in Shanghai", issued on 10 February 2003 (上海市职业教育工作联席会议).
20. China Labour and Social Security News, 12 January 2006.

Bibliography

Cai Zheren (2000), "Objective, Strategy, Policy: A Strategic Program to Build Shanghai as Talent Highland", Jiaotong University Publishing House.

Communist Party Commission of Shanghai (2004), "Action Framework for Implementation of Shanghai Talent Strategy", issued on 11 November 2004.

Ding Xuexiang (2007), "First Resource: Research on Shanghai Talent Strategy 2005", Shanghai Social Science Publishing House.

Pan Cengguang (2006), "Report on the Development of Chinese Talents", Vol. 3, Social Sciences Academic Press.

Shanghai Municipal Government (2006), "Directive for Promoting Vocational Training in Shanghai", issued on 10 May 2006.

Shanghai Municipal Government (2003), "Directives to Promote the Reform and Development of Vocational Training in Shanghai", issued on 10 February 2003.

Shanghai Personnel Bureau (2006), "Study of Establishing Local Regulation for Talent Strategy in Shanghai".

Sun Luyi (2002), "Talent Strategy and International Metropolis", Shanghai People's Publishing House.

Wang Weiyi (2005), "Strategy to Attract Return Talents after China's Accession to WTO", Economic Science Press.

Wu Hanming (1999), "Talent Highland and Shanghai Development Strategy", Wenhui Publishing House.

Ye Zhonghai (2006), "Research on Regional Talent Development", Sanlian Press.

ANNEX 3.A1

Shanghai Data Summary

Table 3.A1.1. **Demographic information**

	2001	2002	2003	2004	2005
Demography					
Local population (million)	13.27	13.34	13.42	13.52	13.60
Age group: ≤ 17				1.70	1.61
Age group: 18-34				3.17	3.23
Age group: 35-59				6.04	6.09
Age group: ≤ 60				2.61	2.66
Migrant population (million)			4.99	5.36	5.81
# of migrants stay less than 6 months			1.16	1.32	1.42
# of migrants stay longer than 6 months			3.83	4.04	4.38
Total population (local + migrants ≤ 6 months, million)			17.25	17.56	17.99
Retired					
Number of retired people (million)	2.40	2.47	2.55	2.65	2.91
% of retired people in local population (%)	18.07	18.51	18.97	19.62	21.37

Source: Shanghai Statistical Yearbook 2001-2005.

Table 3.A1.2. **Employment**

	2001	2002	2003	2004	2005
Employment[1]					
Total number of employee (million)	7.52	7.92	8.13	8.37	8.63
By sector					
Primary sector (million)	0.87	0.84	0.74	0.67	0.61
Secondary sector (million)	3.10	3.21	3.17	3.16	3.22
Tertiary sector (million)	3.55	3.87	4.22	4.54	4.80
By subsectors					
Farming	871 800	842 400	737 200	672 900	610 200
Mining	700	500	300	700	600
Manufacturing	2 697 900	2 834 900	2 760 200	2 720 300	2 753 200
Power, gas and water production	60 200	57 200	56 400	56 200	54 900
Construction	340 300	316 700	354 300	382 500	414 600
Transportation and warehousing	322 300	323 400	459 000	477 000	484 000
Information, computer service and software			71 000	78 500	94 800
Retail and wholesale	908 200	1 017 900	1 138 000	1 255 300	1 313 100
Hotel and restaurant services	110 500	137 500	235 100	230 500	236 000
Finance	110 700	1 262	173 200	159 200	182 400
Real estate industry	87 700	87 900	288 700	289 400	289 600
Leasing and business service	78 000	76 400	216 000	381 100	458 700
Science research, technical service and surveying	100 100	91 800	123 900	133 500	152 300
Water/environmental/public facility management	8 600	7 000	77 200	67 000	67 400
Resident service and other services	724 200	867 200	734 300	747 300	783 000
Education	291 500	265 700	275 400	273 000	276 300
Health, social security and welfare	171 900	143 200	163 300	176 700	182 900
Culture, sports and entertainment	50 200	45 600	81 400	82 800	82 500
Public administration and social organisations	158 400	165 800	185 600	184 800	196 700
Others	429 400	638 038			
Unemployment[1]					
Number of registered urban unemployed	257 200	287 800	301 100	274 300	275 000
Registered urban unemployment rate (%)	4.3	4.8	4.9	4.5	4.4
Employment agencies[2]					
Number of job/employment agencies			464	458	
Number of vacancies registered			1 458 400	1 514 200	
Number of people registered as seeking a job			1 216 700	1 288 700	
Of which: woman			533 800	551 700	
Laid-off workers			152 500	151 100	
Unemployed			613 100	694 300	
People with job qualifications			87 100	181 600	

Table 3.A1.2. **Employment** *(cont.)*

	2001	2002	2003	2004	2005
Number of people receiving career training			866 400	882 300	
Number of people got a job through employment agencies			425 400	466 500	
Of which: woman			203 100	214 700	
Laid-off workers			73 500	65 800	
Unemployed			223 600	272 600	
People with job qualifications			82 700	111 400	

1. Data from *Shanghai Statistical Yearbook 2001-2005.*
2. Data from Shanghai Municipal Labour and Social Security Bureau.

Table 3.A1.3. **Education and skills**

	2001	2002	2003	2004	2005
Education[1]					
Number of schools	2013	1902	1 839	1 726	1 694
University and college	45	50	57	59	60
Secondary schools	1 084	1 069	1 065	990	966
Specialized secondary schools	82	82	83	82	81
Vocational secondary schools	54	48	55	42	37
Polytechnic schools	83	83	83	44	41
Regular high schools	865	857	844	822	807
Primary schools	852	751	686	648	640
Special schools	32	32	31	29	28
Number of full-time teachers	127 800	125 700	123 000	128 500	131 000
University and college	21 700	22 900	24 400	28 700	31 800
Secondary schools	62 200	61 200	61 200	61 300	60 800
Specialized secondary schools	5 100	5 000	5 300	5 300	5 300
Vocational secondary schools	3 700	3 500	3 600	3 400	3 100
Polytechnic schools	2 300	2000	1 500	1 300	2 300
Regular high schools	51 100	50 700	50 800	51 300	51 200
Primary schools	43 000	40 600	38 800	37 500	37 400
Special schools	900	1 000	1 000	1 000	1 000
Number of graduates	544 100	548 000	529 500	521 500	539 000
University and college	42 800	55 200	71 200	88 600	103 400
Secondary schools	326 400	334 600	328 800	322 400	325 500
Specialized secondary schools	29 400	29 400	33 900	30 800	33 900
Vocational secondary schools	33 600	25 800	22 000	23 500	23 400
Polytechnic schools	14 300	15 500	15 200	11 300	14 300
Regular high schools	249 100	263 900	257 700	256 800	253 900
Primary schools	174 300	157 600	128 700	109 700	109 300
Special schools	600	600	800	800	800
Number of new student enrolment		553 400	532 800	523 200	502 800
University and college		109 200	120 300	130 600	131 800
Secondary schools		342 500	311 300	286 400	266 700
Specialized secondary schools		39 300	43 400	38 700	33 300
Vocational secondary schools		26 600	21 100	18 500	18 400
Polytechnic schools		16 400	16 400	11 100	6 000
Regular high schools		260 200	230 400	218 100	209 000
Primary schools		101 100	100 500	105 500	103 600
Special schools		600	700	700	700
Number of student enrolment	2 052 400	2 045 400	2 039 400	2 027 900	1 975 800
University and college	280 000	331 600	378 500	415 700	442 600
Secondary schools	1 044 100	1 035 900	1 007 100	1 069 400	993 000
Specialized secondary schools	121 200	126 600	136 900	140 500	136 700
Vocational secondary schools	75 200	75 600	70 400	64 300	57 600
Polytechnic schools	45 400	44 000	45 100	36 800	28 500
Regular high schools	802 300	789 700	754 700	827 800	770 200

Table 3.A1.3. **Education and skills** *(cont.)*

	2001	2002	2003	2004	2005
Primary schools	722 800	672 400	648 300	537 400	535 000
Special schools	5 500	5 500	5 500	5 400	5 200
Vocational education/Training[1]					
Adult education of university/college level					
Number of schools/college	31	30	27	22	21
Number of graduates	27 600	30 800	42 400	49 100	56 400
New students enrolment	53 800	67 300	72 200	72 200	65 000
Students enrolment	138 300	170 900	198 000	147 000	147 200
Number of full-time teachers	2 400	2 200	2 100	1 800	1 500
Adult secondary education					
Number of schools	439	345	106	93	65
Number of graduates	140 300	127 100	38 700	51 400	27 800
New students enrolment	207 800	177 300	5 000	3 800	3 700
Students enrolment	173 400	130 600	71 300	65 700	41 100
Number of full-time teachers	4 500	3 300	1 000	1 000	900
Adult vocational training					
Number of training schools	822	630	726	612	901
Number of graduates	718 200	144 600	174 200	105 200	198 200
New students enrolment					
Students enrolment	264 500	75 100	193 700	133 200	354 300
Number of full-time teachers	4 100	3 600	5 500	4 200	7 400
Education budget[1]					
Total annual education budget (Y billion)	21.29	24.49	29.17	35.97	40.43
Allocation from Central Gov's budget (Y bn)	4.59	6.05	7.21	9.01	9.72
Allocation from local Gov's. budget (Y bn)	11.00	10.35	11.30	13.61	16.97
Funds of private sector for running schools (Y bn)	0.71	1.01	1.33	2.04	2.02
Donations (Y bn)	0.31	0.54	0.58	0.58	0.24
Tuitions (Y bn)	2.68	3.40	5.04	6.48	7.47
Other funds for education (Y bn)	2.00	3.15	3.71	4.25	4.01

Table 3.A1.3. **Education and skills** *(cont.)*

	Local residents		Migrants	
	# of people	%	# of people	%
Skill Levels: education attainment[2]				
Total number of people	**1 321 6300**		**3 500 200**	
With education of primary school and below	3 863 000	29%	1 046 700	30%
With education of junior high school	4 864 000	37%	1 933 500	55%
With education of senior high school	3 042 000	23%	391 800	11%
With education of university and above	1 446 000	11%	128 200	4%

1. Data from *Shanghai Statistical Yearbook 2001-2005*, Note 2: Data from Shanghai Municipal Labour and Social Security Bureau.
2. Data from Shanghai Municipal Labour and Social Security Bureau.

PART II

Chapter 4

Michigan Regional Skills Alliances: A Statewide Initiative to Address Local Workforce Needs

by

Randall Eberts and Kevin Hollenbeck

The Michigan Regional Skills Alliance (MiRSA) Initiative, launched in 2004, offered thirteen local regions one-year start-up grants to develop local strategies to increase the skills and labour market success of individuals, and provide a collaborative approach through which local employers would benefit from a more skilled workforce. The state's labor market information agency helped applicants by providing a cluster-type analysis of the local labour market and forecasts of employment trends and occupational needs. The implementation strategies varied by region and were based upon the identified needs of the targeted businesses as well as the collective thinking of the local partnership. This chapter reviews the success of the initiative, evaluating how it has impacted on working practices in the state.

Introduction

In May 2004, Governor Granholm announced that the state of Michigan would launch a new initiative designed to "help employers and workers in Michigan improve their competitiveness and economic security"[1]. With the financial assistance of the Charles Stewart Mott Foundation (a charitable foundation located in Michigan), the state of Michigan offered one-year start-up grants totalling over USD 1 million for the initial development of up to 12 Michigan Regional Skills Alliances (MiRSAs)[2] across the state. The purpose of these partnerships was to bring together key local entities to address workforce issues affecting firms operating in a targeted industry in a distinct geographic area. As stated in the initial press release, the prospective bidders for the grants "must clearly demonstrate the problem or set of problems facing their regional industry and how their alliance will focus on meeting employer needs and improve the ability of people to gain employment". The overall goal of MiRSAs is to provide Michigan employers with a highly skilled workforce and to provide Michigan citizens with jobs that offer good wages and opportunities for career advancement.

The objectives of MiRSAs are consistent with the three elements of a skills strategy emphasised in Chapter 1 (attracting and retaining talent, upgrading the skills of the low qualified and integrating the disadvantaged into the labour market). MiRSAs are business-driven, business-focused partnerships that address workforce needs in a specific region and industry sector at least partly through attracting and retaining talent. They are focused on developing a workforce qualified to fill the current and future needs of businesses in specific sectors by training current workers and preparing future workers with the appropriate skills and career aspirations. MiRSAs, by their emphasis on meeting the needs of business, focus on upgrading the skills of current workers by forging partnerships among key regional stakeholders to provide workers with the skills training that business in their region seek. A priority of MiRSAs is also to prepare less qualified workers to fill the needs of business.

To meet these objectives, the MiRSA initiative depends upon the ability to bring together key organisations and leaders in order to form effective partnerships, to identify the pertinent issues facing business, to develop and agree upon an effective strategy to address those issues, to find the funds to provide training and other services to workers, and to support the administrative infrastructure necessary to keep the partnership together and functioning effectively.

The purpose of this chapter is to describe the partnership initiative in Michigan and to provide insights, through evaluating the experience of these 13 MiRSAs, into the attributes of MiRSAs that lead to successful and effective partnerships. The analysis draws in part from an evaluation of the programme conducted by W.E. Upjohn Institute for Employment Research in 2005. While the MiRSAs studied for this report are located in a single state, the regions in which they operate differ in the structure and vitality of their economies, in the size of businesses, and in the types of organisations and institutions that are potential key partners. The variation in circumstances and experience provides an opportunity to assess the various ways in which stakeholders from diverse regions come together to identify and address the specific workforce issues that they have identified. By being spawned through a single initiative with the same rules and procedures and roughly the same amount of funding, the 13 MiRSAs provide a useful "laboratory" to study which approaches work better than others.

Profile of Michigan's economy

Michigan is located in the heartland of the United States. The eleventh largest state by land area, its 96 000 square miles touches four of the five Great Lakes. The state is divided into two distinct regions, the Upper and Lower Peninsulas, which are separated by the Mackinac Straits connecting Lakes Michigan and Huron. The Upper Peninsula holds vast tracts of forests and rich deposits of minerals. The economy there depends upon forest products and resource extraction. The Lower Peninsula also is heavily forested, particularly in the northern parts, but in the southern third of the state the land opens to rich agricultural land, which grows large quantities of the nation's apples and cherries in addition to producing other crops and dairy products. More than 11 000 lakes dot Michigan's terrain, covering nearly 40% of its land area. That, along with the 3 100 miles of shoreline, makes tourism a leading industry in many parts of the state.

The majority of Michigan's 10.2 million people reside in the lower third of the state, where a relatively large proportion of the workforce is employed in manufacturing. Michigan is one of the nation's leading manufacturing states. It was the centre of the industrial boom in the United States during the first part of the 20th century with the development of the mass production of automobiles and other manufacturing processes. Today, the economy is still highly dependent upon goods-producing activities, with the auto industry dominating, although not as much as in previous years. Manufacturing accounts for 18% of Michigan's output and 14.5% of its employment, both significantly higher than the national average of 12.1% and 10.3%, respectively.

The predominance of high-value manufacturing has provided Michigan workers with a relatively high standard of living. Manufacturing wages are among the highest in the country and the highest among the Great Lakes states, averaging USD 22 per hour compared with the national average of USD 16. The high wages and the concentration of manufacturing jobs have resulted in per capita income in 2005 of USD 32 804, which is slightly below the national average of USD 34 471. A decade ago, Michigan's per capita income exceeded the national average, but the decline in manufacturing, particularly the auto industry, has led to a decline in Michigan's living standard.

Michigan has been bombarded in recent years by global competition and the inability to generate and attract other high-value-added activities to replace the declining auto industry and other traditional industries. At the time the Regional Skills Alliance initiative was announced in May 2004, the performance of Michigan's economy was among the worst in the country. The 2001-2002 recession hit Michigan particularly hard. Its unemployment rate reached 7.1%, 2 percentage points higher than the national average and tied with Mississippi for the highest rate in the country. Only five years earlier, Michigan registered one of the lowest unemployment rates in the nation. Prior to the recession, Michigan's employment grew at a rate only slightly below that of the nation. However, while much of the rest of the country was emerging from the recession by 2003, Michigan's employment continued to fall. By 2005, Michigan's employment declined 5.7% from its peak of 4.85 million in 2000. Hardest hit was the manufacturing sector which shed 24% of its workers during that five-year period, while the nation lost only 7.5% of its manufacturing workers. Even Michigan's service-providing sector continued to lose jobs. While this sector helped to pull the national economy out of the recession, Michigan's service-providing sector was unable to stimulate the state economy.

Michigan's economic problems are concentrated to a large extent in the transportation sector. Highly dependent on the "Big Three" domestic automakers – General Motors, Ford and Chrysler-Daimler, Michigan's economy suffered significantly from their accelerated loss of market share since the beginning of this decade. During the 1990s, the auto companies contributed a positive 1 000 jobs per year to the state's employment base, but in the current decade this turned around to a loss of 10 000 jobs per year. With the large indirect effects of the auto industry on Michigan's economy through supply chains and the demand for services (the employment multiplier for motor vehicles is about 5), the loss of jobs in the motor vehicle sector has spilled over into the service-providing sectors, contributing to its poor performance relative to the nation.

Michigan's economic condition has worsened during the recession that began in December 2007. The state's auto industry has continued to suffer job losses, with both General Motors and Chrysler declaring bankruptcy in the spring of 2009. During the 12-month period ending in May 2009, employment at the state's motor vehicle assemblers plunged by 42.8% while its auto part manufacturers cut 35.5% of their workers. At the beginning of the decade, Michigan's share of auto assemblers was around 33%; in 2009 it is below 25%. Auto parts employment in Michigan follows a similar trend: its share fell from 27% in 2000 to below 20% in 2009. Put more starkly, Michigan has lost more auto assembly and parts jobs from 2000 to the present than what currently remains. Job losses extended into almost every other major sector of Michigan's economy. As of June 2009, the state's unemployment stood at 15.2%, the highest in the nation.

Michigan is a microcosm of older industrial economies that are experiencing the confluence of global competition, an aging workforce, a more diverse population, and a workforce that faces difficulty in meeting the needs of business for highly educated workers. For example, Michigan has been known as having one of the best qualified workforces in the world. Yet even today, a significant portion of Michigan's current workforce lacks the education and skills required for the current demand occupations, let alone the new jobs that might be generated by the R&D and University cluster. For example, only 27% of adults possess the necessary quantitative literacy skills for "today's" jobs, only 26% meet the *prose requirements*, and only 23% can meet the document requirements.[3] If current trends continue, while 34% of the current workforce have an AA degree or higher today, the workforce of 2020 projects only 20% with AA degree or higher. This projection is driven by the increase in ethnic groups who do not have the tradition of seeking post-secondary education and an aging population in which many of the skilled workers are retiring.[4]

These issues arise not because Michigan lacks a good education system to prepare its workforce to compete successfully in a world economy. On the contrary, Michigan boasts one of the best public university systems in the world, with the University of Michigan and Michigan State University considered to be world-class research institutions. Michigan also has 13 regional universities, and in total more than three-quarters of a million students are enrolled in these 15 colleges and universities. Michigan also has an extensive community college system, with nearly a half million students enrolled in 28 community colleges located across the state. Community colleges offer a wide range of courses and curricula, ranging from academic courses that prepare students to enter four-year colleges to certification courses that provide them with specific occupational skills to meet the needs of business.

The difficulty facing Michigan is that fewer students are applying to college and fewer are completing degrees. The chance that Michigan's youth will enrol in college by age 19 declined slightly from 41% in 1992 to 38% in 2006. High income students are almost twice as likely to enrol in college as low income. 55% of Michigan students who do attend college complete a bachelor's degree within six years of enrolment. The completion rate is slightly lower than what it was in 1992. Minority graduation and retention rates are about 20 percentage points lower than whites. Yet the percentage of college students returning for their second year has declined from 80% to 74%, which will eventually lower graduation rates even lower. Michigan also experiences a brain drain in the sense that more students enrol in colleges or universities outside the state than students from out of state enrolling at Michigan colleges and universities.[5] The decline in enrolment has led to a reduction in resources for colleges and universities, since the state funds these institutions based on the number of student credit hours. To compound that problem, the state's poor economic performance has left the state with a budget deficit, which has forced the state to cut funds to its entire educational system, including K-12 schools.

Development of the Michigan Regional Skills Alliance initiative

In response to Michigan's economic circumstances, the Governor initiated the Regional Skills Alliance programme to help improve the effectiveness and efficiency of its educational system and its workforce development activities in order to better meet the needs of a struggling state economy. The alliances were put in place also in response to the reduction in federal funds to support the workforce system, which left few if any funds available to support coordination and partnering activities. The state government has pursued other measures, such as a USD 2 billion fund to invest in life-science and other high-tech ventures in order to move Michigan's economy from dependence on declining traditional industries to fast-growing, high-tech companies. Michigan has also unveiled a 21st Century Workforce Strategy. It includes much of what it already provides in terms of workforce and economic development activities, but it further emphasises coordination and collaboration among various government agencies and business. The strategy also provides some scholarships to students who seek to enter high-demand occupations, and it provides additional resources to educational institutions that provide the courses to train persons to fill high-demand occupations, such as nurses in the healthcare industry and selected engineering and technical skills in the manufacturing sector.

The intent of the MiRSA initiative encompasses the overall themes of this workforce strategy. DLEG's goal for the MiRSA initiative is to increase the skills and labour market success of individuals in a region and to provide a collaborative mechanism through which local employers would reap significant benefits in having access to a more skilled workforce. For workers, the potential benefits of a MiRSA include outcomes such as an increase in skill levels, increased employment entry rate and job retention, progression along a career ladder, higher earnings levels and benefits, and earnings growth. For employers, the expected benefits are lower labour turnover, greater productivity and profitability, and fewer job vacancies. While not patterned after any one prior initiative, the MiRSA concept follows several previous activities across the nation that established workforce intermediaries, often referred to as sectoral, skill, or employment initiatives, to help bring together businesses and workforce development and educational systems. A unique feature of the MiRSA initiative is the partnership between the state government and a charitable foundation. Such collaboration is not unusual at the local level, particularly between educational institutions and foundations, but it is not that common for a state government to work closely with a foundation to design the initiative and then to share in its funding. The Mott Foundation had designed and funded sectoral employment initiatives at the local level, providing support to local workforce intermediaries. But this was the first time that they extended this approach to a state-wide initiative. To help localities develop their proposals for selection as MiRSAs, DLEG distributed material describing several examples of workforce intermediaries and offered links to websites of networks of such organisations.[6]

Purpose

MiRSAs, as described in DLEG's Request for Proposals (RFP), are intended to be locally initiated and managed partnerships formed to address workforce issues that affect firms operating in the same industry in a distinct geographic area. The partnerships are expected to resolve challenges facing local businesses such as worker shortages, skill shortages, training mismatches, employee recruitment, and retention and organisational design. The description in the RFP also emphasised the benefits that would accrue to businesses by continually upgrading the skills of their employees – promoting increased productivity and competitiveness. These benefits would also spillover to other businesses within a local labour market, through a healthier business climate and a more highly-skilled local workforce. The description further targets efforts to improve conditions and opportunities for lower-wage workers or potential workers. Finally, the collaboration seeks to resolve systemic and structural problems by working at the multi-firm and industry-based levels.

To achieve these objectives, MiRSAs were expected to undertake activities such as analysing, designing, and implementing improvements to the sector's human resource practices. These practices may include employee recruitment, development of career ladders, training, and mentoring. Other activities that MiRSAs might pursue are revisions and coordination of training curricula, attention to non-workplace issues such as transportation and other supportive services, and the improvement of supplier relationships. The initiative provided very few additional resources that could be used for job training or job search assistance. It was expected that these services would come from existing programmes, such as the Workforce Investment Act (WIA) programmes for adult, youth, dislocated workers, and set-aside funds for incumbent worker programmes. The relatively small amount of funds available to each regional alliance under the MiRSA initiative was used for administrative costs to form and support the alliance and small programmes outside the services allowed under WIA.

DLEG required that MiRSA partners include businesses within the targeted industry, local educational institutions, and workforce development and economic development agencies. Industry and trade associations, organised labour, chambers of commerce, and community-based organisations were also possible partners. The convener of the MiRSA was intended to be an entity with expertise on the issues being addressed that could also act as an organiser of the alliance. Conveners were expected to be key players in the region with the clout to bring together the appropriate partners. The proposed partnerships could build upon existing networks and consortia.

Application process

DLEG received 26 applications for MiRSAs. An interagency review committee evaluated the applications according to the criteria listed above and recommended 13 applications for funding, one more than originally intended. Throughout the review process, the intent was to fund 12 MiRSAs in the first phase of the initiative. A thirteenth initiative, the Lake Michigan College Emerging Technologies RSA, was designated as a MiRSA but was not funded from MiRSA funds. Each funded MiRSA received approximately USD 100 000 for a two-year period, with the expectation that the partners would contribute during the initial two years and then provide funding to sustain the alliances after that.

Throughout the entire process, DLEG staff provided technical assistance to prospective bidders and then to selected grantees. Staff conducted information sessions, answered questions regarding the concept of a MiRSA and the application process, and provided custom assessments of local labour markets (compiled by the Labour Market Information division of DLEG). Technical assistance was also provided for selected applicants during the grant negotiation process by introducing the selected applicants to a peer networking group and scheduling the first set of meetings of the group. During the first 12 months of the grant period, DLEG staff convened a mandatory meeting of grantees to provide a forum for networking and to offer grantees feedback on their progress in convening their stakeholders. Dissemination of information to MiRSAs was aided by the establishment of a dedicated website, which was available at the time of the initial announcement.

However, while the state provided technical assistance, it did not intervene in the decisions of the local partnerships. The local partnerships identified the targeted industries and occupations and came up with the prescribed solutions. Of course, DLEG staff did participate in the final determination of which proposals would be selected, but their selection was based upon whether the proposals followed the prescribed steps of demonstrating commitment among the partners in the formation of the MiRSA and undergoing a rigorous analysis of the needs of local businesses in the targeted industries, among other criteria. Leaving these decisions to the local partnerships follows the premise of sectoral initiatives that local entities know their needs and can derive appropriate courses of action to address those needs better than people who operate at some distance from these local markets. By selecting MiRSAs from across the state, the amalgamation of individual efforts collectively comprises a "grass-roots" approach to regional and state-level issues. However, the state did not make any systematic effort to determine whether or not the bottom-up approach was consistent with a top-down skills gap analysis at the state level.

The selection criteria used are included in Box 4.1 above. The state did expect local partnerships to use cluster analysis to identify the targeted industries and occupations, and the state provided technical assistance by compiling the data needed by each applicant for their analysis. Applicants were at various stages of the planning process at the time they submitted their proposals. Those from existing partnerships had an advantage over those creating a new alliance, since much of the analysis and commitment from partners was completed before the application process began. Those forming new partnerships spent much of the first year assessing business needs, deriving solutions and forming alliances.

Overview of the 13 selected MiRSAs

The 13 MiRSAs that were selected came from various regions of the state and focused on various industries and identified different solutions. Two were chosen from the Upper Peninsula, two from the upper half of the Lower Peninsula, and the remaining nine were representative of the southern third of the Lower Peninsula. As shown in Table 4.1, the majority of MiRSAs (9 of the 13) chose to target the healthcare industry, which is consistent with other US initiatives, such as the US DOL's sector employment demonstration.[7] Only one (and a half) focused on manufacturing, while the rest addressed issues facing construction, nanotechnology, and public utilities. Many of the MiRSAs pursued activities related to training, but only one or two actually became involved in training efforts. Most addressed issues regarding curricula or with acquainting students with occupations in their industries, particularly within the healthcare industry.

Box 4.1. **Selection criteria**

Each applicant was required to include the following items in their proposals.

1. Demonstrate how leading a MiRSA is a core element of the applicant's current mission and a narrative on how the principal stakeholders actively participated in the development of the project plan prior to the submission of the application. Also include letters from all partners signed by their president agreeing to the role of the applicant as grantee and identifying in-kind and cash resources provided.
2. Identify the industry focus and document how this industry contributes significantly to the local economy and workforce.
3. Define the universe of employers in the MiRSA, describe the process of obtaining employer input, the portion of local employers in the industry involved in the application development, and how employers will be involved in the MiRSA.
4. Describe the key partners in the application.
5. Provide a clearly articulated statement of the problem or sets of problems affecting the regional industry which the MiRSA will address.
6. Demonstrate that the targeted industry has a human resources-workforce need that can be addressed by the MiRSA.
7. Provide measurable outcomes for the impact on businesses and workers and system changes that improve the ability of people to gain employment. Outcomes must support the state's goals and objectives of *i)* increasing the use of and participation in the public workforce development system, *ii)* having employers see the MiRSA as an integral part of the community and the success of their businesses and the industry, *iii)* providing solutions for entry level through senior level workforce needs, *iv)* and self sufficiency of the MiRSA from local public and private funds.
8. Describe how the objectives in the RFP will be addressed.
9. Provide a description of the applicant's ability to meet the terms of the RFP.
10. Provide a three-year line item budget that includes all sources and uses of funds.

Unlike sectoral approaches elsewhere, Michigan's initiatives tended to include multi-county areas instead of narrowly defined geographic areas, such as single local labour markets.[8] In particular six of the healthcare RSAs covered very large, multi-county areas. Five of the other MiRSAs operated in a single labour market area (county or urban area), and the other two were

Table 4.1. **Synopsis of the MiRSA regions and targeted industries**

MiRSA	Industry focus	Occupation focus	Jobless rate %	Industry job growth 2001-2003 %		Forecast job growth 2000-2010 %
			US: 6.0 MI: 7.3	Overall	Focus Industry	Overall
Capital Area Mfg. MiRSA	Manufacturing	Production workers	4.9	–0.7	–8.4	+7.5
Flint Career Alliance	Health care	Nurses aide training, LPN, physical therapy assistants	8.9	–4.9	+4.1	+6.4
East Central Health Care Alliance	Health care	Nurses, certified nurses assistants, medical transcriptionists	8.9	–4.9	+4.1	+6.4
Grand Rapids Community College	Manufacturing and health care	Entry-level positions	7.7	–4.9	–14.3 +4.1	+12.0
Detroit Long Term Care	Long-term Health care	Entry-level unlicensed caregivers, certified nurse assistants	+6.9	–4.7	+4.0	+9.9
Mid-Michigan Construction Alliance	Construction	Electricians, bricklayers, plumbers, pipefitters	4.9	–0.7	–11.5	+7.5
Midwest Skills Development Center	Utilities	Line technicians	7.7	–1.0	+7.3	+7.8
Emerging Technologies	Nano-technology	Clean room technicians	7.3	–4.2	n.a.	+9.3
Northeast Michigan Health Care Workforce Alliance	Health care	Radiography technicians, medical assistants	10.4	–3.4	+3.0	+7.4
Northwest Michigan Regional Health Care Industry Skills Alliance	Healthcare	Process-basic skills, foundation skills, home health aides and nurse aids	8.4	–1.9	+8.1	+15.0
Southwest Michigan Health Care Alliance	Healthcare	Nurses aides and other entry level workers	6.0	–1.2	+11.0	+9.6
Upper Peninsula Health Care Roundtable	Healthcare	Certified nurses aides, LPN, home health aides	7.7	–1.0	+6.3	+7.8
West Central Michigan Health Care	Healthcare	Certified nurses aides, LPN, medical record clerks	7.7	–4.9	+7.7	+12.0

Note: The employment projections were made long before the current economic recession and thus may reflect a more optimistic view of future growth than would be the case if the projections had been derived more currently.

essentially specific occupational training programmes (nanotechnology and line technology) at a postsecondary institution that could encompass the entire state. Seven of the MiRSAs fit the description of being an existing collaboration/ partnership prior to the grant award, whereas the other six involved forming new collaborations. Nine of the 13 MiRSAs were convened by workforce boards; the other four were convened by a labour organisation, two postsecondary training programmes, and a community-based organisation (CBO).

Box 4.2 provides more information on different MiRSA activities by objectives.

Box 4.2. MiRSA activities by objectives

Attraction and retention of skilled workers

- School career fairs.
- Summer camps for youth.
- Career information for students, including online video clips.
- Marketing campaigns to bring "retired" nurses back into the workforce.
- Internet-based clinical calendar that reduces wait time for clinical job opportunities.
- Electronic transactions among member businesses.

Skill upgrading

- Collaboration among community colleges to coordinate training curricula.
- Promoting training for workers.
- Computer and Internet training seminars.
- Modularisation and standardisation of curricula among various educational institutions.
- Invest existing WIA incumbent worker funds into long-term care facilities, and other businesses.

Integrating the hard-to-serve into the workforce

- Develop career ladder programme for entry-level nursing-related occupations.
- Work to change the attitude of the construction industry toward minority workers.
- Training to prepare for high school Graduation Equivalence Degree (GED).
- Remedial literacy and numeracy training.

Specific examples of MiRSAs

Four specific examples of regional skills alliances in Northeast and Northwest Michigan, Detroit and Lansing provide a representative overview of the types of activities undertaken by the MiRSAs.

Northeast Michigan Healthcare Workforce Alliance

The Northeast Michigan Healthcare Workforce Alliance encompasses an eleven-county area in the upper northeast corner of the Lower Peninsula. With a 10% decline in manufacturing in the past three years, specifically in machinery and wood products, the unemployment rate reached 11% at the time of the initiative. Many of the skilled workers who could find jobs elsewhere have left, leaving other industries concerned about maintaining a quality workforce. One of the growing industries, healthcare, experienced an acute shortage of nurses and other skilled personnel.

The alliance took a two-pronged approach to address this issue. The first addressed the immediate workforce needs of the healthcare industry by working closely with local educational institutions and others located downstate to offer training. Being a sparsely population rural area, workers must travel long distances to find proper training, and the MiRSA partners attempted to coordinate and align curricula so that individuals can take courses at nearby institutions instead of travelling to institutions located hours away. The interest in developing a state-wide nursing curriculum was shared by other MiRSAs. Such agreements among educational institutions promote education mobility and facilitate the seamless transfer of academic credits between associate degree and bachelor degree nursing programmes. An articulation agreement typically binds all nursing schools to common admission requirements, curricula, and graduation requirement.[9] With the support and encouragement from the Northeast Michigan Healthcare Workforce Alliance, institutions within the region also talked with institutions outside their region about developing common nursing school requirements and curricula. Furthermore, other MiRSAs joined forces to push for a state-wide agreement, which the Governor included in her Nursing Agenda for Michigan: 2005-2010.

The second prong developed a future workforce. Specifically, the MiRSA sought to increase the awareness of middle and high school students about the wide array of available healthcare professions through a series of summer health exploration camps and supportive marketing material. By acquainting students with jobs that are available in the area, the MiRSA hoped to retain qualified and needed workers. MiRSA partners also put together a directory of community college and university programme offerings in northern Michigan for the healthcare professions. As with other MiRSAs, the Northeast Michigan Health Care Workforce Alliance facilitated the use of WIA incumbent worker training (IWT) funds in the healthcare sector. These funds helped to continue and expand a tuition reimbursement programme for incumbent healthcare workers.

Healthcare Regional Skills Alliance of Northwest Michigan

This alliance also identified a shortage of qualified workers for the healthcare industry in their region of Michigan. More specifically, they found a lack of trained, entry-level workers and Certified Nurse Aides, a shortage of Registered Nurses, not enough young people choosing healthcare fields for their career choices and too few and too expensive training opportunities for healthcare employees who need to continually update and upgrade their skills.

In response, the regional skills alliance of Northwest Michigan partners also developed summer camps to attract new workers, including a week-long residential camp for high school students where a variety of medical careers were explored with hands-on, interactive lessons and activities, and tours of local hospitals. At the same time, a 60-hour training course was prepared to help students gain entry-level healthcare positions, and investments were made into Certified Nurse Aid training and staff development for incumbent workers. In order to ensure that employment is accessible to all and to raise employment retention rates, this MiRSA also initiated a health professional recovery programme. The alliance partnered with public health agencies to address job retention for healthcare workers with substance abuse, chemical dependency, and/or mental health programmes. Specialised services were provided to licensed or registered healthcare personnel to help them deal with their problems while remaining on the job.

Southeast Michigan Long-Term Health Care Alliance

The Detroit area formed a coalition, referred to as the Southeast Michigan Long-Term Health Care Alliance, to address worker needs in the *long-term* healthcare industry. Plagued by a steady decline in manufacturing jobs (particularly the large decline in the auto sector in the past several years) and by the lack of opportunities for low-skilled workers to find decent wages, the area turned to workforce issues related to entry-level and moderately skilled workers. The local Michigan Works agency convened the Alliance and for the first time began to emphasise the needs of healthcare providers and their workers. Collaborating with the workforce agencies opened up opportunities for grants, networking, and access to the other resources that the job training agency could provide. Respondents believed that the MiRSA was instrumental in achieving about 250 placements in long-term care since the programme(s) began and in initiating two new nursing programmes to expand the training capacity of area institutions. Another accomplishment of the MiRSA was the prioritisation of needs developed through the strategic planning process, which led to standardising entry-level nursing training.

Capital Area Manufacturing Council

Finally, the Capital Area Manufacturing Council, located in the state capital, focused on production workers in the manufacturing industry. The Lansing area's unemployment is below that of the state and nation, but its core industry, transportation equipment production, has experienced serious declines in the past several years. The MiRSA serves as a council of manufacturers, providing a forum for member employers to report significant trends that could affect manufacturing's competitiveness in the area. It also provides support to explore workforce development issues that are common among manufacturers. The accomplishments to date include establishing a governing council, holding well-attended forums, facilitating e-business transactions among members, and securing funding after the two-year grant expires.

Governance issues

The following section explores how the MiRSAs have been governed (as of the summer of 2006 when the research was completed), looking at collaboration and partnership, communication, resourcing and ongoing state support and technical assistance. The *raison d'etre* for a sectoral approach is for the key entities involved in workforce development – training agencies, educational partners, and employers – to collaborate synergistically. Effective collaboration requires structure, which the MiRSAs established during the formative stage and then carried out in the implementation stage.

Collaboration and partnership

Many of the MiRSAs adopted a formal structure. They created committees to pursue the several tasks that they had identified as important in addressing the workforce issues facing employers in their regions. To administer the activities of the MiRSAs, a few took a more informal approach and relied on the efforts of loaned staff from another organisation or staff they hired through their funding to do much of the work. However, most of the MiRSAs that had paid staff also pursued a structured approach, and the combination proved to be the most successful, as reported by the interviewees.

For the most part, the conveners were well-satisfied with the engagement of partners in the alliances. In many instances, this was the first time that their trio of partners – education, employers, and workforce agencies – had been brought together. The engagement of educational institutions was somewhat less common, although there were several instances where solid collaborations had formed, even though it might have been the first time that the educational institutions had been engaged in formal regional collaboration efforts with employers.

Stakeholders generally felt that it was particularly critical that employers participate in the decision-making process, since the fundamental motivation of regional skill alliances is to bring together the relevant regional stakeholders to address the workforce needs of business. Nearly everyone interviewed as part of an evaluation of the MiRSAs was satisfied that employers had taken the lead in determining their needs and how to address them. However, when surveyed, employer partners were among the least satisfied with their roles. It appears that many of the MiRSAs were challenged with finding a wide representation of employers within the targeted sectors to become involved in the partnership and with garnering financial support for the MiRSA from employer partners. Not surprisingly, the MiRSAs that seemed most successful in bringing in employers were those where the convener was a Michigan Workforce Area (business-led Workforce Investment Board) or included such an area, which occurred in the majority of cases.

Communication

Communication appears to be a key factor in determining the success of MiRSAs. Success requires that each MiRSA create awareness among the employer community, recruit employer participation and communicate ongoing administrative items such as meeting times, agendas, and background materials for consideration by staff and decision makers. Finally, it is important that MiRSAs report their plans and accomplishments to the public, to state administrators, and to all other stakeholders. Obviously, communications are effective when they are clear, timely, and appropriately disseminated.

For many MiRSAs, formal meetings were the primary means of communication. Satisfaction with attendance ranged from poor to excellent. Several factors affecting attendance were offered. One of the issues for some of the more rural MiRSAs was the distance that the partners had to travel to attend meetings. While e-mail was used extensively and websites established, most agreed that in-person contact was necessary to form the bonds for successful interaction. Some MiRSAs were faced with the decision to reduce the size of their geographical area in order to increase attendance, since some participants were driving three or more hours to attend meetings. They recognised that limiting the number of participants could reduce the critical number of participants necessary for an effective collaboration. A few MiRSAs convened subgroup meetings that involved participants from smaller geographic regions. Another important facet of engaging partners was the manner in which meetings were conducted. Many partners expected the meetings to be run "crisply" with a set agenda. This request was expressed most often by employers. Also, partners appreciated meeting regularly, instead of on an as-needed basis.

Resources

Resource adequacy is an important determinant of the effectiveness of the MiRSAs and their continued impact. The grant funds are intended to be a catalyst for forming partnerships, but these funds must be supplemented by in-kind and cash resources from other sources in order to provide the client services that are necessary to improve workforce quality. Sustainability beyond the initial grant also depends on finding adequate resources from partners and other funders.

Each employer partner was asked to sign a letter of financial commitment as part of the application for selection as a MiRSA. It is interesting that the employer partners were the least satisfied with employer investment, while the MiRSA director/convener and staff were the most satisfied. The state, in a newsletter to MiRSA participants, stated that more than USD 14.5 million in public and private resources have been leveraged, which includes the value of the services received from federal and state workforce development programmes such as Work First (job search assistance for the economically disadvantaged), the Workforce Investment Act adult, youth, and incumbent worker programmes, as well as from businesses.[11]

It was expected that the more partners became involved in their MiRSA and the more value they received from their participation, then the more likely they would be willing to contribute to the future operation of the MiRSA. There is a relatively high correlation amongst the MiRSAs between employer engagement and resource adequacy. However, engagement does not always lead to sustainability. Several MiRSAs that reported high satisfaction with employer involvement were not confident that employers would be willing to contribute financially to sustain the operation after the MiRSA grant funds were depleted. Furthermore, employers who expressed high satisfaction with the benefits received from their involvement in the MiRSA did not necessarily support or commit to support the MiRSA with cash contributions.

One MiRSA instituted a system of membership dues for participants. It was set up as an association that put together programmes and services of interest to a group of manufacturers. The MiRSA reported that it covers 85% of the second year's budget. Other MiRSAs experienced similar problems eliciting employer support for several reasons. One is the reluctance on the part of business to spend money on providing basic training, such as literacy and numeracy, on entry-level workers because of their perception that such training generates low returns to the business and that many workers will simply switch to other employers after receiving the instruction.

Some MiRSAs considered other means to address sustainability. Several applied for grants from outside sources, and two tied into a sizable, community-wide grant from the federal government for several years. A few others counted on their "parent" organisations to provide future funding. Another MiRSA relied on the partnering Michigan Workforce Area for additional funding, by selling services to the MWA as contractor. However, halfway through the second year only a few of the MiRSAs had a solid commitment for future funding.

Ongoing state support and technical assistance

As noted above, staff from the Department of Labor and Economic Growth offered technical assistance to the MiRSAs both before and after the selection process. Staff offered help in resolving issues that might arise with contracts or state funding so that local staff did not become mired in administrative trivia. State workers also shared ideas and innovations and were advocates for success. During the grant application process, staff conducted several information forums around the state, which attracted a large number of participants. After the grantees were selected, staff worked closely with each MiRSA to ensure that they had access to resources such as labour market information and examples of other regional skill alliances. The state also provided customised labour market information analysis upon request.

In general the alliances found the technical assistance to be helpful and appreciated the attention given to their needs. They recognised that, due to the quick ramp up of the programme, staff knowledge and expertise evolved along with that of the MiRSA staff and participants. One issue of concern that grantees raised was the seemingly unrealistic expectations on the part of some state staff regarding the pace of progress and the significance of their accomplishments. Some respondents believed that much of what was expected before the grants were submitted in terms of forming partnerships and gaining commitments should have been considered part of the formation process after the grantee was selected. In one or two instances, MiRSAs expressed concern about the appropriate balance between local control and state involvement in the MiRSA planning process, which was triggered by the state questioning the priorities set by local employers. Several interviewees praised the state's effort to convene a forum of healthcare-related MiRSAs so that they could share best practices and common concerns.

Outcomes and value added

It appears that most of the activities that were planned by the first set of MiRSAs were implemented by the end of the second year of the programme. It is not possible to assess independently the net impact of those activities on the employees and employers within the targeted industries, for several reasons. First, many of the activities, such as the summer camps, had long-term consequences, so that their effects would not be observed for many years. Furthermore, some of those interviewed identified systemic change as their main goal, which is difficult to identify and quantify. Second, most of the activities that could have generated more immediate effects, such as short-term training, are funded by other workforce programmes such as Incumbent Worker Training. Attributing the success of those programmes to a MiRSA is not appropriate. Third, activities related to curricula changes were intertwined with the benefits of educational programmes, the benefits of which would be difficult to apportion to the MiRSA, to the educational institution, and to the students attending.

Those interviewed generally confirmed the satisfaction with the progress of activities. They cited accomplishments such as committing incumbent worker training (IWT) funds to train 87 workers in long-term care facilities, placing 250 in long-term care facilities, taking credit for reducing vacancy rates to below 5%, providing scholarships from WIA money for incumbent hospital workers, obtaining a grant to develop career ladder programming in nursing, holding a regional summit on health care, organising summer camps, and developing and implementing an Internet-based clinical calendar software to reduce wait time for clinical opportunities. While each accomplishment is specific to the needs of the employers of the targeted industries, the accomplishment that was mentioned most often was collaboration and networking – the ability to bring together partners that had not interacted before.

When asked about the value added they received from the MiRSA, employer partners in particular first mentioned collaboration and networking. Many stated that those organisations would not have come together without the MiRSA. Establishing the MiRSA provided the opportunity and the convening organisations supplied the clout to bring the appropriate stakeholders to the table. Some people who were interviewed also talked about transforming a competitive environment, in which employers and in some cases educational institutions would not cooperate, into a collaborative environment in which those same organisations were willing to share information, standardise curricula, and work for solutions to the workforce development issues that they held in common. While many of the pre-existing organisations had established the foundation for those networks, it appears from the comments that in many instances it was the MiRSAs that brought the Michigan Workforce Areas, educational institutions, and employers together for the first time.

Many employer partners also stated that the establishment of such a network and the creation of a collaborative relationship with other partners were important for the economic viability of their businesses. The healthcare organisations, particularly in rural areas, viewed the economic future of their regions as tied to the economic health of their organisations. In many rural labour markets, the decline of manufacturing had elevated the healthcare industry as the number one employer in the region. Unless they have access to an ample pool of qualified workers, according to those interviewed, they faced higher costs, higher vacancy rates, the inability to staff positions, and consequently the inability to generate the revenues needed to yield the operating margins required for those entities to remain economically viable.

An overall assessment of the progress of the MiRSAs by the state government[12] concluded that the "MiRSAs established in the first round of grant funding are doing very well" (p. 7). The state report also identified some programmatic issues, which arose from conversations with MiRSA participants. They included the short funding cycle, the use of traditional workforce outcome measures that may not reflect the more systemic outcomes expected of MiRSAs, problems of employer support and sustainability, and stakeholder fatigue in participating in too many regional collaborations.

Other communications from the state indicated that more than 2 100 individuals received training and 813 individuals were placed into employment through MiRSAs. Business leaders were quoted to say that it contributed to their businesses' bottom line and makes Michigan a more attractive place to do business by attending to the specific needs of business. They commented that MiRSAs improved their profitability through job training grants that flowed through MiRSAs, through providing a team-like environment that encouraged companies to flourish, allowing local communities to customise programmes to meet their local needs rather than having programmes handed down and mandated from state government, and providing a vehicle for employers to understand each other's business challenges and to find solutions.

Conclusions

Overall, during the first years of their operation, MiRSAs appeared successful in identifying key industries that face labour shortages and other employment issues, in designing skills strategies, and in implementing them. The networking and collaboration that occurred through the MiRSA activities seemed to be an unqualified benefit of the MiRSA initiative. Nearly all employer partners were committed to remaining engaged with their MiRSAs, although they were not as committed in offering direct financial assistance.

The evaluation process produced several observations and recommendations for establishing successful partnerships.

- The commitment of key stakeholders/partners is essential. It is particularly important that the CEOs of the employer partners be actively involved, at least initially, so that they can provide the clout to attract and keep appropriate stakeholders in the alliance and provide the buy-in within their own organisations.

- The presence of a director and a staff dedicated to the concept and objectives of the MiRSA is an important asset.
- MiRSAs should be funded within a single, well-defined labour market of a manageable size so that partners can focus on and identify with specific initiatives and so that all can meet regularly without travelling great distances.
- The formation stage is crucial, particularly the development of a strategic plan. It needs to reflect the diverse needs of the participating organisations and requires broad consensus of the partners. The strategic plan should also be based on a rigorous assessment of the local labour market and include quantifiable outcome measures.
- As the entities move into the implementation and operation stages, they need to continue to engage partners so that all participants contribute and remain committed to the initiative and can benefit from the collaborative efforts of each partner.
- With intense competition for funds and given the importance of accountability, it is vital that alliances establish performance measures and commit to tracking those measures and using the outcomes as a means to engage the partners and to keep them focused on their mission and purpose.

Arguably the success of MiRSAs is built more on establishing a platform or infrastructure that supports the partnerships than in providing additional services to workers or businesses. MiRSAs provide little, if any, additional funding for traditional interventions, such as worker training or job matching services. Most of the funds that the MiRSAs use for such purposes would be available to the workers even if MiRSAs did not exist, and many of the funding sources have eligibility rules and other restrictions on how the funds are to be used. In fact, some of the MiRSAs were reluctant to use workforce programme services because of the restrictions placed on their use. In addition, the lack of additional funds to tackle local problems identified by the MiRSAs may have limited the scope and breadth of the solutions that MiRSAs derived to address their problems. Businesses did not provide significant funds to augment the public workforce development dollars. Summer camps, job shadowing, information forums, curriculum development do not appear to be cutting edge solutions for businesses in a state that is experiencing significant economic malaise.[13] Yet, it is what businesses wanted with the limited funds available and restrictions on many.

Have MiRSAs achieved the objectives set forth by the state? It is clear that the MiRSAs have helped direct resources to fund activities that the consortia identified as important in helping businesses in their areas. For example, they have developed programmes to acquaint youth with career opportunities in the region in order to encourage them to train for jobs and launched marketing campaigns to attract nursing candidates to the area; they brought together training providers and workforce development agencies to work with businesses to meet their workforce needs; they developed training programmes for entry-level workers and career ladder models for advancement and created programmes for workers with problems that may lead to their dismissal if not addressed. These programmes are aligned with the objectives, and are in line with the priorities of local stakeholders. Obviously, these programmes do not have the capacity to meet all the needs, and as mentioned earlier, stakeholders may have chosen activities that required less funding because they were aware of the limited funding available for additional programmes.

From a state-wide perspective, it is not clear whether the compilation of local initiatives addressed the state's overarching needs. Michigan is losing a large number of manufacturing jobs, but only one MiRSA targeted a manufacturing sector. Life sciences and biotech are leading export industries and Michigan has a significant presence in these areas. Even the state has launched an initiative to promote these sectors, but none of the MiRSAs in the initial phase identified those areas. Rather, they focused primarily on local service sectors, principally healthcare. While a dominant employer in many areas, albeit offering entry-level jobs, it does not have a large potential to stimulate growth in a region. But 9 of the 13 MiRSAs focused on that sector. On the other hand, the fact that many MiRSAs targeted the same industry presented an opportunity for the MiRSAs to share their efforts and concerns.

From a regional perspective, the MiRSAs did offer broader coordination and collaboration than is typically the case with sectoral initiatives that focus only on narrowly defined markets. This has advantages but also costs. One of the problems mentioned was the difficulty in getting partners to travel long distances to meetings, which reduced the alliance's cohesion. Some of this was necessary, given the sparsely population rural areas encompassed by several MiRSAs. But it is important to balance the need for local input and buy-in with the broader coordination that may come from regional initiatives.

As business leaders have stated, the value of MiRSAs is in the networking and the local decision making. To the extent that these factors better identify the issues facing businesses, develop more appropriate solutions, and direct workforce development funds to address the needs, the initiative can be successful. The funds provided to each MiRSA are meagre relative to the funds available through the workforce programmes. However, those funds are important to support the administrative infrastructure that is needed to staff the partnerships. WIA provides no funds for such activities and the budgets of most workforce and educational institutions have little excess that can provide funds to staff the partnerships on an on-going basis. This is one of the problems facing the sustainability of MiRSAs. Without continual funding from the state, it is unlikely that many of these partnerships can be sustainable. Businesses are not likely to contribute unless they see clear contributions to their bottom line. They are reluctant to pay for training of entry-level workers, because of the lack of clear evidence of the benefits received by the firms. Businesses may view the quantifiable benefits of MiRSAs to be equally small and thus are reluctant to offer direct financial support. Moreover, even the state did not finance the full cost of the first phase of the MiRSA initiative; the cost was shared by a private foundation. Given the scarce resources available for such purposes, it would be beneficial to find less expensive ways to form and sustain partnerships, but the reality is that even the initial funds averaging USD 80 000 per MiRSA were not sufficient to sustain most of the alliances. Sustainability requires more funds to support the convener and staff as well as to have sufficient funds to provide innovative solutions.

The state considers the MiRSA initiative to be successful and continues to fund additional ones. Since the initial 13 MiRSAs were chosen, 19 more MiRSAs have been selected and funded. Many have focused on healthcare but others have branched out to address issues confronting manufacturing, construction, forest and timber products, information security, hospitality and tourism, and the life sciences. The focus is the same – bringing together key stakeholders to prepare the local workforce to meet the needs of businesses in these targeted industries. While it is still too soon to evaluate the full impact of such efforts, it appears that with the enthusiasm to form partnerships throughout Michigan, with relatively little initial start-up funds from the state, businesses, workforce agencies, educational institutions, and economic development organisations find inherent value in coming together to address critical issues facing their local economies.

The promise of such initiatives is that the synergies generated from these decentralised efforts will help transform Michigan's economy from one that is dependent on traditional industries that face difficulty competing in a global economy to one that can enhance the competitiveness of existing industries and encourage the formation of new, emerging industries. The reality is that strong leadership and the willingness along with the resources to take bold steps is needed to fulfil this promise. MiRSAs have brought key stakeholders together within various regions of the state to assess their local circumstances and strategise possible solutions. Given the focus with a few exceptions on traditional manufacturing and service sectors, they may be able to improve the competitiveness of the existing businesses. But it may not be their role to transform Michigan's economy from one dominated by slow-growth traditional industries to one driven by more robust emerging industries.

Notes

1. Department of Labor and Economic Growth, press release, 13 May 2004.
2. Michigan Regional Skills Alliances and MiRSA are service marks for the Michigan Department of Labor and Economic Development/Bureau of Workforce Programs. The intention was to fund 12 in the first phase, but a thirteenth was added.
3. As described in the Technical Guide for the National Center for Public Policy and Higher Education (2006), the adult skill levels indicators measure the per cent of the states' populations whose literacy skills are most similar to the skills of college graduates (level 4 or 5 on a scale of 1 to 5 on the National Adult Literacy Survey, NALS). Three types of literacy skills are measured: quantitative, prose, and document literacy. Prose literacy measures the knowledge and skills needed to understand and use information from texts that include editorials, news stories, poems, and fiction. Adults with the highest measured level of prose literacy, level 5, can find information in dense text with considerable distracting information that might seem plausible but is incorrect. Document literacy measures the knowledge and skills required to locate and use information contained in materials that include job applications, payroll forms, transportation schedules, maps, tables, and graphs. Adults with the highest measured level of document literacy, level 5, can use complex documents containing distracting information and make high-level inferences.
4. Roberts T. Jones, Michigan, "The Number One Quality Workforce System in the Nation?", presented at the Town Hall Meeting on Education and Michigan's Economic Future, 17 January 2007, and found on *www.upjohn.org*. High school and college completion rates of Hispanics, in particular, are much lower than whites and African Americans. Only 12.7% of Hispanics receive a BA or higher compared with 17.3% of African Americans and 28.3% of whites. The projected increase of Hispanics as a proportion of US population drives this projection for 2020.
5. National Center for Public Policy and Higher Education (2006), "Measuring Up, A National Report Card on High Education".
6. The specific organisations included in the background material included the Wisconsin Regional Training Partnership, Milwaukee, Wisconsin; Industrial Retention and Expansion Network (WIRE-NET), Cleveland, Ohio; Primavera WORKS, Tucson, Arizona; Cooperative Home Care Associates, New York City, New York; Project QUEST (Quality Employment through Skills Training), San Antonio, Texas. The DLEG website links included in the informational packet were for the National Network of Sector Partners, US Department of Labor's Sectoral Employment Initiative, Aspen Institute, and Public/Private Ventures.
7. One of the MiRSAs is a multi-sector approach with healthcare and manufacturing. So it would be most accurate to say that eight and a half of the 13 target healthcare and one and a half target manufacturing.
8. The six projects in the Aspen Institute's Sectoral Employment Development Learning Project (SEDLP) were Asian Neighborhood Design, San Francisco; Paraprofessional Health Care Institute, South Bronx, NY; Garment Industry Development Corporation, New York; Focus: HOPE, Detroit; Jane Addams Resource Corporation, Chicago; and Project Quest, San Antonio.
9. Unlike some states, Michigan does not have a state-wide articulation agreement among nursing schools within the state.
10. Michigan Workforce Areas is the term used for the area served by the local Workforce Investment Boards, which were created under the federal Workforce

Investment Act to administer the federal and state workforce development programmes. There are around 600 local workforce investment boards in the country and 25 in Michigan.

11. It is fair to say that a large share of the funds came from workforce development funds, which would have gone to individuals in the state without the MiRSAs. The source of the information is a DLEG newsletter entitled "Michigan's 21st Century Workforce Strategy", 27 November 2006.

12. The report entitled "'Michigan Regional Skills Alliances': Report on Site Visits Made to the Original Grantees Prepared for Participants" (16 May 2007) was available was the DLEG/MiRSA website.

13. State officials questioned a few MiRSAs as to whether summer camps were the solutions identified by businesses, and the MiRSAs assured them that businesses did indeed come up with that activity. Many businesses, particularly healthcare providers, offered summer camps periodically on their own, and the partnerships gave them an opportunity to leverage their private resources used to fund the camps.

PART II

Chapter 5

The Choctaw Tribe of Mississippi: Managing Skills for Workforce Transformation

by

Rhonda G. Phillips

The Mississippi Band of Choctaw Indians (MBCI) provides a case study for the development of local workforce skill strategies to address high rates of unemployment, poverty, and the lack of employment opportunities in a rural area. The MBCI has approached skill development by using a method of self-reliance and self-determination as well as participating with other organisations for collaborative partnerships. The results have been remarkable, with poverty and unemployment rates dropping significantly since the early 1970's from highs of 80% to a low of 2% in 2007. The focus for workforce development is on technology intensive manufacturing as well as the hospitality industry, aimed at upgrading the skills of workers, while also training those without skills. The emphasis is also on tribally-owned and managed enterprises to foster self-reliance.

Introduction

Worker skills are a crucial issue that impacts community well-being on a variety of fronts, particularly in areas affected by both social exclusion and economic change. The case selected for this research is the Mississippi Band of Choctaw Indians (MBCI). The Choctaw Reservation is located in east central Mississippi in the south eastern United States, with eight Choctaw communities distributed throughout six counties and encompassing nearly 30 000 acres. There are 9 660 enrolled members, with 8 200 members living in the communities. The majority of these members live on the Neshoba County reservation where the headquarters of the tribe are located as well as an industrial park and other tribal organisations.

Lack of skills and employment were key features of the Choctow tribe until 1969 when they embarked on a strategic and focused community economic development plan. This community plan, incorporating a strong focus on skills, has allowed the tribe to undego significant development transitions from a poverty stricken area dependent on agriculture, to manufacturing, to a tourism/service based economy and now to a technology-intensive economy. This chapter will explore the strategic approach taken by the Choctaw, assess its impact and analyse the reasons behind its success. The principal focus will be on more recent initiatives, particularly those developed since 2000.

The context: rapid economic change

The development of the tribe can be broken down into three timeframes: 1960s-1980s; the 1990's; and from 2000 to the present.

1960s-1980s: transitioning from agriculture to manufacturing

Prior to 1969, the Choctaw tribe, in common with many Aboriginal communities, experienced considerable poverty. Unemployment rates were over 80% and the economy was focused on sharecropper agriculture. The majority of tribal members earned less than USD 2 000 per year. Nearly 80% did not finish elementary school, and only 7% had a high school degree (obtained from boarding schools in other states as Mississippi did not have an Indian high school). Housing was substandard with 90% of homes having no plumbing. Life expectancy was 45 to 50 years and the social trend was for young males to leave for economic opportunity elsewhere. This left the tribal population of 3 000 members in peril and long- term tribal sustainability in question (Ferrara, 1998).

In 1969, federal policy began to shift towards giving indigenous communities greater control over their concerns, and the Choctaws received funding to establish their first company, to construct low income housing. This transition from US government control to local tribal control over reservation activites is significant and enabled more effective and responsive policy decisions.

In 1979, the Packard Electric Company located a branch wire harness assembly plant in the local industrial park. The park had been built in 1971 and it took several years to recruit a company to locate in it. In 1981, American Greetings opened a plant and other companies followed, including joint equity ventures with the tribe and major companies such as Ford, Chryler, AT&T, and Xerox. Unemployment rates were around 20% by the end of the 1980's, down from 80% in the 1960's and 1970's. More young people stayed on the reservation, and the population increased.

1990's: transitioning from low-tech manufacturing to tourism/service economy

By the mid-1990's, manufacturing was the major source of employment and income for the tribe with over 2 200 employees and six manufacturing companies (Rezek and Millea, 2002). Unemployment rates dropped to about 18% by 1992 and average income increased to over USD 13 000. Expansion of the first company to locate on the reservation back in 1979 had grown to four plants, 1 200 employees, annual payroll of USD 12 million, and sales of USD 43 million.

However, change is inevitable and structural changes in the global economy impacted the manufacturing dependent reservation. In the mid-1990's, the North American Free Trade Agreement agreement ushered in major structural changes with low-skill jobs and employers moving south of the US border or off-shore. The Choctaw tribe had operated low-skill wire harness and automobile speaker assembly plants on the reservation and 1 400 jobs moved to Mexico and China. Rather than face decline, the tribe shifted its focus into a tourism and service-based economy. They did this by building a casino and resort hotel in 1994 and adding two golf courses in 1997. This created 1900 jobs (Murray, 2006).

2000 – present: enhancing tourism/service economy and transitioning to technology intensive economy

By the end of the 1990's, it was clear that traditional manufacturing was not a viable option any longer. The tribe expanded its tourism/hospitality industry by constructing another hotel and casino and a recreational water park in 2002. The resorts employ nearly 4 000 people on the reservation. All told, the MBCI is the third largest private employer in the state of Mississippi, providing 9 200 full time jobs; 65% of the employees are non-Indian. 43% of employment is focused on gaming and resort (golf/spa) enterprises while the remaining employment is non-gaming enterprises. The tribe now operates twenty-three business divisions including product lines in the following categories: medical device and pharmaceutical manufacturing, digital mapping, electronic assembly, printing, plastic moulding and distribution.

Designing effective strategies

The tribe have clearly managed to shift their strategic focus over time in response to structural economic changes to replace low-skill jobs with high-skill, technology intensive employment opportunities and operate excellent skill development programmes on-site at the reservation. Additionally, they have developed a hospitality industry that includes both low, average and higher skills to provide a diversity of employment opportunities. How have they achieved this?

The key is an integrated set of strategies focusing on self-reliance and self-determination. As the Tribe describes: "We have used flexibility to capitalise on a number of opportunities that leverage [the tribe's] resources with the resources and experience of its business partners. The tribe has kept its eye on the goal of self-determination, and has grown from the worst economic conditions to the regional leader in economic development" (MBCI, 2007). The ability for self-determination also extends to the area of training and education. Since the 1960s, the Choctaw tribe has assumed control of its educational system, established in 1964 their first high school and improved primary school facilities. They now operate the largest Indian education system in the US, whilst also having responsibility for adult training and workforce development.

While the tribe have attracted some new talent into the region, the majority of efforts outside basic schooling are focused on integrating and upgrading skills of the existing workforce. These efforts form one part of a comprehensive, strategic economic development planning focused on making the reservation an economically viable place to live and work.There are three major areas where attention, policies, and resources are directed: tribal vocational rehabilitation, workforce development, and a college programme. Each of these is described below.

Tribal vocational rehabiliation

The tribe has a unique demographic with many persons over the age of 50. This is significant because until the mid-1960's, tribal members could not receive a high school education in Mississippi, so many have been without benefit of a high school diploma. In 1971 the tribe received funding from the US. Office of Education to establish an adult education programme through the new tribal Manpower Training Centre, providing vocational education and rehabiliation. The focus of this area is to encourage high school equivalency degree education for those over 50, including identification of skills and skills training to gain or enhance participation in the workforce.

Workforce development

In the 1990s, manufacturing was the main source of income for the tribe and the focus of workforce development was basic skills and skill enhancements as needed by the employers. More recently, to support the transition into a technology intensive economy, the tribe has aggressively moved into skill development for technology intensive jobs coupled with active target industry analysis and industry recruitment. This includes development in 2006 of the Integrated Technologies Centre, a state-of-the-art workforce training facility located on the reservation and staffed and operated by the East Central Community College (ECCC).

The centre is located in the *Choctaw Tech Parc*, a master-planned business park with more than 150 acres catering to high-tech companies. ECCC serves a five county region with 60 000 persons in the workforce. The centre provides customised training for employers locating on the park and in the nearby community. The focus of the facility is to select, assess, train, upgrade and transition employees using customised standards for technology intensive industry. The tribe's Office of Economic Development also routinely assesses the types of skills needed for current and prospective employers and works with the training programmes to ensure these needs can be addressed. They find that skill needs are relatively easy to determine, as most enterprises operate on contracts that are 12 to 24 months out in the future, so have time to determine the skills needed and set up training. In 2006, the tribe developed a collaborative relationship with the East Central Community College, which includes the provision of staffing to the centre.

In 2004, the state of Mississippi implemented the Workforce Consolidation Act to serve as an oversight policy for all workforce development programmes with state and federal government funding. Thus, the Integrated Technology Centre became the designated facility for coordinating federally funded workforce programmes. It is one of ten places in the US offering a demonstration training programme for Advanced Manufacturing Integrated Systems Technology[1] with both degree standards and advanced training, and curriculum titled worker training for dislocated workers. The facility certifies to the standards for the National Centre for Construction Education and Research in industrial maintenance and crafts (see *www.crafttraining.com* and *www.nccer.org* for additional information). It also provides training for national skills in advanced

Box 5.1. **Integrated technologies centre**

The Integrated Technologies Centre offers customised training to regional employers to meet technical and professional workforce needs. The centre is staffed by East Central Community College faculty and adjunct faculty (specialists in the major training areas). It is funded by one state of Mississippi and federal programme funding; employers also fund some of the customised training programmes. Services and available training include:

Technical training capabilities

Apprenticeship Program (NCCER — Craft Specific); CNC Troubleshooting; Electric Motor Controls; Electrical Wiring (Residential/Commercial/ Industrial);Electrical (Basic to Advanced); Electronic Drive Systems; Electronics (Basic to Advanced); Heating and Air-Conditioning; Hydraulics-Pneumatics; Industrial Maintenance (Basic to Advanced); Integration of Automated Technologies; Mechanical Drive Systems; Online Industrial Maintenance Training Library; Programmable Logic Controls; Robotics; Welding (Basic to Advanced).

Small business development

Accounting Procedures; Business Plans; Existing Business Expansion; Customer Service; Marketing; Tax Information.

Basic skills

Certified Applicant Training; Personal/Career Life Skills Classes; Spanish Classes.

Human resources

Applicant Assessment/Selection; Conflict Management Sessions; Leadership Skills Training; Motivation Workshops; Quality Control Support; Safety (OSHA Endorsed); Supervisory Skills Training; Teamwork and Team Management; Truck Driver and Fork-Truck Training.

Computer applications

Microsoft Office; Quick Books; Online Training Library; *www.mindleaders.com*.

manufacturing standards in conjunction with the National Centre for Integrated Systems Technology (*www.ncist.ilstu.edu*).

According to the centre, as manufacturing work environments become increasingly high-tech, it is critical that new workers be trained – technologists who can operate, troubleshoot, and maintain today's industrial equipment that involves multiple integrated systems. When the United States retooled its work environments in the 1980s a small segment of the existing workforce was cross-trained to work with new and emerging technologies. Unfortunately, many of these individuals are now retiring and the skilled talent base is depleted. Manufacturers are experiencing an increased urgency to attract and retain highly skilled employees capable of maintaining the high-tech integrated systems found in today's workplace (NCIST, 2007). The facility at the Choctaw reservation focuses on providing both worker skill upgrading and development of new skills for younger workers as well – all with an emphasis on advanced manufacturing and systems technologies. To encourage entry into the workforce, the Youth Opportunity Program provides on the job experience and training for high school students.

The second workforce development programme for training is operated directly by the Choctaws through its Pearl River Resorts. The resorts include two casinos, operated since 1994 and 2002 respectively, a golf course resort, and water park. The Choctaw Hospitality Institute provides skill development for low or no skill workers and "hard to reach" groups. The programme provides an incentive by increasing pay along with training. Approximately 4 000 employees can have access to the training, with 21% of these employees being tribal members. However there is little base for professional workers in the area, so the focus of this training centre is to develop hourly employees targeting young workers or those not currently in the workforce. There is a full-time training staff of five instructors.

Basic training is provided in maths, curriculum skills and work preparation, in addition to different types of vocational training, including management education. The institute works with the programme, Achieve Global, to give training in the principles of quality and leadership to encourage all employees to focus on guest services and pursue higher skill levels. In addition the Institute offers free training to potential future employees in bar tending, dealing and other jobs specific to the gaming industry, with those who successfully complete the courses being selected as employees. Trainees receive starting wages that are higher than minimum wage, attracting potential employees from the broader region. At the higher skill end, tuition reimbursement is also provided for students willing to participate in hospitality degree programmes offered locally through regional universities.

College programme

In the mid-1990's, the tribe also established a wider college scholarship fund for any member wishing to seek a degree. The strategy here is to educate young graduates and work with them to identify job opportunities for them to return to the reservation after acquiring the degree. Each tribal member has a 100% scholarship through post-graduate studies provided once certain criteria are met, and a new programme tracks each of the participants in order to have a job ready for them if they chose to return to the reservation. This programme is targeted to the age 25 and under members (over one-half of the tribe's members).

To date, the scholarship programme has enabled over 1 400 Choctaw students to attend at least one class at a college or university of their choice, and nearly 900 have been enrolled on a full-time basis. To date, 378 Choctaw scholars have completed over 400 degrees.

Other elements of the Choctaw Tribe community plan include:

Attracting new talent

The issue of attracting highly skilled or professional talent to the area has been problematic. It has been difficult to attract highly skilled professionals, such as aerospace engineers, to locate in the area because it is semi-rural. However, the tribe has responded by establishing degree collaborations with universities. Tulane of New Orleans and Mississippi State University both provide on-site educational opportunities, including for obtaining undergraduate and graduate degrees. Also, there are cases where tribal members have been recruited or enticed to return to the area after living away because of new job opportunities on the reservation.

Integrating hard-to-reach groups

For jobs requiring no or low levels of skills, the area has a large potential workforce of nearly 60 000 persons locally so there seems to be ample workers to draw from for these types of positions. However, one of the biggest challenges facing employers in the area is convincing the local population to take advantage of training opportunities and the chance to upgrade their skills and earning potential. In the greater region of east central Mississippi, the workforce participation rate is low, with approximately 40% of eligible workers choosing not to participate. These latent workers represent a potential workforce, but need to gain and upgrade skills. The Choctaw Hospitality Institute works with the Tribal Vocational Rehabilitation programme to identify and place workers with no or low skills into their training programmes. It is on a case by case basis and to date, has resulted in placements for previously unemployed persons. For more skilled jobs, the East Central Community College regularly takes a mobile training unit to rural areas to entice potential workers to explore training opportunities. As several of the employers discussed, there is a need to convince locals of the opportunities to be pursued and community outreach is one such way. The social and cultural organisations in the region also help to distribute information about employment and training opportunities.

Supporting displaced workers

The tribe also supports those displaced by the restructuring of local industries. For example this year 73 employees will be retrained from a plant that is converting to a new higher technology use and hiring 50 or 60 new employees to work on upcoming contracts. There are training programmes in place to transition them to advanced manufacturing systems technology, consisting of a 200 hour curriculum that is approved by a national training centre and implemented on the reservation.

The implementation framework

A policy of self-determination

The Choctaw tribe develops its own strategies and plans for implementation, drawing in technical and professional support where needed, and proceeds to actualise desired outcomes through assertive and determined actions. The tribe maintains an Office of Economic Development to oversee the activities and make adjustments as needed to optimise effectiveness. They work in close collaboration with the Missippi Workforce Development Board and with the regional educational system of the community college system in Mississippi.

The US Bureau of Indian Affairs provides funding to the Choctaws, as it does to other tribes throughout the country. However, as described above in the 1960's, the tribe struck an agreement with the bureau to directly manage schools, medical clinics and other services. This level of local control is not typical for tribes yet is highly effective for the Choctaws. A further turning point came in 1972 when the MBCI Tribal Council passed a resolution stating: "The Tribal Council seeks to position itself to administer and operate on a contractual basis all federal programmes that are now conducted by other agencies for the benefit of the tribe. Such a policy will enable the Choctaw tribe to gain effective control of key socio-political institutions which affect the Choctaw people."

In 1975, this wish was granted when the US Government passed the Indian Self-Determination and Assistance Act which codified the right of Indian tribes to contract out Federal programmes and services (Ferrara, 1998, 90).

Another aspect of the MBCI is unique – the willingness, beginning in the 1970's to reinvest individual tribe members' share of revenues/funds in the community. The chief and council decided to pursue a self development strategy, investing in their community rather than dividing up the majority of revenues to individual tribal members. This is not typical with most Native American tribes. For example, the Seminole Tribe of Florida shares revenues at a rate of over USD 5 000 per month, per family member. The MBCI members each receive USD 1 000 per member, per *year*, in contrast. The remaining revenues, from the US Bureau of Indian Affairs and the substantial revenues generated from the tribal business enterprise division, are reinvested into the community. This includes a variety of social and cultural facilities and services as well as enhanced educational systems, healthcare, and business enterprises.

Why did the MBCI take this radical departure from the standard way of tribal operations? Chief Phillip Martin, who assumed that position in 1962 has been the key in this approach. He convinced tribal members that the old way of doing business, with the Bureau of Indian Affairs controlling decisions, was not in the best interest of the tribe long term. They were not thriving, and indeed, their survival was at stake. It required a departure from convention. Chief Martin has been instrumental in leading the tribe to try new and innovative approaches, with a focus on investing in members' education, training and skill development. This strong leadership and "championing" of the community cause has also been a key component of positive change.

A business-led approach

The Choctaw's business-led approach is another key factor in their success, enabling them to maximise the return on their investments and as such make a relatively large social impact. The tribe's enterprises generate nearly USD 500 million per year in revenues and profits from this are reinvested in the enterprises and other areas of the tribal operations. While a majority of these revenues emanate from the gaming and resort enterprises, many profits are reinvested directly into other enterprise development. For example, gaming revenues have helped fund the new technology business park on the reservation, and also support the workforce training skills programmes. This business investment started with the development of the first industrial park in the 1960s, when the tribe began Chahta Enterprises and recruited an assembly plant from the Packard Electric Division of General Electric. Chahta Enterprises diversified its activities when assembly left to cheaper locales in other countries, and grew to be one of the state's ten largest employers by 1994 with nearly USD 85 million in revenues. Note the substantial amount of revenues generated *prior* to beginning gaming enterprises. In 1994, they opened a casino and hotel and hired employees left without jobs because of the movement away from low-skill manufacturing. In 2002, the tribe expanded its hospitality venues with another hotel and casino along with a golf resort and water park, making the area a "destination travel" location. This has caused employment in these sectors to increase dramatically, to a total of 4 000 employees on the reservation in 2007. Again, note that while tribal members hold many of these positions, the tribe does not have enough members available in its labour force to meet employment demand. Thus, the tribe's enterprises draw from the regional workforce shed for additional workers, and serves as the fifth largest private employer in the state of Mississippi with 7 000 employees currently. Historically, about 35 to 50% of employment by the tribe's enterprises are gaming and resort related. In 1996, 38% were employed by the gaming enterprises (1 900) while 3 000 employees were employed in the other enterprises (at the time, a greetings card manufacturer employed 237, while electronics assembly employed 161, etc.) These enterprises have sinced changed, reflecting the transition to a more technology intensive enterprise base, along with continued construction and development enterprise.

Along the way, the tribe has attempted to balance its business objectives with the welfare of its workers. While hospitality and tourism are growing industries, many of the jobs in this industry are not high skill or high pay. The MBCI decided to enhance the jobs in this area, by establishing a higher than minimum wage (a "living" wage with starting levels at USD 10 per hour) and offering more opportunities to move into higher-skilled jobs through education and job training.

Strong collaboration with business and between policy areas

Close working between those responsible for different policy areas, and between these actors and local employers is another factor important to their success. The close relationship which the tribe maintains with employers is crucial to their being able to forecast future skills needs and respond with the training system in place to meet those needs. Additionally, the Office for Economic Development for the tribe is co-located with the Integrated Technologies Training Centre so that industry prospects can be shown the training facilities and capabilities when they visit the reservation.

The importance of local information and data

Further, the Choctaw tribe has based their activities on a strong and continually updated set of data and information focusing on employer needs, demographic change and related issues. The MBCI's Office of Economic Development tracks demand by employers and prospective employers through its activities. When a business is interested in locating in the tribe's industrial/business park, the office will perform a review of skills available in the workforce and determine the match between the business' needs and those skills. They also commission various studies periodically to review the labour market situation. Such studies have been conducted in 1983, 1986, 1996, and 2006.

In 2002, an additional study, "Workforce Development: A Plan for the Mississippi Band of Choctaw Indians" (Rezek and Millea, 2002) was performed to look at specific industry sectors and skills required for those areas. Using the US Department of Labor's Occupational Information Network (O*NET), each occupation represented in the workforce is matched with occupational descriptions to characterise the knowledge, ability and skill level of the workforce. This type of information is then used to guide potential occupational or industrial mix modifications to more closely match the skills of the workforce. O*NET[2] is a federal database that describes 1 122 occupations by a set of job characteristics. It is used for a variety of purposes related to training programmes, career counselling, job matching and referral, and other human resources functions, with each of the occupations described in terms of the knowledge, skills, and abilities necessary for the job (Rezek and Millea, 2002). These data are used by the tribe in conjunction with other information, such as the US Bureau of Labour Statistic "Career Guide to Industries" which forecasts labour market conditions in 42 industries.

More recently, in 2006, a report, "Jobs Outlook on the Choctaw Reservation", looked specifically at future skills demand (see Box below).

Box 5.2. **Jobs outlook on the Choctaw Reservation: analysing skill gaps**

Jobs Outlook on the Choctaw Reservation, *2006* found the following professions areas would be needed:

- Teachers at all levels; nursing; computer science/information technology; physicians; accounting; engineering; and social work.

In technical areas, the following will be needed:

- Electrical technology and electrical technology; heating, ventilation and air conditioning technicians; auto and diesel mechanics; gerontology; hotel management; culinary arts and food services; truck driving; and carpentry (Murray, 2006).

Implementation

The tribe is the primary actor for implementation. Plans and activities are established by the tribal council with oversight from the chief. The structure for implementation is provided by the tribe's professional offices and is periodically reviewed, with oversight by the Government Services Division and Legislative Branch. Each year, the Tribal Profile is compiled, and there is also involvement with the US Bureau of Indian Affairs, although it is important to note that the entire programme is one that is designed, implemented, and managed by the Choctaw tribe.

The tribe is organised with an Executive Branch (tribal chief), Government Services Division (administrative offices and independent agencies such as the Choctaw Tax Commission), Legislative Branch (tribal council) and the Business Enterprise Division. There are a variety of committees under the legislative branch, including economic development and community services. These committees coordinate with the Business Enterprise Division and the Administrative Department of Employment and Training under the Government Services Division. The chief and staff serve the executive function, with the two other major divisions reporting directly to that office (Government Service and

Business Enterprise). It could be compared somewhat to the "checks and balances" system in that the legislative branch does not report directly to the executive branch.

The professional structure of the tribe has been much strengthened since the 1960s. From 1960 to 1975, the emphasis was on creating a sophisticated professionalised tribal administrative structure. In 1960, the tribe had no service facilities and one employee and was reliant on the US Bureau of Indian Affairs (BIA). Resources were invested in recruiting and training high quality administrative staff and taking over control from the BIA. The staff served as the planning core, and drafted proposals for federal contracts and grants and new business enterprises, under the direction of the chief (Ferrara, 1998). In 1975, the tribe restructured and established separate legislative and executive branches, with elections for chief by tribal election every four years. The 16 members of the tribal council are elected to staggered four year terms, and committees help provide oversight and policy direction in each of the areas (Ferrara, 1998, 88).

It is also important to note that professional staff members manage and are employed in the departments. These are permanent employees of the Tribe and work with a series of "oversight councils" to make sure desired results are achieved. For example, the Office of Economic Development has professional, industry certified economic developers managing the office. Oversight is by a corresponding committee, Employment and Training, as well as collaboration with the economic development committee of the Legislative Branch. Consultants are periodically employed as well for special assignments, for example, to conduct workforce assessments. Additionally, the tribe collaborates with the East Central Community College and other organisations to provide workforce development. For example they have worked closely with the Mississippi Workforce Development programme (a state-funded programme) to customise labour force training requests and provide skill upgrading. They also work with this programme to develop apprenceships.

Budgetary considerations

Currently, education and training receive a relatively high level of funding in the reservation, with an average of USD 3 700 per employee being spent in the high skills area. Less is spent for the low skills jobs. The East Central Community College provides funding as well, via its training programmes, and the primary source of its funding is via the state and federal workforce programme dollars. Specific percentages of tribal revenues are not released, but it is important to note that the majority of profits from revenues are reinvested in the MBCI enterprises and supporting social organisations. The origin of the funding for workforce development is from the enterprise revenues as well as some funding via state and federal workforce development training programmes.

The latter are channelled predominately through the Integrated Technologies Centre at the East Central Community College.

Performance management and evaluation tools

The MBCI's Office of Economic Development tracks outcomes for the skill strategies, focusing on employment levels and employer development needs. While federal or state monies are attached to outcomes, the Choctaws generate large amounts of revenues itself and are thus able to retain more control in how they reinvest those funds for achieving desired outcomes. The MBCI is held accountable for spending funding as allocated via its tribal council, representing the tribal members. Also, each office is reviewed to ensure that funding is allocated and spent according to tribal goals and objectives. The Executive and Legislative Branches review progress towards goals and revise as needed, in terms of resource allocation and new initiatives if necessary. This is the major oversight structure for internal performance monitoring and evaluation.

Collaboration and regional co-operation

It is important to note that while the Choctaws have a policy of self-determination, this has not led a purely inward looking approach. The Choctaws collaborate extensively with other public agencies, non-profit groups, and the private business sector. For example, they participate in the Rural West Alabama-East Mississippi Enterprise-Ready Programme. This 37-county area, known as the WIRED zone, focuses on innovative programmes in entrepreneurship, workforce development and wealth creation. Using asset-based economic development strategies, the region has the mission of skill development through training, financing, facilities to support entrepreneurs and to support skill development for attracting growth industries and higher paying jobs. The WIRED region initiative is supported by grant funding from the US Department of Labor's Workforce Innovation in Regional Economic Development programme (Workforce Development Centre, 2007). The initiative has helped the MBCI further define its workforce needs in terms of skill enhancement needed to meet employment opportunities. Conversely, the MBCI has helped form the focus for the WIRED programme, as can be seen in the stated goals, each of which relates to MBCI initiatives. These goals are: 1) stand up and embed the capacity to identify key assets and strengths, target opportunities, and recruit champions to build an enterprise-ready region; 2) cultivate community and regional entrepreneurship; 3) credential, certify, and transform regionally-branded workforce; and 4) engage K-12 schools and youth development programmes in regional branding and enterprise-ready activities.

Impact

The modern history of the tribe is striking, with progression from one of the worst pockets of poverty in the poorest state in the US to becoming an admired model of self-sufficiency, strategic collaboration and asset based development. This economic expansion benefits not only the tribal members but also the residents of surrounding communities. An economic impact study of Choctaw employment was conducted in 2001. It determined that for every job created on the reservation, another .44 was created in the regional economy (Millea and Rezek, 2001).

Unemployment rate

The tribe was recently at full employment, with the unemployment rate at 2% as of 2007. This compares with the county (Neshoba) level rate of 5.1% as of the fourth quarter 2006, a state rate for Mississippi of 6.2%, and a country rate for the US at 4.2% (Federal Deposit Insurance Corporation, 2007). The following illustrates the changes in unemployment rates over a five year time-frame to 2007.

Table 5.1. **Unemployment rates 2002-2007: MBCI, Neshoba County and Mississippi**

Place	Year	Rate (%)
MBCI	2007	2.0
	2006	2.0
	2005	3.0
	2004	3.0
	2003	4.0
	2002	4.0
Neshoba County, MS	2007	5.4
	2006	4.6
	2005	6.3
	2004	4.5
	2003	5.9
	2002	7.9
Mississippi	2007	6.8
	2006	6.4
	2005	7.1
	2004	5.5
	2003	6.5
	2002	7.0

Source: Compiled from data from the Mississippi Department of Economic Security, 2007; Federal Deposit Corporation, 2007; and the Mississippi Band of Choctaw Indians.

Employment demand

Employment demand continues to be high, as the MBCI expands its operations. This in turn attracts more employees to the area to participate in the employment opportunities. For the hospitality side of the business enterprises, demand continues to be high, and is expected to grow as tourism increases. The tribe regularly advertises in the region to attract new employees, and thus far has been able to meet needs.

The skills, knowledge and abilities of an area determine its attraction to types of firms and businesses. Approximately 60% of the tribal members now have a high school degree or higher. The skill levels of the tribal members vary within the workforce vary from no skill to highly skilled. However it is estimated that approximately 20% of the workforce is highly skilled in advanced manufacturing or professional skills such as those skills required by tribal companies such as Applied Geo Technologies (working with speciality engineered fabrics for water and fuel tanks, for example).

Analysis suggests that the Choctaw's reputation for high "trainability" is seen as a key factor for employers and is evidenced by the operation of highly advanced manufacturing facilities on the reservation, employing tribal members as well as others from the region. As mentioned an example of this is Applied Geo Technologies, Inc. (AGT) a 100% tribally owned enterprise with headquarters at the reservation and other operations at the Stennis Space Centre, Kelly Aviation Centre in San Antonio, Texas, Huntsville, Alabama, and Oro Grande, New Mexico. The company provides advanced manufacturing for systems integration, electronics fabrication, and electromagnetic controls. While the skill sets may not already be present in the local workforce, the workers are highly trainable with the programmes available and it has not been a deterrent to hire workers for this facility. A regional workforce that has low skills is a challenge, yet if they are willing to be trained, it can be key to successful workforce outcomes. Special skills to work with sophisticated materials and assembly of hydraulics for military equipment are examples of technology-intensive training that is provided to employees of AGT. As of 2007, AGT employed 159 workers, 19 at the Choctaw, Mississippi location. Of these, half were tribal members.

Demography

There is now a stable population base now in the Choctaw tribe, with current population at 9 660 enrolled members of whom 8 200 live on reservation in Mississippi. All have at least 50% quantum degree of Choctaw blood. The fact that half of the tribal population is under the age of 25 also promises a sustainable demographic trend and population growth for the future.

Conclusions

The Mississippi Band of Choctaw Indians has overcome extreme poverty via its focus on self-reliance, self-determination and asset based economic development approaches. The tribe has focused heavily on education and economic development, with the idea that both are mutually supportive. The economic development revenues provide funding for continuing educational activities while the latter supports skill development for supporting additional development outcomes. A key strength is that rather than resist change or wait for others to determine what should be done, the MBCI tailored its strategy to changing conditions.

The specific strategies have changed over time but the underlying theme is constant: invest in people via education and skill upgrading while at the same time developing enterprises to provide jobs matching those skills. The first phase was to develop low-skill, low-wage manufacturing assembly jobs. After this type of jobs declined, the move was to the hospitality/tourism industry with some improvement in job skills and generally higher wages than minimum. More recently, the strategy has shifted to developing technology intensive jobs that require a higher level of skill while paying higher wages.

Training and workforce development has focused on three areas to serve its unique demographic of over 50% under the age of 25, and many of the remaining over the age of 50: tribal vocational rehabiliation, workforce development and the college programme. The strategies have worked well, with nearly full employment now on the reservation. The key focus now is to help current workers upgrade their skills while attracting additional employees as enterprises expand. Their strategy in this regard is to both encourage employee development from within the tribe while also working with others in the larger community. Still, there are many others not in the workforce in the greater region, and this represents a challenge. As the MCBI expands its business enterprises, it will need to draw in additional workers from the greater region to satisfy demand.

A further lesson to consider from this case is the importance of a management and implementation structure which provides a strong, local control over decision making processes. As noted, not every community can achieve this type of autonomy in decision making, given the unique governing structure of the tribe. However, others can take away that local control is important, and not rely too heavily on outside or external sources to make results happen. Conversely, while retaining strong local control, the tribe has reached out for collaborative relationships for workforce training and development, benefitting both themselves and the larger community.

The Choctaw case demonstrates that investing in worker skill upgrading and development is crucial. Not only will it yield benefits regarding employment opportunities, it will enable the community to have greater choices regarding their economic future. Further, it is critical to note that strong leadership has been provided by the chief since the 1960's. Chief Martin's role as a champion for the tribal community has made a significant difference in accomplishments. This holds true for any community – there must be someone or a core group of people who believe that positive change is possible and work for those changes. Without the leadership component, it is difficult to actualise desired outcomes. Providing leadership in the case of the MBCI did not imply one person making all decisions; rather, it incorporates building a strong community governing structure. This includes hiring talent and professional permanent staff, so that the tribe is able to fully develop its capabilities.

The Choctaw tribe's success with community economic development is admired by other tribes throughout North America, as well as other cities and regions. The Choctaws are visited frequently to learn about their high level of success and how some of these lessons can be used to help others. The tribe also provides advice and guidance to other tribes in the Western US to help address issues of chronic poverty. The lessons learned about its success can be transferrable to other places, particularly the practice of self-determination – communities and regions actualising their desired outcomes with strategic approaches and a mindset of investing in their citizens. The Choctaw tribe illustrates that effective and innovative practice in designing local skill strategies can achieve desired outcomes and benefit not only the local community but the greater region as well.

Notes

1. Integrated systems technology is an adult learner programme providing a variety of features to accommodate diverse learning styles of adults. This includes: modular instruction with content and tasks broken into small applied segments; industry-designed curriculum specifically based upon industrial tasks to be performed in future jobs; self-paced learning; authentic assessment for learners to demonstrate skills acquired; web-enabled curricula available via the Internet; hands-on training; multi-media instruction; and group activities in teams of two to attain specific competency levels.
2. O*NET is a comprehensive database that divides the three main categories of knowledge, skills and abilities into multiple subcategories: 33 for knowledge; 35 for skills, and 52 for ability. For each occupation, a standardised score of 0 (irrelevant) to 100 (essential) for each subcategory is given, which indicates the value of that attribute for any occupation. For example, postsecondary college teaching as an occupation would indicate a 100 in the knowledge category of education and training, while in the skills category, a score of 0 may be indicated for skills such as repairing a machine. See *http://online.onetcenter.org/* for additional information.

Bibliography

Applied Geo Technologies, Inc. (AGT) (2007), "Economic Development Update", AGT Inc., Choctaw, MS.

Federal Deposit Insurance Corporation (2007), "Report for County Overview", retrieved *www.fdic.gov/recon/*, accessed 10 May 2007.

Ferrara, Peter (1998), "The Choctaw Revolution, Lessons for Federal Indian Policy", Tax Reform Foundation, Washington, DC.

Millea, Meghan and Jon Rezek (2001), "The Economic Impacts of the Mississippi Band of the Choctaw Indians on the State of Mississippi", report to the Mississippi Band of Choctaw Indians.

Mississippi Band of Choctaw Indians (MBCI) (2007), "A Tribal Profile", MBCI, Choctaw, MS.

Mississippi Department of Economic Security (2007), "Labour Market Data", MDES, Jackson, Mississippi.

Murray, Steve (1996), "Choctaw Reservation Labour Market Survey", report to the Choctaw Vocational Education Programme.

Murray, Steve (2006), "Job Outlook on the Choctaw Reservation", report to the Mississippi Band of Choctaw Indians.

National Centre for Integrated Systems Technology (2007), *www.ncist.org*, accessed 23 March 2007.

Rezek, John and Meghan Millea (2002), "Workforce Development: A Plan for the Mississippi Band of Choctaw Indians", Mississippi State University, Starkville, MS.

Workforce Development Centre (2007), "West Alabama-East Mississippi Building an Enterprise-Ready Region", East Central Community College Decatur, Mississippi.

PART II

Chapter 6

Addressing Skills Shortfalls in Mackay, Australia

by
Cristina Martinez-Fernandez*

The region of Mackay in Australia has experienced unprecedented growth and wealth creation since 2004, putting significant pressure on company development. In response, manufacturing companies in Mackay have formed an industry cluster named "Mackay Area Industry Network" (MAIN) with the purpose of addressing skills shortages quickly and effectively. The result was the MAIN CARE programme – a programme designed to recruit, select and manage apprentices in the workplace. The main success of the scheme has been improving retention rates within the apprenticeship programmes which previously had high drop-out rates. This chapter situates the approach within wider skills strategies in Queensland, and assesses whether an employer-led approach can fully integrate hard-to-reach groups into the workforce development system.

* Dr. Tamara Weyman and Merete Bjorkli collected and computed statistical data for this paper. Melissa Telford and Helen Easton provided proofreading services. Many thanks to managers and professionals of organisations from Mackay and other parts of Queensland. Their participation in face-to-face telephone and e-mail interviews provided the insights recorded in this paper.

Introduction

Mackay is a city of 112 607 habitants located on the central coast of the state of Queensland in Australia. Mackay has the distinction of being the largest sugar producing region in Australia, and has the largest bulk sugar facility in the world (737 000 tonne capacity). In addition, the Mackay region has one of the largest coal loading terminals in the southern hemisphere (Hay Point) with a capacity of over 50 million tonnes per annum. Mackay's mineral and mining industry accounts for more than 20 coal mines operating in the region. Most of this growth occurred since 2004, putting significant pressure on company development; skills-shortages in particular are still a constant threat to industry growth, even in times of economic downturn.

Mackay's extraordinary growth draws attention to the mismatch of talent in the area, as well as the lack of skilled people. Skilled workers from the sugar industry needed re-training for the mining boom; there was a shortage of school-leavers wishing to enter a trade; and the available large Maltese and indigenous populations were a wasted source of un-tapped talent. This situation is not unique to Mackay; the state of Queensland is experiencing an economic boom with rapid business growth and a general shortage of skills in many areas.

A new report shows wealth in the Mackay region in north Queensland continues to grow, despite the global financial crisis. The State of the Regions report, by National Economics, shows the mining boom has had a significant impact on the overall wealth of the region. It shows on a per capita basis, each person earned more than AUD 23 000, a 35% jump from 2003. In the same time frame, the percentage of people who were unemployed almost halved to 4.4%. More than 20 000 people have moved to the region in the past six years; those between the ages of 30 and 54 remain the biggest portion of the population. With the mining boom continuing, construction of non-residential buildings jumped almost 60% since 2003, while residential buildings increased by 26% (ABC Tropical Queensland, 2880).

This chapter discusses how Mackay's skills issues are being addressed through a combination of national, regional and local strategies; in particular the Australian framework for skills, the state of Queensland's Skills Plan, and chiefly a business led strategy in Mackay relating to the manufacturing industry. The Queensland Skills Plan, established in March 2006, is particularly relevant to the Mackay region in that it has a particular focus on trade shortages.

In parallel, as Mackay was experiencing strong growth, the private manufacturing sector developed its own strategy in collaboration with local organisations to quickly deal with skills shortages. The latter initiative is particularly innovative in adjusting the national Australian Apprenticeships scheme to local market needs, although unlike the broader Skills Plan it does not actively target disadvantaged groups.

This study has used desktop research, analysis of databases and interviews as the main methods of investigation. Data sources used in this paper are: census data from the Australian Bureau of Statistics (ABS); local government databases; data from the Australian Department of Education, Employment and the Arts (DETA); data from the Bureau of Transport and Regional Economics (BTRE); from the Queensland Office of Economics and Statistical Research (OESR); from the Queensland State Development and Trade; from the Department of Immigration and Citizenship (DIAC); and from the Department of Employment and Workplace Relations (DEWR). Interview data from MAIN, Mackay City Council, Mackay Whitsunday Regional Development Economic Corporation (REDEC), Queensland Government State Development and Trade, Technical and Further Education Institutes (TAFE), the Department of Education, Training and the Arts (DETA), migration consultants, and private companies provide further explanatory detail.

This paper begins with a description of the national policy context for skills development in Australia. This is followed by a discussion of the context of the state of Queensland and the Skills Plan. The remainder of the paper examines the local socio-economic context of the Mackay region, and presents skills strategies in Mackay. Finally some concluding remarks and good practices are highlighted.

The national context

The Australian economy has been a long period of high economic growth from the mid 1980's to 2006, registering a small recession in 1990-1991 and a limited impact from the economic crisis in 2008. Among the factors that contributed to this economic prosperity are low inflation, an openness within the national economy towards the global economy, increased productivity driven by technological development, the emergence of knowledge-based sectors and economic policies associated with trade liberalisation, deregulation and micro-economic reform (Larcombe, 2005).

This high economic growth has had impressive economic outcomes for Australia with official unemployment rates declining from 11% rate in early 1970's to the low 4.2% rate in 2008. Incomes per capita have increased by 50% over the past 15 years due to high productivity and a favourable trade with Asian neighbours, especially China. Australia's resources sector has experienced strong demand from China which imports Australian minerals and energy commodities. Analysts warn, however, that in a global period of economic uncertainty, the Chinese economy is over-heating[1] and therefore Australia's economic bonanza might not last.

One of the consequences of strong economic growth with full employment is the emergence of skills shortages as the economy grows. It also needs to be taken into account, however, that in Australia a person is defined as "employed" if they work more than one hour per week. Therefore, there are a large number of adults that are under-employed or in employment conditions below the poverty line. In many cases this pool of under-employed persons would prove difficult to reintegrate because their skills do not match employment demand. For example, unemployment rates for managers, professionals, associate professionals and advance clerical workers have reached historically low levels in the last decade – between 1% and 2%. The trend for unemployment rates for tradespersons and related workers is also declining and significant skills shortages are emerging in these areas. On the other hand, unemployment rates of service workers and labourers continue to increase despite high growth rates during this period.[2]

Within this context the Australian government funds a number of programmes addressing the skills needed to secure a sustainable economic future for the country. This includes the promotion of skilled migration, Skilling Australia (an agreement of the Commonwealth and the states[3] for skilling Australia's workforce), and the Australian Apprenticeship Scheme. These programmes are briefly discussed below.

Skilled migration

The Australian Department of Immigration and Citizenship has established the Skills Matching Database[4] (SMD) to help match skilled immigrants with skilled vacancies or skill shortages in Australia. This database is used by employers for employer sponsored migration categories, as well as by state and territory governments. The Department of Immigration and Citizenship (DIAC) funds Regional Outreach Workers to assist employers in regional areas with the migration process. Regional outreach workers also help local agencies to use the migration system to meet specific local skills needs.

Skilling Australia

In broader terms, the long term planning and strategic directions for vocational education and training (VET) in Australia were identified in "Shaping our Future", Australia's National Strategy for Vocational Education and Training 2004-2010. Reinforcing this commitment, the 2005-2008 Commonwealth–State Agreement for Skilling Australia's Workforce created the basis for a partnership between the Australian, state and territory governments to work together to support new national training arrangements on a consensus approach (Australian Government, 2006).The agreement established national priorities and a new national training system (see Box 6.1). The agreement provided close to AUD 5 billion over the 2005-2008 quadrennium with the potential to create up to 128 000 additional training places Australia-wide.

Box 6.1. **Skilling Australia framework**

National priorities

- Improving the system's responsiveness to rapid changes in demand for skills development and addressing skills shortages, especially in traditional trades and in emerging industries.
- Delivering improved outcomes for employers, individuals and communities.
- Improving quality.
- Increasing participation and up-skilling mature age workers.
- Encouraging greater re-engagement in training by Australians who are not fully participating in the labour market.

The new national training system

- Industry and business needs drive training policies, priorities and delivery.
- Better quality training and outcomes for clients, through more flexible and accelerated pathways.
- Processes should be simplified and streamlined to enhance national consistency.
- Young people have opportunities to gain a wide range of lasting skills that provide a strong foundation for their working lives.
- Training opportunities are expanded in areas of current and expected skills shortage.
- National governance and accountability framework: establishes the decision-making processes and bodies responsible for training, as well as planning and performance monitoring arrangements to guide the operation and growth of the training system.
- National Skills Framework: sets out the system's requirements for quality and national consistency in terms of qualifications and the delivery of training. The National Quality Council monitors quality assurance procedures in the vocational education and training sector.

Source: Australian Government (2006).

A new national training infrastructure, Australian Technical Colleges (ATCs), also commenced operations in 2006, in addition to the state based TAFE Technical Colleges. The ATCs are an AUD 351 million Australian Government initiative to encourage and prepare more young Australians for traditional trades. There are 28 ATCs across Australia in areas where there are skills needs, a high youth population and a strong industry base. These colleges cater for students in years 11 and 12 who wish to study for their year 12 certificate and start an apprenticeship whilst still at school. The colleges target five priority industries where skill shortages are acute: metal and engineering, automotive, building and construction, electrotechnology, and commercial cookery. An innovative component of the ATCs is the leadership role that local industry and business is playing in the operation and governance of the colleges, a model already used in the state-based TAFE colleges.

Australian apprenticeships scheme

Australian Apprenticeships is a scheme directed to attract people to trades. It combines training and employment that leads to a nationally recognised qualification. Apprenticeships are accessible to anyone of working age and do not require any entry qualification. In March 2006, there were 403 600 Australian Apprentices in training (National Centre for Vocational Education Research, 2007). Since 1 July 2006 the Australian Apprenticeship Incentives Program provides financial incentives to employers who employ and train an apprentice or trainee. A summary of the scheme and the latest incentives is provided in the Annex (see Box 6.A1.1).

In addition to the Australian Apprenticeship Incentives Program, the government released the Skills for the Future package on 12 October 2006. This package, worth AUD 837 million over five years, involves a set of initiatives focusing on the need for continuous upgrading of the skills of the workforce. These initiatives include:

- Apprentice Wage Top-Up – a tax free payment of AUD 1 000 per year for first and second year apprentices under 30 in trades facing skills shortages.
- Business Skills Vouchers worth up to AUD 500 available to apprentices or newly qualified tradespersons in traditional trades as a contribution towards the cost of undertaking accredited business skills training.
- Incentives for Higher Technical Skills of at least AUD 4 000 for Diploma and Advanced Diploma qualifications, particularly in engineering fields.
- Financial Support for Mid-Career Workers (aged 30 or more) to upgrade their skills through an apprenticeship in a trade occupation in high demand. The payment is made to either the employer or the apprentice –

AUD 150 per week (AUD 7 800 per annum) in the first year and AUD 100 per week (AUD 5 200 per annum) in the second year.

- Support for Fast Track Apprentices to help apprentices reach their qualification sooner while still meeting all the requirements of employers and industry (Department of Education, Sciences and Training, 2007).

National priorities in Australia are strongly oriented towards solving the acute skills shortages in many trades, a disappearing core talent, especially in manufacturing regions. Trades are quickly vanishing in Australia as occupations related to the knowledge economy (such as managers and associated professionals) more successfully attract youth. Apprenticeship programmes have been the traditional way to attract new talent in this sector but the absolute number of apprentices is not a good measure for determining responses to labour market demand in the short-term. Instead, the key measure is the training rate – the ratio of apprentices to tradespersons, and the average age of on-the-job tradespersons. These measures indicate the extent to which trade occupations are able to reproduce themselves through the domestic training system. The Australian case is an interesting one because, due to the privatisation of government services, there has been a major decline in the training rate over the last decade – down by 16% in aggregate terms but as much as 25% in some trades. This, combined with the fact that the average worker in some trades is in the 50-plus age bracket, highlights a matter of serious concern, in that the training system will not able to reproduce skills lost to retirement (Toner, 2003).

As Toner (2003; 2005) has discussed, the reasons behind this situation are complex and encompass both national and international factors, which translate into an effect on the local labour market. In the case of Australia, prior to the major corporatisations and privatisations of the 80's and 90's, government-owned enterprises in major infrastructure services were significant employers of tradespersons and played a significant role in training people for industry. However, as a result of the privatisation, this training focus was lost, and a reduction of 80% to 90% in their intake of apprentices followed over the next ten years (although there has been an increase in public sector intake in recent years). Another influencing factor in the last 10-15 years has been the pattern of corporate restructuring to outsource maintenance services to labour hire companies, which rarely employ apprentices. In addition, the focus on corporate downsizing and outsourcing has led to a significant reduction in firm size in manufacturing and construction, and mining services. These small firms have less training programmes and lower investment per employee than larger firms.

The implications of a training system that is not able to reproduce skills in demand are of concern at the local level, as well as for the industry as a whole. Economic implications are evident when companies are unable to find tradespersons locally or nationally, and so have to hire from overseas markets. However, there are other critical implications in terms of innovation, which are more difficult to see in the short-term. Many of the trades experiencing skill shortages, such as metal, engineering, electrical, and construction, represent an important source of innovative activity for the manufacturing, transport, and mining industries that cannot be supplied by scientists or traditional research. Technological innovation needs the input of people on-the-job because they provide feedback in the use of machinery or processes, which then goes back to universities, research labs, and firm management. Thus, in reality, innovation activity is fuelled from the floor of the workplace (Toner, 2003). Shortages of these key trade skills have an important effect in reducing the innovation capacity of an area and of the industry in broad terms as there is a collateral reduction of professionals' input on Knowledge Intensive Service Activities (KISA).[5]

The state of Queensland and the skills plan

The whole state of Queensland was driven by strong economic growth of 3.8% in 2006 but has been forecasted to fall sharply to just 0.5% in 2009-2010 before making a recovery in 2010-2011. The gross state product growth was 5.3% in 2005-06, forecasted to drop below 1% during 2009-2010 and making a recovery in 2010-2011 of over 2%. The unemployment rate in June 2009 was 5.4%, up from the 3.5% in May 2007; forecasts predict an increase above 7% in 2010-2011.[6] Population growth is strong, reaching 4.2 million in 2008 and business investment is well over the national average. High level of services, incentives for relocation of business and a pleasant climate have attracted large numbers of people from other states to settle in Queensland in what has been called a "sea change" phenomenon.

Positive economic conditions in 2006, with an unemployment rate below the national average, the strongest competition in the labour market seen within the last 30 years, and major structural shifts across industries and markets fuelled the design of skills strategies and reforms to the training and vocational system state-wide in Queensland. In 2006, the denominated Smart State undertook the most significant reform to Queensland's skilling and training in more than 40 years with the release of the billion dollar Queensland Skills Plan in March 2006, designed to address the emergence of skills shortages (Queensland Government, 2006b).

Prior to this plan, the skills framework in Queensland was under the SmartVET – Skilling for the Smart State strategy. SmartVET was launched in June 2004[7] as a three-year pilot strategy aimed at providing skilled workers for industries central to Queensland's economic growth. From 1 July 2006 the initiatives piloted under the SmartVET strategy became part of the Queensland Skills Plan. The Skills Plan articulates specific mechanisms of action to respond to the loss of skills, to up-skill the workforce, and to integrate hard-to-reach groups. The plan integrates education policies and reforms from the national and state level to respond to present and future challenges of the labour market. The plan is a top-down approach specifically targeting broad skills infrastructure gaps affecting industry competition at the state level. Amongst the structural changes to Queensland's labour market (some of which might be unique to an Australian context) noted in the plan are:

- Decline in traditional sectors such as agriculture, primary industries, and manufacturing.
- Substantial growth of service industry sectors.
- Resurgence of industries such as mining, utilities, construction, transport and storage, and community services.
- Rising demand for skilled trades people and technicians as a result of the booms in resources and building sectors.
- Higher-than-average growth of professionals and associate professionals.
- Non-standard forms of employment occupy up to 40% of the workforce, and include part-time, casual, contractual, seasonal, self-employment, and labour hire agreements.
- An ageing workforce combined with higher levels of people taking early retirement (Queensland Government, 2006b).

Two issues were identified as critical for the design of skills strategies:

1. A serious shortage of trade skills, with current intakes to trade apprenticeships insufficient to meet the projected growth and turnover in trade occupations, and with only two-thirds of current trades people fully qualified.
2. An under-qualified associate professional workforce, with only half of the employees in some of the highest skilled jobs in Queensland holding a vocational education and training, or university qualification.

An analysis of the Skills Plan shows four broad systems for the design of skills strategies: the training system, through the vocational education sector (VET) and the technical colleges (TAFE); the industry and employers; the employees and talent pool; and a strong specific focus on trades as a key occupation that interrelates with the other systems (see Figure 6.1). These four broad systems indicate the "skills ecosystem" in Queensland, and although some characteristics might be common to other OECD growing economies, this ecosystem is strongly tied to local and regional conditions of Australia's development, and particularly the recent Queensland economic boom. The particular components of the model might not be transportable, but the model

Figure 6.1. **Queensland's skills ecosystem**

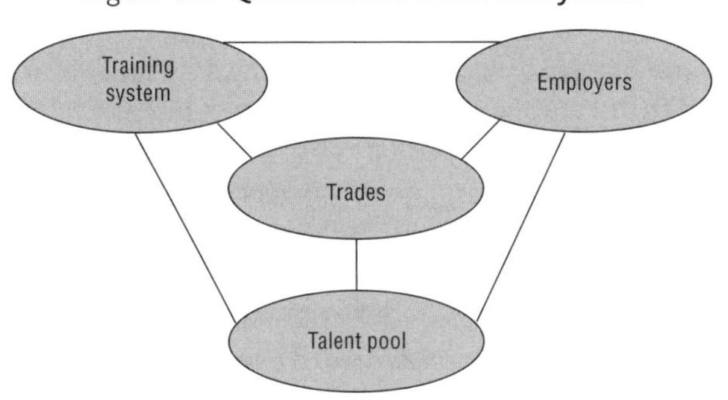

itself is interesting as a toolbox for designing skills strategies elsewhere. Skills ecosystems provide different analytical lenses in a local context for the complexity of systems involved (Martinez-Fernandez, forthcoming).

The total budget for the Skills Plan is AUD 1 billion from 2006 to 2009 (Queensland Government, 2006a). A full list of the 24 actions of the Skills Plan are found in the Annex (see Box 6.A1.2). A range of actions in the Skills Plan are dedicated to assessing training needs, skilling and labour market development at the *local level* through partnerships with industry groups. These actions include:

- *Skills Alliances* – autonomous organisations made up of major industry stakeholders, unions and employers that provide strategic advice about industry skills needs through monitoring the demands of the industry and fostering open communications with stakeholders on skilling issues. Among the services these alliances provide are the identification of the causes and effects of skill shortages, planning for future skill needs, promotion of their industry to schools and regions and encouraging each industry to take control of its skilling future.
- *Industry-Government Partnerships* – these capitalise on existing industry networks and address the industries' skilling and workforce development needs through a "whole-of-government" approach.
- *Direct Engagement* – this involves consulting with industry representative organisations to obtain specialised advice on workforce development and skilling requirements for industries. Formal agreements are put in place in certain industries for on-going consultation.
- *Centres of Excellence* – the centres' mission is to identify skills requirements at the local level, so that training priorities, products, and methods of delivery are tailored to local employers. A strong focus on development partnerships is supported by AUD 1 932 million over four years, with specific actions targeted, such as holding annual industry forums to discuss skills issues (see Box 6.2).

Box 6.2. **Centres of excellence**

Key goal: to better partner with industries on their skilling needs to lead and influence targeted industries in skills-related matters.

Existing centres: Aviation and Mining.

New centres from July 2007: Energy, Manufacturing and Engineering, Building and Construction.

Key objectives

- Provide a "one-stop-shop" for coordinating the industry sector's vocational education and training.
- To provide strategic leadership for the industry's skilling and training.
- To ensure a coordinated approach to skills formation.
- To supply crucial information to government on the sector's training needs.
- To identify skill needs at the local level, ascertain training priorities, suitable training products and ideal training delivery methods.
- To undertake workforce development planning with major firms.
- To assist government to direct its investment in training areas of greatest need.

Added value

- Develop strong and enduring links with employers and other stakeholders including unions and professional associations, education and training providers, and labour market intermediaries.
- Expand industry and enterprise focused innovation in the development of advanced training strategies.
- Future orientated in addressing skills formation issues.
- Avoid duplication of effort and attain efficiencies through specialisation.

Source: Queensland Government 2006b.

As at the Commonwealth level, attracting people into trades is an important priority for the Queensland government. Over one-third of the actions proposed in the Skills Plan are directed towards improving the trades system, with actions such as funding of AUD 159.39 million being allocated to the apprenticeship system, or 14 000 places each year up to 2010 in high level training. The development and modernisation of trades as a high profile occupation is embedded in the strategic development of the other parts of the ecosystem, and therefore monitoring of this aspect would constitute a good indication of the effectiveness of the Skills Plan.

Skills for disadvantaged groups

Despite the strong economic growth of Queensland and the low unemployment it was estimated that in 2006 around 102 000 people were jobless or looking for work. Action 21 of the Skills Plan introduced Skilling Queenslanders for Work, a new initiative that built on the successful Breaking the Unemployment Cycle initiative initiated in 1998 for disadvantaged groups in the labour market. The initiative provides a "toolbox" of mix and match strategies that can be customised to the individual, including job preparation training, mentoring, accredited vocational education and training, internships, post-participation support for up to six months, cadetships, employer wage subsidies and contribution to transport and child care costs for eligible parents and carers. The initiative is directed to support the following groups:

- People who are employed 20 hours or less per week.
- Long-term unemployed.
- People with a disability.
- Parents and carers.
- Indigenous people.
- Mature adults, aged 50+.
- Young people, aged 15-24.
- Migrants from culturally and linguistically diverse backgrounds.
- Queenslanders living in rural and remote areas.
- Ex-offenders (Queensland Government, 2006a).

For people with a disability, the government has contracted the services of Disability Works Australia (DWA), which coordinates disability recruitment for employers for free, in many instances through sub-contracting of services to other companies available in the local area.

In relation to Indigenous Australians, Skilling Queenslanders for Work expanded the number of Indigenous Employment and Training support Officers from 20 to a minimum of 40, specifically to improve the retention and completion rates of Aboriginal and Torres Islanders apprentices, trainees and vocational students.[8]

The Mackay Region

Demographic and economic figures for Mackay point towards a growing and well-performing economic region. This section provides an overview of Mackay's socio-economic profile.

Demographics

The population of the Mackay region increased from 84 856 in June 2006 to 112 607 in June 2008. The rate of increase rate is larger than the Australian average, in addition, the overall change in employment from 1991 to 2001 was 25% for Mackay compared with 17% for Australia overall. The unemployment rate has remained below the national average since 2006 (see Table 6.1).

Table 6.1. **Demographics of Mackay and Australia**

Indicators	Mackay	Australia
Estimated resident population at June 2008	112 607	20 600 856
Change in working age population (1991-2001)	20%	14%
Change in population 2001-2004	0.05%	0.03%
Median age at June 2005	35.1	36.6
Average individual annual taxable income, 2003	39 279	40 829
Population location quotient (2000-2003)	1.02	1.0
Taxable income location quotient (2000-2003)	1.04	1.0
Percentage change in employed person (1991-2001)	25%	17%
Unemployment rate 2002	8.1	6.6
2003	7.7	6.2
2004	7.1	5.7
2006	3.5	4.6
2007	2.8	4.1
2008	3.3	4.2

Source: Computed using ABS, Journey to Work 2001, ABS National Regional Profile, 2000 –2004 and BTRE Industry Structure Database, 2003. Queensland Government, 2007.

As part of this study, a Location Quotient (LQ) technique was employed to identify growth or decline in two variables: population and taxable income, between 2000 and 2003, using national figures as the reference region. The LQ encapsulates the concept of competition by considering a location's share of the national population. Mackay has an estimated residential population and income of LQ > 1, which indicates that it is growing faster both in population and income share than the nation as a whole. Population projections also indicate a consistent growth to the year 2026, with an annual growth rate of 1.7, well over the Australian average of 1.2 (see Table 6.A1.2 in the Annex).

In relation to the age structure of Mackay's population, the median age at June 2005 was 35.1 years for Mackay, which is below the Australian average of 36.6 years. The age structure from 2000 to 2004 shows a consistently higher percentage of youth (0-14 years) and working population (15-65 years) in Mackay, while the over 65 group is smaller than Australian figures.

The Mackay-Whitsunday region has grown from 247 586 estimated residents in 1991 to 294 748 people in 2005. Although Mackay city and the region as a whole are clearly growing, there are acute differences in the performance of the eight Local Government Areas (LGAs); in fact, some of them are shrinking or expected to shrink after the mining boom starts to decline. The shrinkage of the towns Belyando, Bowen, Broadsound, and Nebo is historical in nature, and although some of the towns have picked up slightly due to the coal mining in the last few years, regional agencies predict that they will fall again when the mining sector starts to decline (Interview, December 2006). A further analysis of age structure would allow a better understanding of this shrinkage in an overall hyper-growth economic region, but interview data with local agencies reveals that it is the youth and working population who are attracted to the new cosmopolitan lifestyle of Mackay city and by the demand for workers in several industry sectors.

Employment

According to the 2001 census, 43.7% of Mackay's population were employed, the same percentage as the overall Australian population. Total employment has increased by 9% for Australia and 6% for Mackay for the period1996-2001.[9] The increase in total labour market participants for the period 1991-2001 was above that of the nation in all knowledge intensive and non-knowledge intensive occupations and more acute in the "associate professionals" category, with a 98% increase (see the Annex, Table 6.A1.1).

Overall, there has been an increase of 33% of employed persons in technology and knowledge intensive industries, compared with 37% increase of the Australian working population[10] during the period 1991-2001. Of these occupations, employment of computer professionals has increased to 170% in Mackay, while other groups such as health, teaching and building engineering professionals all experienced higher increases than the national level (see Table 6.A1.2 in the Annex). Tradespersons in particular have a 20% employment increase in Mackay, but declined Australia-wide.

Even in the context of the economic downturn, employment rates are looking even higher in 2009. Participation rate in the March quarter of 2009 is 72% for Mackay region, above the figure of 65.5% for Australia and 67.8% for Queensland. The unemployment rate in Mackay declined from 8.1% in 2002 to 7.1% in 2004. This is higher than the Australian average of 6.6% and 5.7% respectively, but the rate has continued to decrease reaching 3.5% in December 2006 and 2.8% in 2007, which is below the national average of 4.6%. Latest unemployment figures show an increase to 3.3% in 2008, below the state (3.7%) and Australia (4.2%) (see Table 6.A1.1 above).

The overall ratio of workers to jobs is smaller in Mackay than in Australia, indicating skills shortages, although there are differences at the regional and local level. Mackay's city rate has gone up slightly during the period 1996-2001 while Mackay's Statistical Division (SD) rate has gone down (see Figure 6.2).

Figure 6.2. **Ratio of workers to jobs (1996 and 2001 census)**

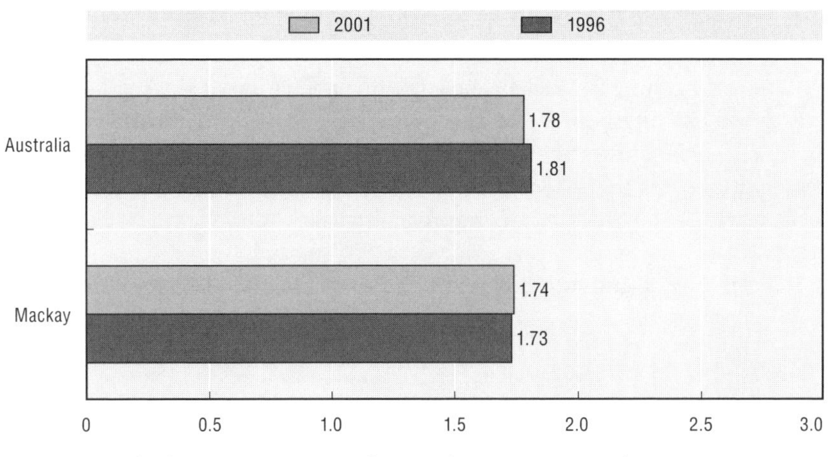

Source: Computed using ABS Census Data and BTRE Industry Structure Database, 2003.

A disaggregation of the data by occupation also shows differences in the type of jobs in demand. Associate professionals have a higher ratio than the nation (especially in Mackay's statistical area) while tradespersons and intermediate clerical and service workers and labourers have a smaller ratio especially in Mackay city (see Figure 6.A1.1 in the Annex).

Industry

At the industry level, there is evidence of structural change in Mackay for the period 1996 to 2001, while Australia as a whole has undergone little change away from the areas of business services, health services and education. The top three employing industries[11] for Mackay in 1996 were: agriculture; accommodation; cafes and restaurants; and food, beverage and tobacco manufacturing. The top employing industries changed in 2001 to: education; personal and household good retailing; and business services. The top industry specialisations also changed in Mackay from agricultural services, hunting and trapping, agriculture and commercial fishing in 1996, to coal mining, rail transport, and mining services in 2001 (see Table 6.A1.4 in the Annex).

The three ANZSIC industry subdivisions with the highest Location Quotients are identified in the database for 1996 and 2001, and labelled as the region's top (or 2nd or 3rd) specialisation. Location Quotients (LQs) are used here to relate an industry's employment share in a region to the industry's national employment share. A ratio of more than one indicates a higher degree of specialisation than the national average, while a value of less than one indicates a lower degree of specialisation in that industry. LQs can provide insight into a region's comparative advantages. It is important to recognise that an industry can be a top specialisation for a region, but account for a very small share of regional employment. The three largest LQ values for Mackay were used to identify its three top industry specialisations.

Industrial shifts in Mackay show the diversification of Mackay's economy due to the mining boom and the overspecialisation in mining services. Figure 6.3 below shows the Industrial Diversity Index (IDI), which indicates Mackay has diversified its economy in a very significant way from 1996 to 2001 because its IDI is increasing and approaching 100.

Figure 6.3. **Industrial diversity index (1996 and 2001 census)**

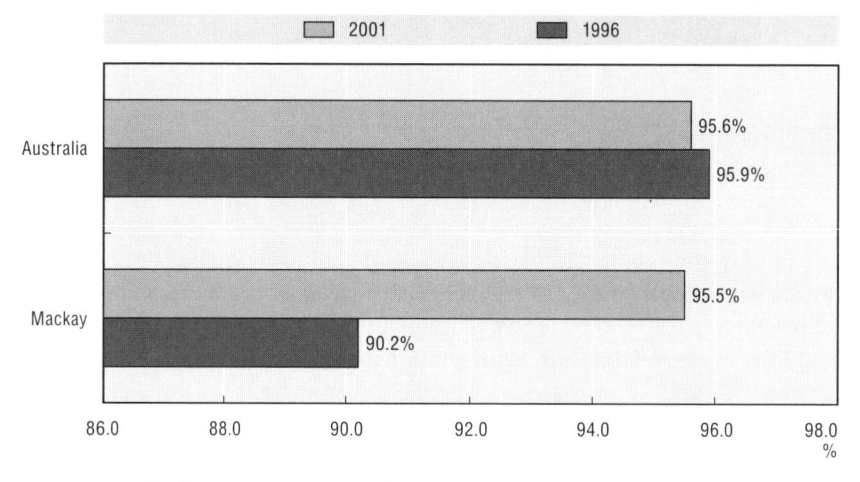

Source: Computed using ABS Census Data and BTRE Industry Structure Database, 2003.

Six industries are acknowledged by the Queensland Government (2006a) as high performing industries in Mackay: mining, agriculture, engineering services, construction, marine, and tourism. The mining industry produces over 35% of the region's output, and 76% of Queensland's coal exports. There are approximately 20 open cut and underground mines operating in the region. Advanced manufacturing and engineering represent 27% of all industrial output to the local economy with over 220 companies providing mining services. Agribusiness is a traditional sector in the region, producing goods worth a gross value of AUD 625 million in 2001. Industries include: beef cattle, sorghum, sugar, wheat, mangoes, lychees, and wild-caught fish. The region also hosts the major ethanol distillery, with bi-products utilised as stock feed and fertiliser. The gross regional product in 2003-4 grew significantly due to substantial expansion of the coal and mining industry, transport and storage, and some recovery in agriculture (see Figure 6.4).

Figure 6.4. **Percentage gross regional product at factor cost 2003-04**

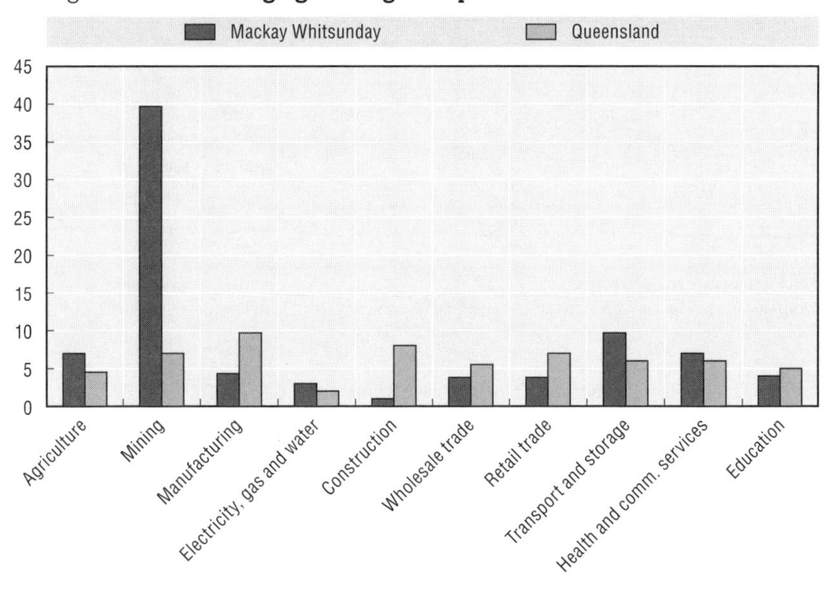

Source: Queensland Government, Department of State Development, *www.sd.qld.gov.au.*

The major contributor to employment decline for the period 1991-2001 in Mackay was food, beverage and tobacco manufacturing while the top industry specialisation was food retailing. Australia-wide, the major contributor to employment decline was the finance sector and the top industry specialisation was business services.

Skills

Mackay's education attainment has increased more than the national average in all levels except for the "diploma or advanced diploma" level over the period 1996-2001. The education attainment of trade's certificates is also significant in that it has shown growth in Mackay but declined in the nation (see Table 6.2).

Data on the number of trainees per Local Government Area (LGA) shows that the number of apprentices in training has increased significantly from 2001 to 2006 but this increase varies depending on the LGA. Table 6.3 below shows the number of apprentices from 2001 to 2006 and average commencement age for the years 2001 and 2006.

Mackay city has the highest number of apprentices in training (2001-2006) with 84.3% of all apprentices from the eight LGAs. This indicates the strong growth of the city and the increasing demand for skills in a variety of sectors from retail manufacturing, business services and hospitality. Mackay and the

Table 6.2. **Increase/decrease in total employed persons, education attainment shares (1996-2001)**

Percentage

Region	Bachelor degree or higher	Diploma or Advanced Diploma	Certificate III or IV	Certificate I or II Certificate nfd[1] and/or completed year 10 or above	Total respondents[1]
Mackay	120	8	61	11	26
Australia	95	32	44	–5	15

1. Nfd = not further defined.

Source: Computed using ABS Census Data and BTRE Industry Structure Database, 2003.

Table 6.3. **Number of apprentices per LGA (2001-2006)**

LGAs	No. of apprentices in training by calendar year as at 31 December						Mean* Com. Age	Mean Com. Age
	2001	2002	2003	2004	2005	2006	2001	2006
Belyando	45	47	78	129	208	264	18.49	18.66
Broadsound	22	82	71	78	74	139	17.82	19.08
Bowen	57	61	108	140	164	268	18.41	18.8
Mackay	940	1 109	1 364	1 627	2 053	2 671	18.16	19.14
Mirani	22	30	28	19	22	35	19.42	18.22
Nebo	7	10	11	26	53	118	19.67	19.67
Sarina	30	149	112	111	93	137	16.94	18.4
Whitsunday	117	132	113	149	209	287	17.93	18.5

* Average Commencement Age of the contract.

Source: DETA collected statistics (unpublished).

surrounding LGAs of Whitsunday, Mirani and Sarina have succeeded in attracting individuals working in the service industries, the international coal terminal and port infrastructure, and tourism. The shrinking areas of Bowen, Belyando, Nebo and Broadsound all have significant mining infrastructures and new coal mines but the population is either not stable or expected to decrease after the mining boom. Figure 6.5 shows a map of the Mackay region showing the shrinking LGAs with the number of apprentices in training. The number of apprentices in training in the shrinking areas are significantly smaller than in the Mackay LGA (scale 1:5); but indicates the investment of each of these areas in retention and upgrading of local talented people that otherwise might leave and search for jobs in more prosperous areas such as Sarina or Mackay. It is unclear if further investment in apprentice training and skills upgrading will influence remission of the shrinkage but it is a valuable strategy to explore by local agencies.

Figure 6.5. **Map of Mackay showing number of apprentices (2001-2006) and shrinking LGAs**

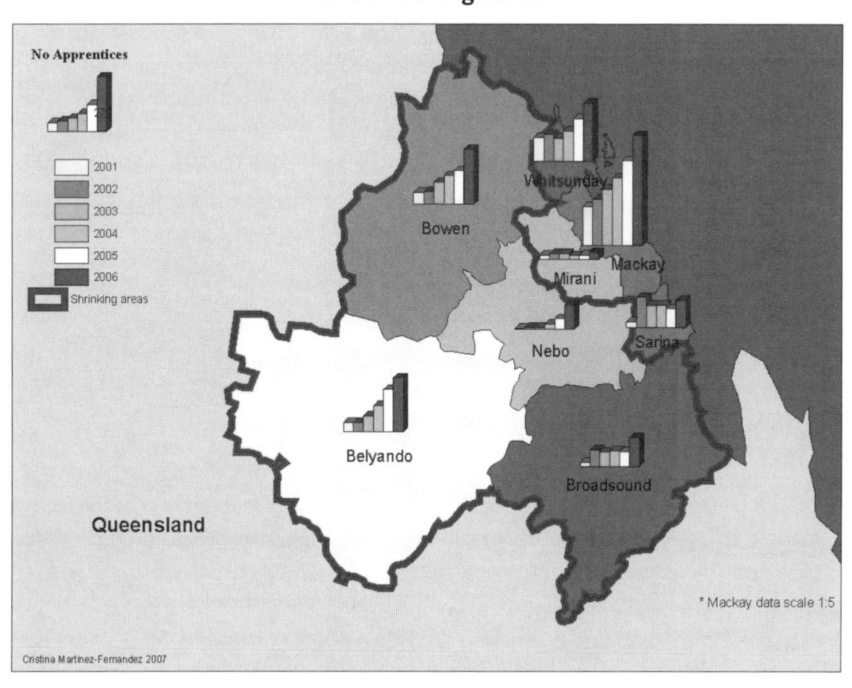

Strategies for tackling skills shortages and skills strategies in Mackay

Evidently, Mackay is a strongly performing region in a strongly performing state. An analysis of skills shortages in Mackay shows skills needs in most industry sectors except for sugar production and tourism. The industries where skills shortages could lead to a loss of opportunities are:

- diversification of horticulture production;
- forestry and associated value-added products;
- aquaculture industry;
- machinery manufacturing;
- coal and shale mining production;
- alternative energy sector;
- growth and export of business services in mining, education and health-care;
- research and development in strategic industries; and
- e-commerce and electronic operating systems by industries (Queensland Government, 2001).

The private sector has experienced difficulties with filling vacancies at many levels, but especially at the trades level in some of the main employment industries such as manufacturing, agriculture, forestry and fishing, mining, transport and storage, and construction. The shortages were across the board, with electrical and electronic trades, and metal and engineering trades being part of the main employment occupations in Mackay,[13] and consistently noted as "skills in demand" for the state of Queensland (DEWR, 2006).

Highlights from the 2007-08 regional budget indicate the following initiatives:

- AUD 70 million over four years to provide state schools and technical college teachers with computers.
- AUD 39.9 million to develop SkillsTech Australia's specialist trade training campus working closely with industry to address the skills gaps of existing workers.
- AUD 160 million for industry development and trade services.
- AUD 82.5 million for Biosecurity Queensland – coordinates the government's efforts to prevent, respond to, and recover from pests and diseases that threaten the economy and the environment.
- AUD 31.2 million for fisheries management.[14]

Skilling Solutions Queensland customer centres have also recently opened a branch in Mackay providing skills-related services to both employers and employees. Skilling Solutions Queensland is a network of centres across the state. The first centre was launched in March 2005. This type of centre provides interface services between employers and employees such as knowledge-intensive services related to labour market information, labour market research and human resources management in a more locally coordinated manner than in previous state strategies.

The MAIN CARE scheme

Public sector interventions in the area of skills have been complemented in Mackay by a significant private-led initiative. During the mid 1990s the shortage of tradespersons, and challenges of the apprentice training system were considered risk-factors for the manufacturing sector in Mackay. A group of companies joined together in a cluster type organisation – the Mackay Industry Network (MAIN) – to attempt to solve the skills shortages in their companies and the lack of needed skills associated with the national apprentice training system, which was not responding fast enough to the growth of the manufacturing industry. Under the national apprentice scheme, the skills areas of trainees were not well adjusted to the set of skills needed in the sector and there was a high rate of non-completions.

MAIN[15] was formed by manufacturing and engineering firms in 1996 in response to the industrial changes occurring in Mackay. Engineering firms have dominated the sugar industry in the past, and there is a strong tradition of manufacturing and engineering services in the town. In the early to mid nineties, the sugar industry started to decline, due to some years of drought and insect infestations in the crops. As a consequence, the industry as a whole started to slip away. The concern then for some of the companies in the engineering sector, was that if the revival of the economy was going to be dependent upon the mining industry, the majority of Mackay companies will not be able to compete with the big companies normally associated with mining. There was concern that the local companies would not have enough capacity to cope with large scale demand, and would consequently not be able to attain the bigger contracts. MAIN admininistrators recall from that period:

> These companies realised that if they come together as a cluster of companies they will have much more access to good information, timely information, and relevant information. Also they realised that if they could work together and trust each other they would be able to look much greater and that the chances of spinning-off work from one to another was greater. This is a big step because the history of these companies was not to work together at all. There was a big deal of secrecy about what each company did and which might be the deals they were involved in. Most of them are small companies, usually an ex-miner or an engineer, anybody that has been on the ground out there and was shown an opportunity to set up a business. Individually they didn't show much room to move forward in the mining industry boom but together they showed kind of a future. So the idea of the cluster was born. (Interview, December 2006)

> Our companies are within the mining manufacturing services sector; they supply safety equipment, electronic equipment, welding machinery. Some of the manufacturing companies working first for the sugar cane industry came across to work for the coal industry and they become bigger and searched for opportunities beyond Mackay. Companies in the cluster are at very different levels of the value-chain, there is a huge range of what they do. Mackay is a very interesting place for doing a cluster because it is very insular; the first thing people would think is "you can't do that, you cannot change that". It was important for companies to see that things could improve by working as a network. (Interview, December 2006)

The network started operations with an industry forum and a feasibility study of the coal industry funded by the state government. The 1997 study collected information from different mining corporations operating in the area, and the results showed that there was an expanding demand on manufacturing services for the coal industry, but it was very hard to determine if the local industry was going to respond to or participate in that demand. At that point, the Regional Economic Development Corporation (REDEC), an organisation financed by the state government and the city council, supported the cluster initiative by offering office space for the network, and funding of AUD 120 000 for three years. There were 45 companies in the beginning and six "champions" driving the process. The first action of the network was to apply for funding for a general manager. The Federal Government's Department of Transport and Regional Services (DoTARS) provided AUD 130 000 to engage a general manager to coordinate the network.

Early analysis by the general manager indicated that the network would be very useful for accessing big contracts, and that companies would be able to do business better together and have better access to information about how to improve their businesses. In the first 12 months, the network organised monthly events to provide information on "how to do good business". At the same time, the network set up the structure of the business as an incorporated not-for-profit organisation with a board of directors and membership fees ranging from AUD 700 to AUD 2 000 annually, depending on the revenue of the company.

The companies involved in the network analysed the strategic needs required to remain competitive in Mackay during the mining boom, and how they would be able to maintain their level of employment under stiff competition. They decided to have three major areas of focus: 1) networking information; 2) skills; and 3) exports. The identification of "skills shortages" as one of the key areas of work led to the establishment of the "CARE programme" – the most succesful activity of the network, as highlighted by MAIN staff:

> "Skills" was highly significant because the employment of apprentices had dropped dramatically, the good training skills that came out in the late 80s-90s under the federal government didn't satisfy the needs of the engineering sector. They have skills that didn't work for most companies and so they just stopped taking apprentices. Thus the network identified that there was an opportunity for them to offer "apprentice management" and to go further and become a good training organisation. So a company employs the apprentice and we come in and take over the administration; let's say that we become the "apprentice master"; we solve all the problems that need to be solved to get the apprentice in place. The company is happy because they have the employee, they own their loyalty and they only deal with an organisation to get all the administration sorted out.
>
> This has been a big success and ensured our sustainability as a network because that is from where we get all the income. We work with many companies, not just the ones that are part of the network. It is a good

> arrangement because the companies do not need to put on extra staff to do the administration side for the federal government; they can put their people to doing their job and we get the extra burden of the administration of apprentices. Things like training them to work on the floor space, going to TAFE [technical college] for training etc. We have 2-3 staff working on this. The programme resulted in a stronger workforce, especially it stopped the drop-off apprentices, which was a problem over here. The retention rate is 90-95% which is nothing like the average. Alongside this, we developed very useful relationships with other training organisations such as TAFE. (Interview, December 2006)

The relationship with the technical colleges deserves further analysis because they have an important role and tradition in the delivery of industry training in Australia. The companies in MAIN used to liaise directly with the Mackay Technical College for training purposes, however, this was identified as an extra burden on top of their core business activities. MAIN documented the types of barriers and went back to the technical college with the issues the employers identified in relation to policies of orienting the trainees. For example, there were issues with the inductions: the way they were conducted; the involvement of employers; and the understanding of apprentices of what their responsibilities were. This lack of knowledge of the working conditions and expectations of the trade is cited as one of the reasons for rising non-completion rates in apprenticeships at the national level (Toner, 2005), so it is a relevant concern identified by the Mackay Network that had not been previously addressed by goverment policy.

MAIN acts as an intermediary agent connecting industry with education agents; they organise all bookings for all of their apprentices, and they also focus on the sort of gaps prospective employers might have in the near future. The role of the programme is not to train – other organisations such as the technical colleges do that – but to organise the logistics of training courses and inductions that the technical colleges or other organisations deliver. MAIN also take care of the basic information needs of apprentices, explaining the expectations of the job from inside the workplace; important information on which companies are usually too busy to expend time on. This information is part of the "induction" programmes that MAIN delivers (subcontracted by the Mackay Technical College):

> This arrangement is convenient for them [technical college] because they don't have much time to do it and so they are free to do what they are supposed to do, which is training. Also, the cost for them to have someone going to the workplace to do the induction is very high because usually they are there just one at a time while we are there all the time; so it is cheaper for them to use us. It is also more effective because we know where the apprentice might be having problems or why problems have arisen, etc.,

> just because we are there all the time, so we can look after the small problems arising in the workplace. The result is a significant fall in the number of apprentices dropping off the programme, and a high rate of completions. (Interview, December 2006)

MAIN CARE programme has also been able to introduce hard-to-reach groups (the long-term unemployed, people from indigenous backgrounds, and women) into the workforce, although this is not the focus of the programme. MAIN staff noted that the engineering sector by large would be able to employ only a small part of these groups. In particular, it would be very difficult to employ people with physical disabilities due to the type of jobs in the sector. However, one of MAIN's strategies is directed towards placement of indigenous people:

> We got special funding (STEP) to employ indigenous people, we have just made an application to employ six of them. However, this group is hard. We have a couple graduating but there are difficult barriers. It is nothing to do with the employment or the job conditions or anything else. For example, we had an Aboriginal kid that was going to be nominated "Apprentice of the year" for the whole programme but halfway into year three he walked out because his family needed him. (Interview, December 2006)

In the case of MAIN and the CARE programme, the driver of the network is really the General Manager who is responsible for putting together the infrastructure needed to ensure the office is a focal point, but also producing the "jelly of the organisation" and realising the "nexus between industry, government and education" (interview, December 2006). The main difficulties in the forseeable future are centred around attracting the big companies to utilise MAIN's services, so that MAIN can capitalise from the high value chain opportunities. MAIN had a turnover of AUD 700 000 (1/3 is generated by CARE fees; 1/3 is from state government grants and 1/3 from membership fees)[16] with seven staff in December 2006. Some of the challenges ahead are:

> The challenge for MAIN is to engage with the mines, because mines have been a dying source of the shortage of skills and the supply of services for the growing demand. Actually, the mining companies do not care about where the services they need come from – they really don't care – if they cannot find the service here they will get them from elsewhere. For financial reasons we now need these mines on board and also for practical reasons. We need them to start thinking about the impact they have on manufacturing companies in the region, and we need to work more closely together with them as a cluster. We also think the big companies in town should be engaging with smaller companies in a much more communicative way. This in fact would also reduce stress in poaching

staff. We are having trouble getting professional staff for our industry. (Interview, December 2006)

Local partnerships

The MAIN CARE programme, although driven by the private sector is a strategy designed in co-operation with the Australian Industry Group, the Mackay Regional Development Economic Corporation (REDEC),[17] DETA, and the TAFE Technical College. The implementation of the strategy is coordinated by an Apprentice Master who liaises with public and private organisations, coordinating all inductions into apprentice programmes in collaboration with the technical colleges. The programme also looks after all management and health and safety aspects of the deployment of apprentices into the workplace. MAIN CARE uses a "consortium" type model of delivery, where the professional services of educational institutions, support from government, and partnerships with industry, result in recruiting new apprentices, managing apprentices and trainees in the companies, and training the workforce. Although no forecasting data is used by members, future skills needs are dictated by introduction of technologies in the workplace and the need for skills to use those technologies:

TAFE training is accessed and MAIN does make recommendations to TAFE on both the content and delivery methods of some of their programmes. Currently a relationship is developing between some member companies and the Central Queensland University as well to provide better undergraduate programmes for the industry. (Interview, June 2007)

The technical college in Mackay has different agreements with companies in the region for delivery of trainees and apprentices. Demand for these services has significantly increased since mid 2003-2004; mainly triggered by the demand for mining and manufacturing services to support the growing mining industry. Locally in Mackay, the technical college has financial arrangements with 35-40 Registered Training Organisations (RTOs) for training delivery that is increasingly held on-site and tailored to the demands of the company, not at the technical college campus. The role of the technical college is to act as an umbrella organisation looking after the quality of education provision, and monitoring delivery of training programmes. Curriculum development is adapted to the needs of companies and the apprentice programme is designed in collaboration with companies. The Skills Plan is significant for the Institute's operations, but there is currently no performance review against the strategies proposed in the Skills Plan:

The Skills Plan is extremely significant for us. It is a response to changes in the market conditions and provides strategies for how we will meet the skills needs and demand. The plan is an important investment in Mackay

> because it provides funding for new infrastructure of the institute to locate new facilities closer to Mackay's industrial district so we can interact better with our companies. (Interview data, 2007)

The success of the MAIN network and the CARE programme follow a "cluster business model", with a general manager and a board making financial decisions and member companies and organisations providing strategic directions. The role of the executive manager has been instrumental for the success of the CARE programme, together with a strong driving force provided by the companies that constitute the network and the support of public organisations. Some of the mechanisms used to encourage local partners to agree to a common skills strategy are exemplified by one of interviewees:

> Key activities for the cluster are found through some common need. For example, for MAIN it has been the need for skilled workers; companies needed an apprenticeship programme because they didn't have the capacity to manage this on an individual basis. The cluster has to identify what the potential benefits are, and they need to show that the investment in developing the cluster is going to assist the development of that industry in the region in a way that individual companies on their own would not be able to do. This is exactly what the CARE programme has done and the model they have developed can be applied across the board to other starting clusters.
>
> It is very important for government to assist clusters to get established, because it is very hard to ask businesses to invest in another business structure that might die, or that they don't know whether it is going to help to built their own business; so I think it is appropriate that governments provide some start-up – about two years' assistance in some form to get them up and running and to help them to transition to self-management. (Interview data, 2006).

The case of the MAIN network highlights the importance of providing the private sector with mechanisms for participation in designing solutions to their labour market imperatives. MAIN started to address the skills shortage in trades some years in advance of the Queensland Skills Plan, although the analysis the MAIN companies did on the impact of the mining boom on business was much less sophisticated than the analysis conducted by the government. However, as these companies based their strategic analysis and planning on the direct local market impacts of their day-to-day work, they were able to move quickly and design a solution that targeted trades as the core skills of their businesses. As the network includes state and local organisations involved in the Queensland Skills Plan, they now benefit from the analysis and strategies proposed in the plan and are aware of the opportunities for extended partnerships with local agencies such as Skilling

Solutions Queensland that might provide a more tailored service for apprentice programmes for SMEs. Nevertheless MAIN CARE is likely to continue operating for the manufacturing sector in Mackay, as most of the companies are small and the benefits of the cluster model are evident. Enhancing local partnerships for a common local skills strategy would further strengthen the competitiveness of companies in MAIN as well as the broader industry and community in Mackay.

A key initiative impacting larger institutional training that could be part of this forum are the Trade and Technician Skills Institute (TTSI); and the Australian Resources and Infrastructure Institute (ARIIT). TTSI will lead the technical college training in the industry sectors of automotive, building and construction, manufacturing, engineering, electrical, and electronics. Mackay Technical College campus is one of the major delivery points for the TTSI. ARIIT will operate when and where major projects materialise; it is a virtual institute with no campus infrastructure, and flexible delivery on the job site. The concept is that ARIIT will contract out the technical college and other training organisations when training resources are needed. ARIIT targets major projects in central Queensland (Mackay's region) in designated industries: energy and water, minerals processing, mining services, civil construction for rail, road and port, and infrastructure (Queensland Government, 2006c).

One way to develop the model led by MAIN could be to establish a common skills strategy as a Mackay Skills Partnership Forum including the different local, state, industry and community organisations dealing with skills development in Mackay. This type of regional network model has worked well in other regions facing step economic shrinkage, such as the Hunter Valley closure of the BHP Steelworks in the late 1990s (Martinez-Fernandez, 2001; 2004). Its strengths in strategic planning and regional coordination of efforts can be applied to growing regions just as well.

Integrating the disadvantaged into the labour market

While the MAIN CARE scheme has not itself actively targeted disadvantaged groups, the broader Queensland Skills Plan focuses on customising training for different groups, including disadvantaged people that are finding it harder to secure sustainable employment even in a hyper-growth economy. For example, providing training tailored to Indigenous Australians, to the needs of older workers or young people looking for their first job, migrants from culturally and linguistically diverse backgrounds, people from remote communities, people with disabilities, and ex-offenders.

In the case of Mackay, indigenous and foreign born people constitute over 12% of the population (see Table 6.4), with the Maltese and South Pacific Island populations being the largest outside of their homelands. In the 1920s, these nationalities were brought as slaves to work in the sugar cane industry; now they have second and third generations well settled in Mackay. However, their participation in the labour market is still below average.

Table 6.4. **Indigenous and overseas born (percentages, 1991-2001-2006)**

Category	1991 census		1996 census		2001 census		2006 census	
	Mackay	Australia	Mackay	Australia	Mackay	Australia	Mackay	Australia
Indigenous persons	2.4	1.6	1.8	1.8	2.1	1.9	2.2	2.0
Born in Australia	86.4	75.5	84.6	73.9	81.8	71.8	77.4	70.1
Born overseas (b)	10.1	21.9	10.1	21.8	9.7	21.6	10.0	22.0

Source: Computed using Census of Population and Housing; different census.

As Mackay grows in importance as a regional centre, indigenous populations from outlining towns move in, searching for jobs and better education and health services. A recent study shows that almost three-quarters (72%) of the population growth of these regional centres was due to an increase in the number of indigenous people moving to more accessible areas (Taylor, 2006). Unemployment is, however, much higher among these groups; a situation considered of "extreme labour-market disadvantage" by the Queensland Government (Queensland Government, 2006a).

Mackay has a lower share of welfare recipients than the nation as a whole. The only category higher than the national average is in the area of provision of support for new workers, but the long-term recipients are lower again than the national average (see Table 6.5).

Table 6.5. **Percentage change in welfare recipients**

Category	Mackay		Australia	
	2002	2003	2002	2003
Age pension	6.7	6.8	9.0	9.1
Disability support pension	3.1	3.1	3.3	3.3
Newstart allowance	3.7	3.5	3.0	2.8
Parenting payment – single	2.3	2.3	2.2	2.2
Youth allowance	1.8	1.6	2.1	2.0
Other pensions and allowances	3.3	3.2	3.3	3.2
Total welfare recipients	**20.8**	**20.6**	**22.9**	**22.7**
Percentage of long-term Newstart allowance recipients	**52.3**	**52.8**	**58.8**	**60.6**

Source: Computed using ABS National Regional Profile, 2000 to 2004.

One of the difficult adjustments of Mackay's population has been the rising value of housing. As the economic boom and the city attract more high-skilled and high paid professionals, the availability of housing has been dramatically reduced, leaving a rising demand. The result has been that disadvantaged groups are forced to move from their houses as they cannot cope with new rental prices. The instability of housing affordability only adds to the disadvantages already experienced by these populations to access sustainable employment, as they are moved further away from the centres of employment. The issue is complex, and city agents do not have a clear or rapid solution to the problem:

> People have problems getting accommodation or paying for accommodation. The prices have gone up astronomically in the last couple of years, so the people with high income jobs, people that are in the mines, they can pay the rents but there are people of lower economic levels that have to leave the town for other places where they can afford to live basically. That is not healthy for any community as we need all of the socio-economic levels to have a functioning society, so that is a concern for all government agencies. This is an issue not just for Mackay, it is an issue for the whole of Queensland – full stop – but it is exacerbated here due to our phenomenal growth. It is a problem for Mackay, and it is a problem for some of the hinterland towns such as Moranbah where housing that were AUD 250-AUD 300 a week are now AUD 800 a week for a 2-3 bedroom house.
>
> Real estate is a big business here, people raise the rents to the roof. A lot of the developers in this town are taking advantage of the situation, buying properties and not putting them back into the market, holding them back until the demand is high and the prices are up. They can afford to do that because they are companies with big money, they don't have mortgage stress, they sit on those properties and manipulate the demand-supply situation. This is not something anyone can do anything about. The council is aware of this, the government is aware of this, but it is a very complex problem, because we have to make sure that by addressing the problem we don't build social ghettoes. These are issues that especially indigenous and South-Islander populations, people with disabilities, young people, single parents, and the elderly are facing every day. (Interview, December 2006)

This situation is very different from what is experienced in places where the economy is not that buoyant; it also suggests a different, rapid, urban gentrification that is normally only experienced in the big urban centres where the housing stock is greater and more diverse. The Skills Plan and the local strategies emerging in Mackay do not deal with the housing situation and the extent to which disadvantaged groups can benefit from the current economic boom, or how sustainable and transportable the skills that they might be acquiring are is uncertain.

Mackay City Council provides information on the multicultural resources available in Mackay through the Local Area Multicultural Partnership (LAMP) Program. The initiative envisages strengthening the links between cultural groups and mainstream sectors of the community. LAMP also provides information on the cultural diversity of the Mackay region through the collection of statistics related to birthplace of origin and Indigenous Australians residing in the region. Among the organisations operating in Mackay are the following:

- 10 Australian South Sea Islander Organisations such as the South Sea Islander Association, the Mackay and District South Islander Association (MADASSIA)[18] and the Mackay South Island Community.
- 13 Aboriginal and Torres Islanders Organisations such as the Department Aboriginal and Torres Strait Islander Policy, the Gumbi Gumbi Aboriginal Corporation Ltd and the Yuibera Aboriginal Corporation.
- Adult Migrant English program (Technical College).
- Migrant Settlement Services Scheme.
- Filipino Australian Community Association.
- Islamic Centre.
- Mackay Hellenic Association.
- Mackay Maltese Club.
- Multicultural Community Worker Program.

As an example, the Mackay Maltese Club is a social group that bring the Maltese community together for bi-monthly dinners and an annual traditional festa on or around 8 September each year. The club estimates that one in four residents in the Mackay region are of Maltese descendent whose origins go back to 1883. One of the many aims of the club is to act as the focal point to foster and promote Maltese cultural awareness in the district. Maltese dinners are hosted on a regular basis to provide opportunities for members to meet and socialise as a group. These functions are also frequented by visitors from other Australian states and foreigners, often by people from Malta who are on holiday. The club however, does not provide any service related to skills development or matching service.[19]

Although LAMP coordinates cultural activities and disseminates information it is not a skills matching service or a service under the Skills Plan. Specific support for hard to reach groups is provided through the Skilling Queenslanders for Work initiative under the Skills Plan. The Queensland Government is engaging community groups through an "engagement strategy" to address the different situations faced at the local level. In particular a "disability plan" is being prepared and expected to be finalised by the end of 2007. At the moment, for people with a disability, the government has contracted the services of "Disability Works Australia" (DWA), which coordinates disability recruitment for employers for free, in many instances through the sub-contracting of services to other companies available in the local area, as is the case for Mackay.

Attracting new talent

Looking at the impact of migration, 1 809 migrants settled in Mackay from 2001 to 2006. The majority of settlers came through skilled migration visas (1 104), family reunions count for 694 people, and humanitarian entrants count for 8 people (DIAC, Settlement Database, 2006). The top five countries of origin are: South Africa, United Kingdom, Zimbabwe, Philippines, and the United States (see Table 6.6).

Table 6.6. **Top 20 countries in the migration stream to Mackay (January 2000-December 2006)**

Country of birth	Humanitarian	Family	Skilled	Special	Total
South Africa	0	24	392	0	416
United Kingdom	0	160	206	1	367
Zimbabwe	1	9	170	0	180
Philippines	0	110	16	0	126
USA	0	34	21	0	55
Thailand	0	52	1	0	53
Canada	0	29	17	1	47
Germany	0	21	21	0	42
India	0	8	28	0	36
Indonesia	0	24	10	0	34
Unknown	0	10	22	0	32
China (ex Taiwan)	0	26	2	0	28
Netherlands	0	15	6	0	21
Fiji	0	7	12	0	19
Ireland	0	10	6	0	16
Pakistan	0	0	16	0	16
Former USSR	0	13	2	0	15
Papua New Guinea	0	5	10	0	15
France	0	5	9	0	14
Sri Lanka	0	5	9	0	14
Others	7	127	128	1	263
Total	**8**	**694**	**1 104**	**3**	**1 809**

Source: Department of Immigration and Multicultural Affairs Settlement Database. Extracted on 11/4/07.
Note: New Zealanders' permanent visas not included.

The Skills Plan specifies that migrants from culturally and linguistically diverse backgrounds will receive assistance to become competitive in the job market through a new multicultural strategy; however, there is no further specification of the elements of this strategy. There is no evidence of the linguistic barrier being addressed since the federal government stopped support for

English classes in the mid 90s. Current immigration policy in Australia requires English language proficiency for most of its visa options, and therefore the top countries of origin are English speaking countries. Migration agents and consultants in specific areas focus on providing links to specialised pools of talent from overseas, and facilitating sponsored applications. For example, interview data (December 2006) suggests that there is an informal network attracting South African workers, a group that has significantly grown in the city in the last 12 months.

> The mining industry in particular is targeting workers from other countries where there might be a downturn in mining, such as Germany and South-Africa. Individual companies have programmes linking with particular countries to bring workers here. Particularly, some of the mining companies recruite very actively overseas. (Interview, December 2006).

> Workers from South Africa are preferred in town because they speak English, are well educated, and want to leave South Africa. Two hundred and fifty families from South Africa are in town, many of them work in manufacturing and engineering. Sometimes there are problems occurring between black and white South Africans – there is violence in the workplace in a way we had not seen before. Some employers have been forced to split these workers into different shifts so that they do not work together. Other workers are brought from South-East Asia – they are good for short-term work, they are well trained and have a good work ethic. (Interview, December 2006)

At a broader level, migration of skilled workers is highly regulated by the federal government; each case is looked at individually, and therefore cooperation agreements between Mackay and other regions for provision of skilled workers is not contemplated under current policy. However, pools of talent are accessed by employers and migration consultants because they are aware of the excess of skilled workers from an industry that is in decline elsewhere. This can readily affect the mining industry, but also other industries impacted by the mining boom, such as building and construction, manufacturing, or the food industry.

For example a local abattoir, "Borthwicks", brought 60 Brazilians into their workforce under the skilled migrant programme in 2006. The owner of the abattoir acknowledges that the only way to operate at the level of demand was to bring skilled slaughtermen, butchers and boners from overseas because of acute skills shortages in the industry at local, state and national levels. The 60 skilled migrants have enabled the subsequent employment of 130 local people, who are under a trainee agreement with the company. The reason why this company looked towards Brazil was because this country has a big beef processing industry with very similar skills, but a much bigger unemployment rate. The administrative process was easy, and the new workers could start working with no further training (ABC, 2006a).

Another Mackay manufacturing company attended a job exposition in the United Kingdom organised by the Department of Immigration and Multicultural and Indigenous Affairs (DIMIA), where they obtained contacts for potential new employees from South Africa and the UK. They now have around 20 families moving in to Mackay (ABC, 2006b). Local migration agents are also contacted by the building and construction industry in search of particular trades, which may be difficult to find in the local market (Interview data, 2007). Thus, there is some evidence that local markets are able to tap into pools of talent available because of industry decline elsewhere. It might be mining talent pools in South Africa or Germany; or abattoir skills pools in Brazil; or boilermakers and sheet metal talent pools from the UK industrial belt. The mobility of these workers is facilitated by the immigration policy framework in Australia, but also by the employers and consultants who understand that the skills of their business are global, and therefore they can search for these skills elsewhere. The cost associated with bringing in a skilled worker is no higher than the time and resources needed to train an unskilled person, which is why there is the market advantage for searching for overseas talent pools.

Mackay council, under the LAMP initiative, has recently established a Multicultural Reference Group that is developing, among other priorities, a welcome programme intended for skilled migrants and their families. This programme is a whole-of-the-local-government approach and it is anticipated that it will form part of the council's core business in the future. The council ran several activities in the past in an effort to integrate migrants into the community, but this has always been on an ad-hoc basis. Examples of activities run by the council include: various Harmony Day activities; the Migrant Voice Multicultural Newsletter; welcome picnics; and translation and interpretation training for council staff. As one of the officers from LAMP indicates:

> There is certainly more dialogue now more than ever about the need to integrate and "welcome" new migrants and their families into regional centres as it is recognised that the cultural diversity of community's such as ours is growing. (Interview data, 2007)

The council however is not looking specifically at the integration of children into the education and housing system. Other not-for-profit organisations in Mackay that are funded to provide support to migrants and families are:

- Settlement Grants Program – provides support and assistance to migrants and humanitarian entrants, including improving the employment and training opportunities for migrants and humanitarian entrants.

- Multicultural Community Worker Program.

In summary, plans for hard-to-reach groups are still being developed and although some programmes exist, there seems to be more sophisticated mechanisms for reaching overseas talent pools and bringing skilled workers from shrinking industries elsewhere. The associated costs of integration of these new immigrants into the housing, health and education systems has not yet been looked at specifically, at least at the local government level in Mackay.

Conclusions

The case of Mackay exemplifies the skills imperative for cities in Australia that are growing above the national average because of the resources boom. The following conclusions can be drawn:

1. First, facilitating industry clusters to take the lead in addressing skill shortages at the local level can result in the creation of skills-hubs of tailored talent for current and future needs of the industry. In this regard, the case of the MAIN CARE programme is an example of good practice in designing effective local skills strategies. Investing in local employment requires connecting talent with employers in ways that may be more sophisticated than just offering recruitment services or information services. Companies need some support to initiate collaboration structures where "thinking spaces" focused on skills and their business development can take place. It is too hard for companies to obtain capital to create the organisational structure that clusters need, and this is where governments and local agencies can help, by supporting clusters and networks to create skills-hubs. The investment is usually small, and the solutions companies come up with together are usually very well-tailored to the local operating context. This local focus is difficult for agencies at the state or national level, and although they need to provide overarching plans such as the Skills Plan, they also need the companies at the other end of the equation to fast-track solutions for their business. In the case of Mackay, the umbrella reform represented by the Skills Plan, plus the local network initiative, seem to be targeting similar objectives, thereby moving all forces in the same direction even though perhaps not as a planned and coordinated activity.
2. Second, overarching skills strategies such as "whole-of-government" Skills Plans need a clear, local means of implementation connected to industry skills hubs so that the strategies really engage with those who can apply and use them. Businesses and all parts of the skills ecosystem need to participate in the implementation of overarching plans to assure their success. Defined management structures and evaluation programmes are

as important as ensuring that all parts of the skills ecosystem understand the opportunities embedded in the overarching plans.

3. Third, for cities where economic growth is driven by corporations (*e.g.* mining companies), it is important to connect big and small businesses. There are important innovation spin-offs from this connectivity, as corporations often operate at international levels where local businesses do not usually have links. Local businesses do however have local knowledge and local skills to offer. Connecting all parts of the industrial system will help to prevent skill shortages and assist in designing quick local responses.
4. Fourth, pools of local talent from hard-to-reach groups are still difficult to integrate, and more work is needed to ensure the industry sector (including government) is committed to offer work options to these groups. Industry does not necessarily have a good understanding of the different characteristics of disadvantaged groups, including the type of jobs adapted to their abilities, or the type of mechanisms to guarantee their success (*e.g.* peer-to-peer mentoring). Governments have an important role in educating industry, from both private and public sectors, on the skills available from these groups and the advantages of their employment.
5. Fifth, the housing and infrastructure environment in rapidly growing cities needs to be analysed carefully, and included in overarching plans so as not to further alienate disadvantaged groups who are already finding it hard to participate in the labour market. Loss of housing affordability is a significant collateral effect of hyper-growth economies, and a critical challenge for disadvantaged groups attempting to participate in the wealth creation of their city. Local governments have a role in engaging the property and real estate sectors in ensuring a responsible housing market.
6. Finally, international mobility of workers from shrinking cities to growing cities is a growing trend calling for new roles and investments by local governments. More work is needed to understand the pressures occurring at both urban ends, the sustainability of the imported skills, and the significance of informal networks operating across international regions.

Regions such as Mackay show an enormous potential to capitalise from the different collaboration schemes emerging from public and private organisations and for the success of some of the schemes already addressing skill shortages. The main recommendation from this study is the formation of a Mackay Skills Partnership Forum where all stakeholders involved in skills development could come together to discuss their skills needs and initiatives and to integrate their knowledge into strategic plans that can later be implemented at their own organisation level. Public organisations such as DETA, the Mackay Council, TAFE Technical College, the Department of State Development and Trade, Skilling Solutions Queensland, industry clusters such as MAIN, SME organisations (supporting small and medium sized enterprises) large employers, community organisations from the Indigenous and South Islanders sectors, and multicultural and disability organisations, all have different knowledge and skills strategies that can produce the type of synergies needed for a convergent regional skills planning and implementation.

If one lesson can be learnt from the analysis of the Mackay region it is that skills development and strategic skills planning requires a network approach at the local level where different public and private organisations take leadership in different aspects of skills development but all converge in providing targeted development paths for their region or city as a whole. Skills Alliances under the Skills Plan are specific to certain industry sectors while the Skills Forum could take a "whole-of-the-region" approach. A Skill Partnership Forum is a powerful tool for providing cohesive, well-informed solutions to skills challenges.

Notes

1. Larcombe (2005).
2. *Idem.*
3. Australia is a federal parliamentary democracy with six states and two territories: Australian Capital Territory, New South Wales, Northern Territory, Queensland, South Australia, Tasmania, Victoria, Western Australia.
4. *www.immi.gov.au/skills/*, accessed 06/04/07.
5. These are interactions with other professionals around a core problem or issue that needs intellectual input to be resolved. It can imply internal knowledge services for a particular activity or external services from business or technical advisors (Martinez-Fernandez and Miles, 2006; OECD 2006).
6. Australian Bureau of Statistics, Queensland Treasury 2007, 2009.
7. SmartVET was a AUD 1 billion strategy that built on the "Breaking the Unemployment Cycle" initiative created in October 1998 and that helped to create more than 100 000 jobs. Department of Employment and Training, Annual Report 2003-2004, Queensland Government.
8. Ministerial Media Statement, Ho Tom Barton, 7 June 2006, Queensland Government.
9. Computed using ABS census data and BTRE Industry database, 2003.
10. Industries defined as technology and knowledge-intensive (converted to an Amala aware ANZSIC basis) are: Education; Health and community services; Finance and insurance; Communication services; Business services; Services to mining; various detailed high or medium-high technology manufacturing industries (*e.g.* Basic chemicals, Other chemicals, Photographic and scientific equipment, Electronic equipment, Electrical equipment and appliances, Industrial machinery and equipment, Motor vehicles and parts, and Aircraft); and various detailed service industries (*e.g.* Machinery and equipment hiring and leasing, Non-

financial asset investors, Personal and household good hiring, and Photographic film processing, and Photographic film studios).

11. ANZSIC Subdivisions.
12. Total Respondents: for each census, around 75% of census respondents provided complete answers to the education questions.
13. ABS, 2001 census, Occupational and Skills Analysis Section, DEWR – Department of Employment and Workplace Relations.
14. Regional Budget Statement 2007-2008, Mackay-Withsunday, Queensland Government 2007.
15. Information regarding this network was collected through in-depth interviews with MAIN staff and other organisations in Mackay, December 2006 to April 2007.
16. MAIN General Manager, 2007.
17. Mackay REDEC is responsible for facilitating the economic development of Mackay and the Whitsunday region. Mackay's statistical division covers eight shires, from the coast to the hinterland areas where the coal mining is located. REDEC is the region-wide agency, and each of the shire councils have an economic development unit. REDEC is not part of the Queensland government, but is however funded by the Queensland government. The Queensland government has a strong development focus across the state of Queensland, but they do not necessarily have much detail of the situation in each regional area. The government therefore funds REDEC to provide the regional focus for state-wide planning.
18. MADASSIA assists in the recruitment of South Sea Islander people, who are mainly descendents of the predominantly Melanesian people who were brought to Queensland between 1863 and 1904 from eight Pacific Islands. The majority of these people originate primarily from Vanuatu and the Solomon Islands (Queensland Government, 2006d).
19. The Maltese Club President, June 2007, personal communication.

Bibliography

ABC (2006a), "Foreign Workers: an Employer's Perspective", *ABC National Interest*, ABC Radio National, Australia, 23 April 2006.

ABC (2006b), "Importing Skills from Overseas", *ABC Tropical Queensland*, ABC Radio, Australia, 20 February 2006.

ABC Tropical Queensland (2008), "Global Financial Crisis No Brake on Mackay Wealth", available at: *www.abc.net.au/news/stories/2008/12/09/2441254.htm?site=tropic*.

Australian Government (2006), "Skilling Australia: 2005-2008 Commonwealth-State Agreement for Skilling Australia's Workforce", Australian Government, Department of Education, Science and Training, Canberra.

Department of Education, Sciences and Training (2007), *www.dest.gov.au*, accessed 15 June 2007.

Department of Employment and Workplace Relations (DEWR) (2006)," Skills in Demand Lists – States and Territories" 2006, DEWR July 2006.

Larcombe, G. (2005), "Howard's (Di)vision for the Land of the Long Economic Boom", paper presented to the *Advance Australia Fair – Building Sustainability, Justice and Peace Conference*, 30-31 July 2005, Melbourne Trades Hall, Carlton South, Melbourne.

Martinez-Fernandez, C. (forthcoming), "Skills Ecosystems: Fostering Local Talent", OECD, Paris.

Martinez-Fernandez, M.C. and I. Miles (2006), "Inside the Software Firm: Co-production of Knowledge and KISA in the Innovation Process", *International Journal Services Technology and Management*, IJSTM Special Issue Vol. 7, No. 2, pp. 115-125.

Martinez-Fernandez, M.C. (2004), "Regional Collaboration Infrastructure: Effects in the Hunter Valley of NSW", *Australian Planner* Planning Institute of Australia, Queensland, Vol. 41, No. 4.

National Centre for Vocational Education Research (2007), *www.ncver.edu.au*, accessed 10 June 2007.

OECD (2006), "The Role of Knowledge Intensive Activities (KISA) in Innovation", OECD, Paris.

Queensland Government (2001), "State Infrastructure Plan – Strategic Directions", Department of State Development and Trade, Queensland Government.

Queensland Government (2006a), "Growing your Business in the Mackay Whitsunday Region, Australia", Department of State Development, Trade and Innovation, Manufacturing Industries and Investment Division, Queensland Government.

Queensland Government (2006b)," Queensland Skills Plan: A White Paper", Department of Employment and Training, Queensland Government.

Queensland Government (2006c), "Queensland Skills Plan. Presentation to Australian Institute of Training and Development", Department of Employment and Training, Queensland Government, November 2006.

Queensland Government (2006d), "Skilling Queenslanders for Work", *Employment and Indigenous Initiatives*, Queensland Government, Reference No. EII03, Version No. 3, 1 July 2006.

Queensland Government (2007), "The Queensland Labour Market and Training Review – Three Months to December 2006", Department of Education, Training and the Arts, VET Policy Development Division, Queensland Government, January 2007.

Taylor, J. (2006), "Population and Diversity: Policy Implications of Emerging Indigenous Demographic Trends", Discussion Paper No. 283/2006, CAEPR, ANU, Canberra.

Toner, P. (2003), "The Case of the Vanishing Apprentice", broadcast in *The National Interest*, ABC Radio National, Australia, 21 September 2003.

Toner, P. (2005), "Getting It Right: What Employers and Apprentices Have to Say About Apprenticeships", Dusseldorp Skills Forum, Group Training Australia Ltd, Australian Industry Group, Dusseldorp Skills Forum 2005, ISBN: 0 9750250 31.

ANNEX 6.A1

The Australian Skills Context: Background Information

Box 6.A1.1. **Australian apprenticeship scheme and incentives programme**

Key facts

- Combined paid work and structured training that can be on-the-job, off-the-job or a combination of both.
- Training is "competency based" which means training can be completed faster if the required level of skills is reached.
- Existing skills and prior experience are recognised and course credit granted, potentially reducing formal training time.
- Available for 30+ age group.
- Available full-time or part-time (in many schools).
- Led to nationally recognised qualifications and skills which provide the basis for further education and training.
- Available in different certificate levels and more than 500 occupations in traditional trades as well as a diverse range of emerging careers in most sectors of business and industry.
- Free service to employers and apprentices by Australian Apprenticeship Centres in most Australian regions.

Key funding incentives for employers

- For up-skilling Certificate II, III, IV, Selected Diploma and Advanced Diploma.
- To employ an apprentice in an eligible Innovation Training Package qualification.
- To employ an apprentice in an endorsed Australian school-based Apprenticeship.
- To employ apprentices aged 45 years or more; apprentices from rural and regional areas and apprentices from declared draught areas.

Box 6.A1.1. **Australian apprenticeship scheme and incentives programme** *(cont.)*

- To retain school-based apprentices after completion, and for recommencement of trades Certificate III or IV.
- Incentives for mature age apprentices in successful completion.
- Additional assistance for employers of Australian Apprentices with a disability.

Key funding incentives for apprentices

- Up to 36 months of Living Away from Home Allowance (LAFHA).
- "Trade Learning Scholarships provides two tax exempt AUD 500 payments if the Apprenticeship is undertaken with a small/medium enterprise or Group Training Organisation.
- Eligible for Youth Allowance (including Austudy for over 25s and ABSTUDY)*.
- The "Tools for your Trade" initiative provides up to AUD 800 for the purchase of trade tools.

* Austudy and Abstudy are two allowances available for young people to undertake formal training in an education institution.

Source: Australian Government, July 2006.

Box 6.A1.2. **Queensland Skills Plan – summary of actions**

A training system that works for Queensland

Action 1: Developing the Queensland VET sector.

Action 2: Reforming the Queensland TAFE system.

Action 3: Restructuring TAFE across Queensland and creating new specialised institutes.

Action 4: Nominating TAFE lead institutes for key industries.

Action 5: Improving coordination of TAFE's product development.

Action 6: Supporting TAFE Queensland staff.

Action 7: Investing in TAFE infrastructure and ICT.

Training that works for industry and employers

Action 8: Giving industry ownership of skills development through new customised skills strategies.

Action 9: Supporting skills development for small business.

Action 10: Age proofing our workplaces through the new Experience Pays Awareness Strategy.

Training that works for the trades

Action 11: Dealing with the demand for skilled trades people.

Action 12: Reinventing the trades through new occupational pathways.

Action 13: Attracting more people into apprenticeships.

Action 14: Providing improved support to apprentices during their training.

Action 15: Making apprenticeships work better for apprentices and employers.

Action 16: Introducing up-front training options.

Action 17: Subsidising workplace trainer and assessor training for trades people.

Action 18: Reviewing the role of group training organisations.

Training that works for individuals

Action 19: Customising training to meet the needs of our workforce.

Action 20: Preparing young people for work.

Action 21: Maximising our workforce through the Skilling Queenslanders for Work initiative.

Action 22: Introducing Skilling Solutions Queensland services throughout the state.

Action 23: Embedding employability skills in training programmes.

Action 24: Delivering training for the highest skilled jobs.

Source: Queensland Government 2006b.

Table 6.A1.1. **Increase/decrease in total labour market participants**

Occupation and labour force status, 1991-2001 Census

Percentage

Statistical local area	Managers, administrators and professionals	Associate professional	Tradespersons and related workers and advanced clerical and service workers	Intermediate and elementary clerical, sales and service worker; intermediate production and transport workers and labourers and related workers	Not employed
Mackay	31	98	2	23	14
Australia	25	74	–12	17	11

Source: Computed using ABS Census Data and BTRE Industry Structure Database, 2003.

Table 6.A1.2. **Increase/decrease in total employed persons**

Selected professionals and skilled trades people, 1991-2001 Census

Percentage

Professions	Health professionals	Teaching professionals	Computer professionals	Building engineering professionals	Tradespersons – Combined
Mackay	30	33	170	49	20
Australia	26	17	111	10	–1

Source: Computed using ABS Census Data and BTRE Industry Structure Database, 2003.

Table 6.A1.3. **Population projection of Mackay and Australia**

	Mackay[1]	Australia[2]
2001	75 993	18 972 350
2006	84 856	20 600 000
2011	91 980	21 988 000
2016	101 517	n.a.
2021	109 376	24 878 000
2026	116 979	n.a.
2031	n.a.	27 834 000
Annual Average Growth Rate	1.7	1.2

Occ-3 = Tradespersons and related workers and Advanced Clerical and Service Workers.

Occ-4 = Intermediate clerical, sales and service workers; Intermediate production and transport workers; Elementary clerical, sales and service workers; labourers and related workers.

1. Government of Queensland, Office of Economic and Statistical Research (OESR), March 2007.
2. ABS Population Projections, Australia, June 2006.

Table 6.A1.4. **Top three employing industries and their specialisation priorities matrix by SLAs and Australia (1996 and 2001 Census)**

Regions	Major employing industries (ANZSIC industry subdivisions)			Top industry specialisations (ANZSIC subdivisions)		
	I	II	III	I	II	III
Mackay 1996	Agriculture	Accommodation cafes and restaurants	Food beverage and tobacco manufacturing	Services to agriculture hunting and trapping	Agriculture	Commercial fishing
Mackay 2001	Education	Personal and household good retailing	Business services	coal mining	Rail transport	Services to mining
Australia 1996	Business services	Health services	Education	n.r.[1]	n.r.[1]	n.r.[1]
Australia 2001	Business services	Education	Health services	n.r.[1]	n.r.[1]	n.r.[1]

n.r. = not relevant.

1. An industry only qualified as a top three specialisation if the LQ exceeded 1.1 (*i.e.* the industry was at least 10% more important to the region than to Australia as a whole). If there were less than 3 industries with a LQ exceeding 1.1, the relevant specialisation variable(s) are coded "nr" (not relevant).

Source: Compiled using ABS Census Data and BTRE Industry Structure Database, 2003.

Figure 6.A1.1. **Workers to job ratio**

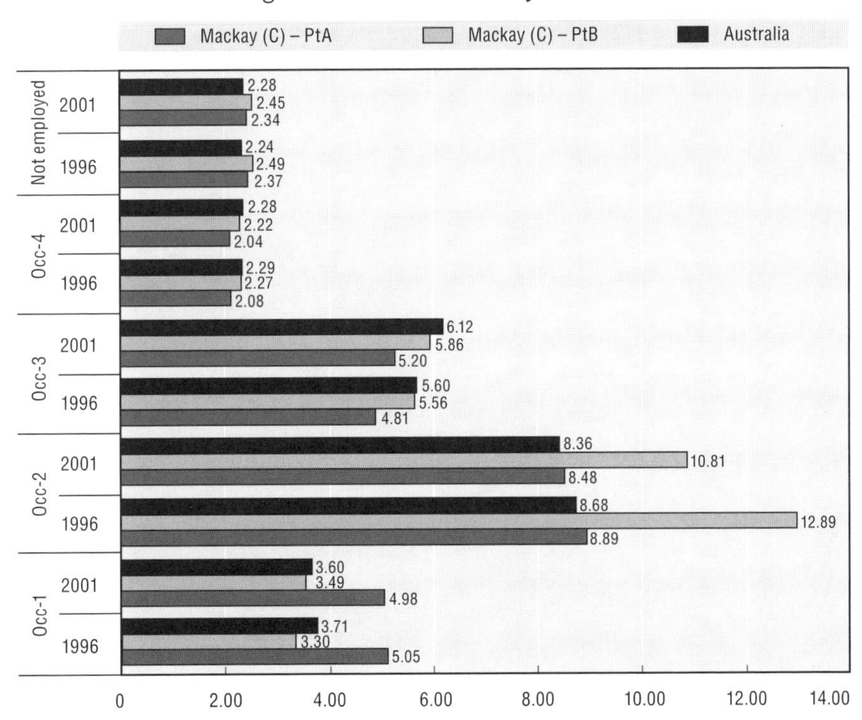

Source: Computed using ABS Census Data and BTRE Industry Structure Database, 2003.

PART II

Chapter 7

From Crane to Torso: Local Skill Strategies in the City of Malmö

by
Pieter Bevelander and Per Broomé

The City of Malmö has drawn on the skills of the city's substantial immigrant population in its recent transformation into a centre for service, trade and finance related industries. In addition to attracting significant numbers of new residents through investment in infrastructure and a new university, the city has developed a range of initiatives to improve the labour market integration of immigrants, including a new "portfolio approach" to recording an immigrant's skills. The city's "Vision 2015" strategy benefits from a high level of direct involvement and co-operation between local education officials, labour exchange offices and employers. The chapter analyses whether the city has succeeded in developing a balanced approach to improving its skills-base and identifies remaining gaps to be addressed.

Introduction

The harbour crane of the Kockum shipyard was the landmark of Malmö for many decades, until its demolition in 2002. Today the "Turning Torso", a 190-meter-high apartment building, designed by the Spanish architect Santiago Calatrava, has taken over this role. The change in landmarks reflects the economic structural transformation that Malmö, like many other former industrial regions, has undergone since the mid 1970s: from being a city dominated by industry to having a dynamic economic scene in which the service sector is playing an increasingly important role. A strategy to raise the city's skills levels has played an important role in this transformation.

When looking at recent actions to raise skills levels in Malmö, it is useful to briefly place them in the context of the economic development path of the city over the last thirty years. To a large extent, the economic development of the region of Malmö can be seen as a magnified example of the national economic development picture in Sweden. However its principle economic activities saw a stronger downturn after the economic crises in the 1970s and the early 1990s, which created a lower employment rate and higher rates of dependence on social security compared to other large cities in Sweden (Bevelander, Carlson and Rojas, 1997; SOU, 1998: 25).

Immigration has always played a role in the local economy, with migration trends reflecting those of Sweden as a whole (Bevelander, 1998). Applying a simplified view, immigration to post-war Sweden can be divided into two eras. The first period (1945-1970) is predominantly characterised by a labour market driven immigration, in which the flourishing Swedish economy attracted workers mainly from neighbouring countries, western Germany and Italy, whereas the second period (since 1970) saw a shift towards refugees and forced migration and family reunions.

For the region of Malmö the immediate post-war period had positive effects on the development of the engineering and shipbuilding industries, resulting in a substantial increase in employment in these sectors in the late 1940s. The shortage of skilled labour was, however, a bottleneck. The consumer goods industry also expanded and the textile industry in particular generated a large demand for unskilled labour. War refugees and women relieved this shortage. In the 1950s the consumer goods industry started to decline but the industrial sector continued its expansion with a demand for skilled labour, raising the general employment in the city somewhat above the national level in this period. The demand for skilled industrial labour was mainly relieved by active recruiting of companies in co-operation with Swedish and foreign labour market organisations. The larger part of this skilled labour came from West Germany, Denmark and Italy (Ohlsson, 1978; 1995).

In the 1960s, the industrial sector in the region of Malmö, as in Sweden as a whole, showed the characteristics of structural change: an intense rationalisation process and declining industry. Automation, division of labour, specialisation and large-scale production in industry made it possible to hire employees without any particular skills. Women and foreign labour filled the vacancies at the assembly lines whereas native workers started to work in the expanding service sector. In other words, these workers, in contrast to their counterparts of a decade earlier, were used more as substitutes for the native workforce than as complements. While earlier immigrants allowed the economy to grow in size, the immigrants of the 1960s facilitated a widening of the economy. The fact that these newly vacated jobs could be filled by unskilled workers is a result of industrial investment aimed at increasing international competitiveness and reducing costs (Ohlsson, 1975; Lundh and Ohlsson, 1999). In the region of Malmö, the shipbuilding and engineering industries dominated this development. Labour force immigrants during this decade came largely from Nordic countries but also from Mediterranean countries such as Greece, Yugoslavia and Turkey.

By the end of the 1960s, however, the situation began to change for immigrants. The trade unions saw immigration as producing a number of negative side effects. One such side effect was the delaying of industrial transformation through the steady supply of workers to replace Swedes who moved into the service sector. This supply of labour also served to depress wage increases in industry, which could otherwise have occurred due to scarcity of labour. In this way, immigration was seen as preserving the traditional industrial structure at a time when it would otherwise have been forced to undergo large changes. The government responded to these criticisms by making entry to Sweden from non-Nordic countries more difficult. According to the new legislation, which entered into force in 1968, applicants for work and residence permits from non-Nordic countries had to arrange for both a job and a place to live before entering Sweden. This dramatically cut down the labour immigration from non-Nordic countries.

Following the oil crisis of the early 1970s, Swedish economic growth dropped from 4% to less than 2% and set off a transformation process in which the decreasing industrial sector was surpassed by an increasing service sector. In the Malmö region, the industrial sector also stagnated. The structure of the region's industry meant that companies faced great difficulties in changing their production processes. Management and the strongly specialised labour force were suited to a specific productive apparatus which was highly inflexible. At the same time, employment was increasing in the public sector, a trend which had already started in the late 1960s. The economic growth of the 1960s gave rise to a demand for public services such as childcare, education, elderly care, healthcare, etc. The large increase in the public sector and a stagnating industrial sector, led to structural problems in the economy, with low growth and high unemployment especially among low-skilled workers. According to Schön (1996), the transformation process towards a knowledge intensive economy did not start until late in the 1980s in Malmö, almost a decade later than in other larger Swedish cities.

Building a local strategic approach

In the mid 1990s Malmö was in the middle of economic restructuring. The consequences were alarming – sharp decreases in employment, tax revenues and a rapid increase in the costs of social allowances – and led to the need for more central budget funding. The socio-economic impact of the crisis also instigated closer co-operation between the two opposing political parties – the Social Democratic Party and the Conservative Party – representatives of local large companies, and private housing companies, which led to the drafting of a local development vision statement, the so-called Vision 2015. The vision was developed through a series of informal meetings led by the mayor, assisted by various local, national and international experts.

Vision 2015 has played, as we will see below, a significant role for Malmö's revitalisation and facilitated major changes in local government action. It contained a number of different visions for the city:

- A business vision – the city of development.
- An environment vision – the green city.
- A city builder's vision – the capital of the Skåne region.
- A cultural vision – the city of many cultures.
- A social vision – the city that gathers socially competent citizens.
- A youth vision – the city that empowers the young.

In moving out of the crisis, Malmö had several favourable local development conditions and opportunities to build on. These constituted key pillars of the Vision 2015:

- EU-membership and Malmö's locational advantage as a port city (reality in 1994).
- Tax equalising system between municipalities in the Malmö region with contributed to filling local budget gaps (reality in 1996).
- Local university (reality in 1998).
- Administrative reforms at regional and city levels promising both economic and democratic governance improvements (reality in 1999).

- Bridge over the Öresund to Copenhagen increasing the level of communication, exchange and co-operation in the Öresund region, and enlarging local and regional markets. Decision to build a city tunnel to ensure better transportation (reality in 2001).

The Vision also had a strong skills focus. At the turning point in 1995, knowledge and human capital were seen as key to future economic development and increased employment. Major challenges included: *i)* a large number of students with missing or incomplete secondary education; *ii)* a low level of educational attainment within the labour force; and *iii)* an outflow of talent.

The city government was confronted with a strategic problem of having two very different target groups for education and skills-based interventions. On the one side there were those who had not finished primary education, that is, with less than nine years of formal education; and on the other side were those in possession of a university degree that were unable to enter the labour market, either because of their background or because of a lack of demand. Labour market measures, such as job centres and additional vocational training seemed to be unsuccessful in integrating people who were lacking basic skills into the labour market. At the same time, the steady stream of immigrants faced increasing integration difficulties.

Changing governance: developing a joined-up approach to skills

Local politicians in Malmö shared their belief in education as a key to economic growth and prosperity with national politicians, seeking ways to adapt existing nationwide education measures; for example, through upgrading the nine years of compulsory education to eleven years, and increasing university attendance rates.

In addition, tackling these problems has required a number of changes in the local governance system. In Sweden, labour market policies, unemployment programmes and local job and skills training centres are usually planned and delivered by national government. In order to create a local approach to skills and workforce development, therefore, the local government had to negotiate and merge strategic responses and resources with those of central government. Successful negotiations resulted in a set of new job and skills training arrangements in the city of Malmö. However this produced a rather complicated and comprehensive network of local organisations and programmes working to support the labour market integration of new immigrants, the long term unemployed, persons on social allowances or incapacity benefits, and young people. It also required an increase in the city's finances, through the tax-equalizing system and increased central state transfers for local labour market organisations and programmes starting in the late 1990s.

In all of this, Vision 2015 has played an important role, in particular by redefining the involvement and responsibilities of public and private actors.

Traditionally, the task of the public sector has been to facilitate infrastructural investment by the private sector. The public sector also had responsibility for providing education, whilst the private sector provided jobs. During the period of economic decline, this relationship was breaking down, as the SMEs (small and middle sized enterprises) and new ventures remaining after restructuring were not able to absorb the labour force released by troubled larger firms. New ways had to be found to relieve the burden this placed on public labour market institutions and the social allowance system. The Vision 2015 was considered a joint blueprint of action rather than a weak political compromise, and a transparent process with open mediation. It enhanced participation and commitment from private sector actors, as they were given a voice in the process without being bound into contracts. The strategy was founded on the idea that the resources from the national and municipal levels could be brought together, and the activities of different public organisations could be merged and better aligned at the local level. To do this it was necessary for local agencies to negotiate with central government for the authority to develop local initiatives, in addition to gaining agreements across the different municipality agencies in Malmö. In advancing these negotiations, the economic crisis was used as an important justification for change, and considerable efforts were made during the period 1997-2003.

The key axes of the strategy

Below we consider the key axes of the strategy.

Making the City of Malmö an attractive place

Malmö has long shown itself open to the forces of globalisation, economic transformation and migration. The future development of the city was seen to depend on its ability to continue to harness these forces, becoming an attractive city and drawing in finances, production, and people. A large number of infrastructure actions were taken in this respect during 1995-2005, among these a new bridge to connect the city with Copenhagen, the development of an underground train system, new up-market residential developments in the harbour, the university and the Turning Torso. In particular, the change in Malmö's skyline with the Turning Torso was a transformation which won international awards and helped to generate the city's image as a creative and progressive place. This also triggered a change of identity, as is underlined by the new city slogan "Diversity, Meetings and Possibilities", which it is hoped will make the city more attractive to new arrivals (both people and firms).

One way of raising both the attractiveness of the city and the level of education was to increase the possibilities of higher education. But to develop a new university a city must have central government and parliamentary support and funding. This was achieved in July 1998, and since then the number of students has increased from around 5 000 to 20 000. Because of the university, more young people now live in Malmö which has also had a positive impact on the city's identity.

Integrating the disadvantaged into the workforce development system

Along with the socio-economic consequences of the economic transformation increasing tendencies towards social and ethnic segregation became evident in Malmö during the 1990s, as in other large cities in Sweden. In response to this, an integrated national metropolitan policy was introduced in 1998 in order to reduce social, ethnic and discriminatory segregation. Key to its implementation are the so-called local development agreements, or Metropolitan Policy Programmes that link together different policy priorities with the aim of achieving collaboration between different levels of government. The first of these agreements dated back to 1999 and covered 24 city quarters and administrative sub-districts in Malmö city.

The city government also received considerable state funding to intervene in four economically weak and ethnically segregated parts of the city (two more areas were added in 2006). Special organisations, so-called Local Work and Development Agencies (AUCs) were established to increase labour market integration and skills development activities for the "hard-to-reach" groups of the local population. The AUCs have a broad range of activities (*e.g.* one-on-one counselling, language courses, vocational training, etc.) that takes into account the needs of the target group as well as those of local firms. The AUCs combine the work and resources of state and municipality agencies and oversee collaboration and resource allocation (horizontal contracting) between the city's Department of Social Services (*Socialtjänsten*), the local state Employment Services Office (*Arbetsförmedlingen*) and the local arm of the Social Insurance Office (*Försäkringskassan*).

As part of the Vision 2015, the local education and training system for disadvantaged groups was re-orientated towards a more bottom-up approach. In the mid-1990s, basic implementation measures to integrate hard-to-reach groups were managed using a top-down approach. During the period 1997-2003 this changed considerably. To start with, there was a move to create a "one-stop shop" approach for particular target groups. Whereas before, different organisations (state and municipality) handled the same target groups differently, using a variety of approaches, authority was passed on to a local organisation with a single broad management framework. At the same time, the city moved from occupation-based, standardised and time-fixed training programmes to individual needs-based learning (formal training, on-the-job training or regular work experience, modular courses); and from an emphasis on passive to active labour market policy.

Integrating the immigrant population

The economic crisis of the early 1990s meant that the policy response to high rates of immigration to the city since 1995 has focused on tackling relatively high rates of unemployment among the immigrant population. A whole range of measures has been undertaken by local authorities in co-operation with state and non-state actors in order to adapt policies and measures to local circumstances, and to develop genuine local approaches to fill gaps in services, to fight unemployment and to support integration.

In Sweden all newly settled immigrants have the right to an introductory period of training for a maximum period of three years. This is financed by the central government and is implemented locally through the AUCs. The different education and training programmes for immigrants combine studies in the Swedish language, culture and society ("Swedish for Immigrants"). The programmes also aim to connect immigrants to the local labour market through on-the-job training and job-specific skills development.

In Malmö the so-called "Local agreement with regard to co-operation in the integration of asylum seekers, refugees and other immigrants to Malmö City" lists and defines the basic services offered to immigrants, such as Swedish for Immigrants, Undifferentiated Introduction (for persons with low-skilled occupation qualifications), Academic Introduction (for persons with higher education) and IntroRehab, a programme for the rehabilitation of traumatised immigrants. The agreement distributes responsibilities amongst the different local organisations involved.

The introduction period should last three years and lead to employment. In Malmö, immigrants that do not succeed in this have access to other AUC training services and are offered experienced counsellors and a more individually tailored service. The services are closely linked with KOMVUX, the national adult learning facility that provides formal education from basic courses up to university level. In this way, immigrants can brush-up and/or complete their education. Furthermore close integration exists with general workforce development activities run by different agencies and focused on professions currently in high demand, such as bus drivers, computer operators, butchers etc. Participation is free of charge and participants can receive a small living allowance.

Highly-skilled immigrants

A number of activities are targeted at highly-skilled immigrants and delivered by city agencies and the university. Some form part of the introduction period, with eligible participants being chosen by AUCs. Others are accessed directly by individual immigrants. The Centre for Widening Participation at Malmö University is particularly active. Two types of courses are offered, an introduction programme of one year, and a shorter course for foreign-trained academics.

The Introduction Programme in Swedish with English and Social Sciences, is a one-year intensive programme which targets immigrants with a completed foreign secondary education, and a partly or fully completed university education. It offers language training in Swedish and English and introductory courses in social sciences. The aim is to prepare immigrants for a university education in Sweden. Entry exams are language tests in Swedish and English. The programme takes in 60 students a year. Over the period 2000-2006, a total of around 400 students participated in the programme.

The shorter course, the Aspirant Education Programme, offers a special theoretical and practical programme and awards 60 university credits. Foreign trained academics with a completed academic degree who want to work in the field of training or in related fields are targeted. Individually tailored study programmes also include company internships, independent project work and career advice. In order to be eligible for the Aspirant Education Programme, applicants need to possess a resident permit and a successfully completed foreign university degree (at least two years) in one of the areas of study taught at Malmö University. Applicants must have also completed the Introduction programme in Swedish with English and Social Science at Malmö University or have the equivalent level of competence in Swedish and English. The programme has a strong labour market integration component, which currently consists of three lines of study. The first is a general option which involves refresher courses, putting things in a Swedish perspective and making contacts with future employers. The second prepares students to work in the Swedish public administration, and the third prepares students to become teachers and trainers. The latter started in autumn 2007 and has the lowest number of students to date (see Table 7.1 below).

Table 7.1. **Aspirant education, applicants, admitted and registered students, 2002–2006**

Year/term	Applicants	Admitted	Registered
2002 (Public administration line)	22	16	14
2003 (General)	13	12	10
2003 (Public administration line)	17	17	16
2003 (Teacher, trainer)	–	12	8
2004 (General)	30	19	16
2004 (Public administration line)	25	16	14
2005 (General)	43	18	12
2005 (Public administration line)	59	28	19
2006 (General)	44	16	8
Total	**253**	**154**	**117**

Validating skills

Getting their skills recognised is a problem for immigrants. Educational, vocational and experiential attainments are not always easily accepted by Swedish employers, educational institutions and public labour market institutions, such as job centres. The government of Malmö has thus established a Centre for Validation. Here education and skills attainments that are based on foreign formal education and training, but also work experience, are validated against an industrial upper secondary curriculum for different occupations, such as that of a childcare worker, electrician, industrial mechanic, carpenter, builder, chef, assistant nurse and car mechanic.

The centre offers three main services. The first is to evaluate the individual's general education. The results of the validation of general and core subjects in the secondary and upper-secondary school curriculum provides the individual with suggestions of which further education and training offers are most suitable. The validation happens in co-operation with local schools in Malmö. The second service includes an evaluation of the acquired work competences and experiences against the Swedish vocational or secondary education. Finally a "competencies portfolio" is prepared, which aims to make the education and skills attainment of immigrants more visible and understandable for Swedish employers. The competencies portfolio is a structured and comprehensive summary of the individual's work experiences, education, training, and other merits. It gives a complete and distinct job-related picture of the job seeker and his/her educational background and work experience and makes the job search and career planning easier for the immigrant. It is thus the key document for job applications and the basis for job counselling and further education planning. The competences portfolio concept has spread to the entire Skåne county, and is being carried out annually for at least 3 000 immigrants (2007), of which at least half are in Malmö (see Table 7.2 below). The validation exercise is an effective approach to document prior education and work experience and gives both the immigrant and the training institution or the future employer more clarity about acquired and needed skills. Table 7.2 below shows the numbers that have been validated by the Centre of Validation so far.

Table 7.2. **Validation 2003-2006**

	Occupational identification	Occupational validation	Merit portfolio
2003		73	160
2004	19	72	190
2005	89	81	630
2006	87	179	555

Source: Centre for Validation, City of Malmö.

The validation activity is restricted to secondary level educational attainments. The validation of higher educational attainments and medical professions can be done only by central state institutions, which can cause delays.

Impacts: The changing local context

From the second half of the 1990s, the Swedish economy saw high annual GDP growth rates. Similar trends can be observed for the region of Skåne and Malmö city. The leading question is therefore – what has been the impact so far of Vision 2015 and the activities described above on employment and skills outcomes in Malmö and its surrounding region?

Since January 2004 the number of new vacancies for both low-skilled and high-skilled categories – as published by the public employment services (labour market boards) in Malmö, Göteborg and Stockholm – has been increasing in all three cities, with Malmö showing the highest level. According to the Malmö Labour Market Board the Öresund Bridge connecting the South of Sweden with the larger Copenhagen region has been crucial for this. The integration of Malmö into the larger economic region around Copenhagen resulted in a high demand of labour and increased commuting into Denmark. In 2004 around 50 000 individuals commuted into Malmö to work while about 22 000 individuals living in Malmö worked outside the city. Compared to 1994, the number of individuals commuting into Malmö increased by 19% and those commuting out of the city increased by 68%. Commuting to work was also a discernable phenomenon prior to the Öresund Bridge. Other consequences of the Swedish-Danish economic region are increased inward investment and new business formation on the Swedish side. These changes to the Malmö economy have resulted in an increase in employment trade activities, transport and communication, and B2B services, such as financing, insurance, and real estate. The city outperforms both the region and the country as a whole in these sectors (Figure 7.1).

Changing supply

The changing labour demand of the city has been matched by a changing supply over the last decade. Over one-and-a-half decades the population grew by 15%, from 230 000 in 1990 to over 270 000 inhabitants in 2006 and the foreign born population almost doubled from about 36 000 to 70 000 people (Figure 7.2). Influential to the latter has been a favourable housing market in Malmö that also attracted people from the Copenhagen region. The renovated old harbour area, the Malmö "Docklands", and the university were additional magnets. Compared to the Skåne region and other large cities in Sweden, Malmö had a faster growth in working age population (20-64), in particular during more recent years.

Since the beginning of the new millennium the trend has been towards a net immigration of the foreign-born population and a net outmigration of the

Figure 7.1. **Employment by sector, City of Malmö, 2006**

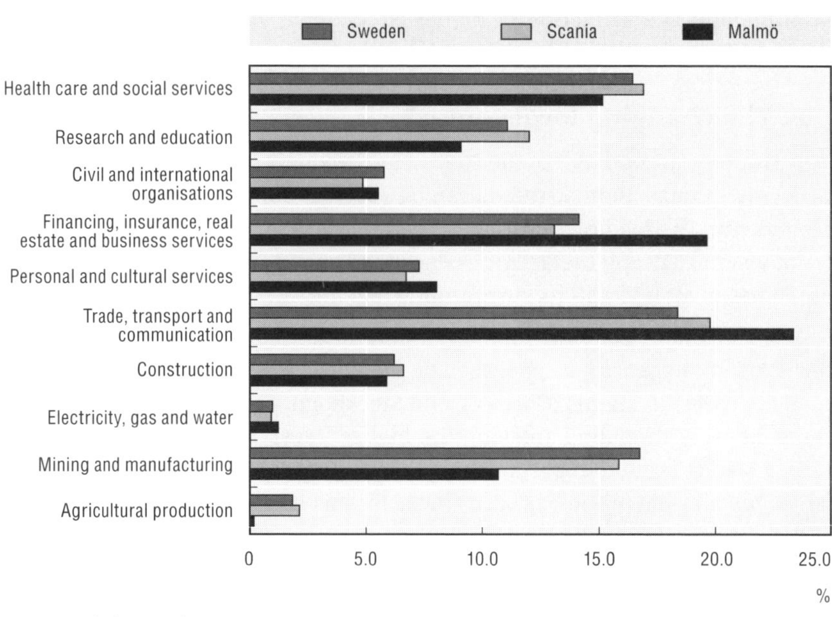

Source: Statistics Sweden.

Figure 7.2. **General population, number of foreign born and number of individuals over age 65, City of Malmö, 1990-2006**

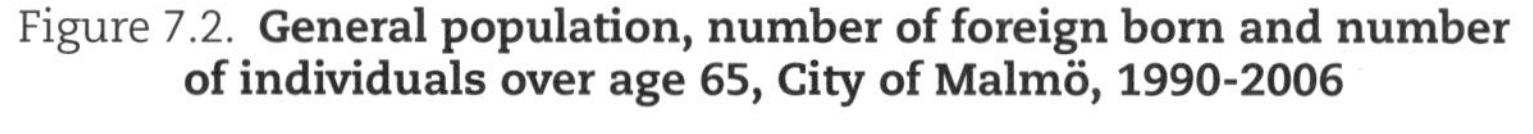

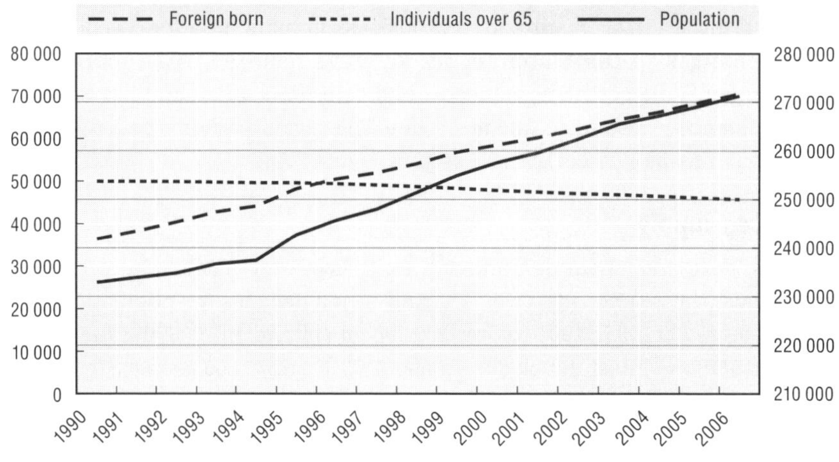

Source: Statistics Sweden.

native population. Malmö has become the city with the highest share of foreign born individuals in Sweden, with nationals from around 171 countries and 36% of the population having a foreign background (Table 7.3). The 1970s

Table 7.3. **Population of Malmö, by country of origin (1999 and 2007)**

	Number 1999	Percentage 1999	Number 2007	Percentage 2007	Change in number 1999-2007	Change in per cent 1999-2007
Sweden	254 904	78	276 244	73	21 340	–5
Foreign born	56 903	22	75 156	27	18 253	5
Yugoslavia	9 239	3.6	8 791	3.2	–448	–0.4
Denmark	3 461	1.4	7 826	2.8	4 365	1.4
Iraq	3 295	1.3	7 101	2.6	3 806	1.3
Poland	5 442	2.1	6 008	2.2	566	0.1
Bosnia-Herzegovina	4 488	1.8	5 637	2.0	1 149	0.2
Lebanon	2 630	1.0	3 309	1.2	679	0.2
Iran	2 670	1.0	2 958	1.1	288	0.1
Hungary	2 009	0.8	1 845	0.7	–164	–0.1
Germany	1 751	0.7	1 767	0.6	16	–0.1
Finland	1 886	0.7	1 678	0.6	–208	–0.1
Afghanistan	767	0.3	1 606	0.6	839	0.3
Rumania	1 352	0.5	1 542	0.6	190	0.1
Turkey	856	0.3	1 445	0.5	589	0.2
Chile	1 253	0.5	1 305	0.5	52	0
Vietnam	936	0.4	1 144	0.4	208	0

Source: Statistics Sweden.

saw changes in the type of immigration flow, with a gradual decrease in immigration from the Nordic countries, mainly Finland. This was largely because of a diminishing gap in the standard of living between Sweden and the emigration countries of Finland and Denmark, and an increasing demand for labour in these countries. While labour migration has dwindled, other types of migration, mainly forced migration and family reunification saw continuous increase during the 1970s and 1980s. This led to a major shift in the countries of origin, with a greater share of non-European immigrants coming to Sweden. In Malmö mainly Chileans, Iranians and people from several Asiatic countries settled.

Skills

At the same time, skills levels in the city's labour force have been changing.

Over the period 1996 to 2003, the overall skills level of the population – in terms of primary, secondary and tertiary education – increased (Table 7.4). For both gender groups of native and foreign-born individuals, we can observe a 10 percentage point increase in completion or attainment of a university education. The increase can be partly explained by a general increase in education in developed countries, and by a replacement of lower-skilled exit of cohorts (born in the 1940s) by higher-educated individuals. A differentiation of

Table 7.4. **Educational level by country of birth, Malmö, 1996 and 2003 (percentage) (25-64-years-old)**

	Males			Females		
	Primary education	Secondary education	University education	Primary education	Secondary education	University education
1996						
Native born	28	45	27	26	45	29
Foreign born	30	47	23	38	40	22
Finland	37	44	19	30	45	25
Denmark	34	45	20	38	40	22
Germany	17	54	29	23	52	25
Poland	18	54	28	21	50	29
Former Yugoslavia	36	55	9	56	35	8
Turkey	51	38	11	70	21	9
Chile	33	46	21	36	45	19
Iran	21	43	36	39	39	22
Iraq	33	26	41	54	20	26
2003						
Native born	17	45	38	14	43	43
Foreign born	21	47	32	28	40	32
Finland	24	48	28	20	43	37
Denmark	18	38	44	20	37	43
Germany	13	50	37	17	47	36
Poland	14	56	30	14	50	36
Yugoslavia[1]	25	57	18	43	42	15
Bosnia-Herzegovina	13	59	28	24	51	25
Turkey	40	43	17	55	31	14
Chile	19	55	25	22	54	24
Iran	11	50	39	13	45	42
Iraq	24	29	47	44	24	42

1. Former Yugoslavia in 1996 became Yugoslavia and Bosnia-Herzegovina in 2003.
2. Unfortunately no statistics are available for where the education was obtained.

Source: Statistics Sweden.

the foreign-born population by country of origin reveals a strong increase in skill levels in the period 1996 to 2003 of individuals born in Denmark and Bosnia-Herzegovina as well as women born in Iraq and Iran; important for the latter is the increase in attainment of a university education. Most other groups show a lower increase compared to natives.

A breakdown of education into vocational/professional *versus* academic education shows that the foreign-born have a higher degree of academic education at the secondary level compared to native-born. At the post-secondary/ university level the native-born have a higher level of university education compared to foreign-born individuals. The foreign-born are more likely to have

Table 7.5. **Percentage in vocational and theoretic education, native and foreign born, 2003, Malmö (age 25-64)**

	Males		Females	
	Natives	Foreign born	Natives	Foreign born
Primary education	17	21	14	28
Vocational secondary education	26	22	25	16
Theoretical secondary education	23	26	19	25
Post secondary education	3	15	2	13
Professional University education	17	10	27	12
Theoretical University education	14	6	13	7

Source: Statistics Sweden.

undertaken post-secondary education however. These differences between native and foreign-born can partly be explained by different educational systems in host and home country as well as by the difficulties in translating foreign educational levels.

Employment development

Employment rates have not increased significantly in recent years. Increasing employment levels were first observed in the second half of the 1990s, after which they have been rather stable up to 2006. In addition, the gap between the employment rate in Malmö, and that of Sweden as a whole, has not narrowed over time. The last decade showed an increase in employment of about 5 percentage points for both the country as a whole and the city of Malmö. However, in 2006, the employment level in Malmö was still about 10 per cent lower than for Sweden as a whole. An increasing proportion of the city's population is employed in the Copenhagen area of neighbouring Denmark, however, which to some extent blurs the actual employment level of the city's population.

While no difference in the gap in employment for the city of Malmö and the country as a whole could be measured between 1993 and 2006, the employment gap between native and foreign born in the city of Malmö narrowed somewhat in this period (Figure 7.3). The native population saw an increase of approximately 5 percentage points, while the employment rate for foreign born increased by almost 10 percentage points. This suggests that the latter profited more from the general positive economic development, especially since the beginning of the new millennium.

Figure 7.3. **Employment rate, native and foreign born in Malmö, 1993-2006, (age 16-64)**

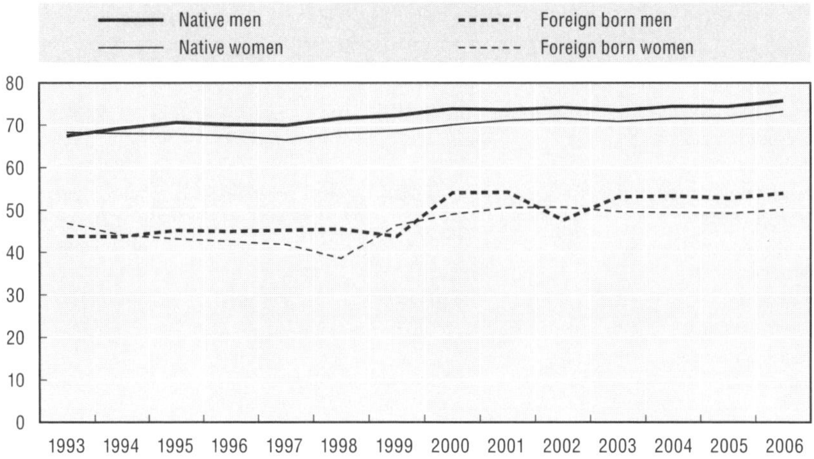

Native men
Native women
Foreign born men
Foreign born women

Source: Statistics Sweden.

Figures 7.4 and 7.5 illustrate the employment rate for the foreign born by continent, based on the local labour force survey. However, care has to be taken when analysing this data since the survey was based on a small number of participants. People born outside of Europe and North America show the strongest increase in employment over time.

Figure 7.4. **Employment rate, according to Labour Force Survey, Malmö, males**

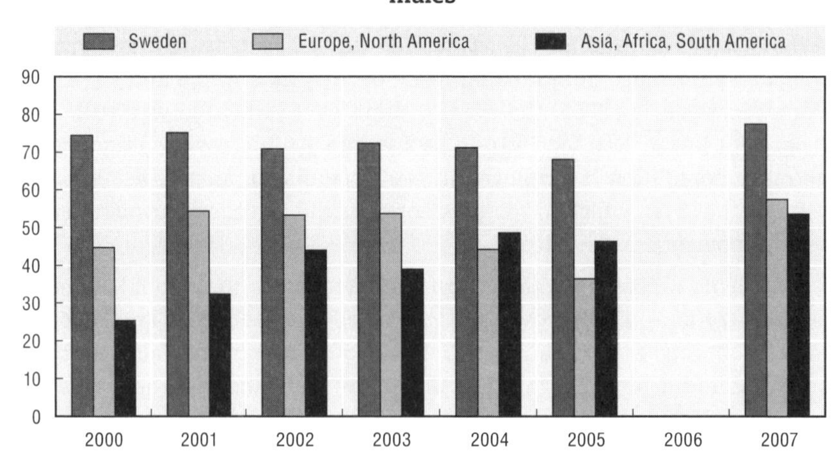

Source: Statistics Sweden.

Figure 7.5. **Employment rate, according to Labour Force Survey, Malmö, females**

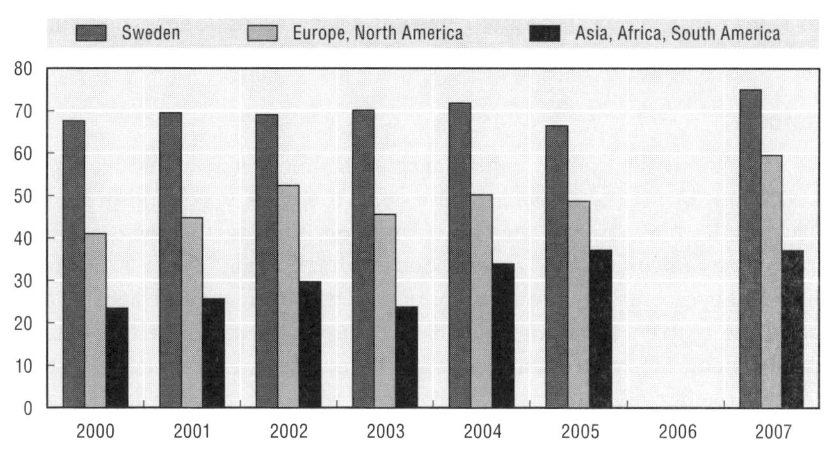

Source: Statistics Sweden.

While wider economic development has been an important factor in stimulating higher labour demand and increasing employment levels in Malmö, a better matching of labour market supply and demand has also played a role. The AUCs in Malmö help those with difficulties to enter and stay on the local labour market. In the period 2000-2006 there has been a more than ten-fold increase in the number of people who have accessed AUCs services (Table 7.6). About one in four clients were employed or started a regular education after having been in contact with the centres. Increased

Table 7.6. **Results 2000-2006 Local Labour and Development Center (AUC) Malmö**

	2000	2001	2002	2003	2004	2005	2006	Total
Number enrolled	4 141	5 151	6 066	7 262	10 540	10 506	10 841	54 507
Number discharged	1 227	1989	2 740	3 045	4 226	5 407	5 618	24 252
Number to employed of discharged	626	759	1 070	1 244	1 782	2086	2 403	9 154
Number to education of discharged	205	250	428	492	877	824	851	3 927
Number to employment and education of discharged	831	1 009	1 498	1 736	2 659	2 910	3 254	13 081
Share to employment of discharged	51	38	39	41	42	39	43	38
Share to education of discharge	17	13	16	16	21	15	15	16
Share to employment and education of discharged	68	51	55	57	63	54	58	57

Source: City of Malmö.

decentralisation, a more individual approach in mediation, competition and co-ordination between different labour market institutions and the centres are key to this, as earlier labour market policy assessments also suggest (Bevelander *et al.*, 2004).

Conclusions

Like many other former industrial cities, Malmö has gone through a period of economic structural transformation since the mid-1970s. And in the mid-1990s, at the low-point of the transformation process, the socio-economic situation became particularly precarious. At the time, the Vision 2015 strategy helped to overcome the growing political power struggle that accompanied economic restructuring and led to a strong alignment of efforts around entrepreneurship, youth, culture, and the environment. Since then these governance changes appear to have contributed significantly to an increase in collective resources and power in negotiation with the state.

Overall, the Vision appears to have been beneficial in helping Malmö to recover from previous economic downturns, and build its new role as an open and attractive global city. Migration flows of Swedes and immigrants have increased the population steadily during this period and changed the ethnic mix of the city. Economic restructuring has also accelerated, and small- and medium sized firms in the new economy have replaced the old industrial plants. Economic growth has returned to average for Sweden, although it was not as high as in the industrial booming days of the 1940s, 1950s and 1960s.

Knowledge and skills were key components of the new approach. The Local Labour and Development Centres in particular have helped disadvantaged individuals to upgrade their skills and gain better access to employment. In addition, newcomers to Malmö have been able to benefit from tailored skills development initiatives that take into account prior learning and work experience. The establishment of a university in Malmö, and the infrastructure development around the Turing Torso have greatly contributed to making the city an attractive place to live and work. The university has, in particular, been successful in attracting highly-skilled migrants, who are able to upgrade their education and skills without having to start from zero. In the future, the university will need to grow and broaden its research areas, while also finding its niche in the Öresund region, which hosts a number of universities and higher education institutions.

Despite this positive picture, imbalances remain. Immigrants still have a problem getting jobs and have a considerably higher unemployment rate than Swedish-born people. And the overall education level in Malmö is still lower than, for instance, the nearby university town of Lund. Three key areas for consideration by local policy makers as they plan future employment and skills for the city include:

Is an education-first approach necessarily best for all immigrants?

The city government has taken an education and skills based approach to the labour market integration of immigrants. Unemployment amongst immigrants is in large part understood to be caused by a lack of appropriate education and training, a belief which is positively influenced by the important priority given to education in general in Sweden. This has permeated the services available to immigrants and the mix of education and labour market assistance. It is evident, for example, in how the AUCs work (trying to integrate those who have not succeeded during the three year introduction period), where participation in formal education is viewed as equivalent to having a job. It is also evident in the introduction programmes run by the local authorities and the university, where all forms of education, from Swedish for Immigrants to "brush-up" courses in childcare, are seen as a primary means of gaining employment. Obstacles to the labour market persist, however, for those immigrants with a good level of education, especially in the current time of global economic down-turn. It may be that other factors need more consideration, including accessibility to employment (for those in certain housing areas) and labour market discrimination. Furthermore, prioritising education has been seen by some critics to encourage passivity. In particular, the possibility of remaining in training after an unsuccessful 3-year-introduction period acts against early labour market integration, and critics warn that prolonged training may cause unnecessary isolation from the local labour market.

Is a one-stop shop approach really best?

Isolation may also arise from the current emphasis on a one-stop shop approach to active labour market policy. This approach sprang from earlier critiques of a fragmented set of public institutions that were not working together. However it also has its disadvantages. While offering a "clearing house" for immigrants may help them to better access education and training, for example, it can cause relative isolation from mainstream services. It may also underestimate the motivation of immigrants to succeed in using the mainstream services available to all residents. Finally, bringing services under public sector leadership risks losing the input of civil society, and associated bottom-up and participative approaches to labour market integration. In the future a merger of public and private responsibilities, with clearly defined boundaries, could potentially make labour market integration and training services more effective.

The missing link: skills upgrading for workers

Finally, while there is a strong focus on both attracting talent, and better integrating disadvantaged groups into the workforce development system in Malmö, there is a limited focus on upgrading the skills of those already in employment. There appears to be an absence of local initiatives to better train those already in work and support career progression, particularly as lifelong learning is traditionally dealt with at the state level in Sweden. The city could benefit from working more closely with local employers to ensure that in-house training and skills upgrading is available. This could go hand-in-hand with a new strategy to dis-incentivise passivity among immigrants and support combined employment and education approaches which make career progression a real option for all those living in the city.

Bibliography

Bevelander, P. (1998), "Employment and Structural Change: Economic Integration of Immigrants in the Swedish and Malmöe Labour Markets 1970-1990", in C. Gorter, P. Nijkamp and J. Poot (eds.), *Crossing Borders, Regional ad Urban Perspectives on International Migration*, Ahsgate/Aldershot, Brookfield.

Bevelander, P. B. Carlson, and M. Rojas (1997), *I Krusbärslandets Storstäder, om invandrare i Stockholm, Göteborg och Malmö*, SNS-förlag, Stockholm.

Bevelander, P., P. Broomé, B. Carlson and G. Lindberg (2004), *Variationer pa framtidsmelodi. Storstadssatsningen i Malmö, Utvärderingen av lokala arbets- och utvecklingscentra*, Lund, Malmö Stad.

Lundh, C. and R. Ohlsson (1999), *Fran arbetskraftimport till flyktinginvandring* (From Labour Import to Refugee Immigration), SNS, Stockholm, second edition.

Ohlsson, R. (1975), *Invandrarna pa Arbetsmarknaden* (Immigrants in the Labour Market), Lund.

Ohlsson, R. (1978), *Ekonomisk strukturförändring och invandring* (Economic Structural Change and Immigration), Lund.

Ohlsson, R. (1995), *Malmö Stadshistoria del 7* (Malmö City history part 7), O. Bjurling (ed.).

Schön, L. (1996), *Malmö, Fran kris till tillväxt, Ett langsiktigt perspektiv pa struktur-omvandlingen och en konstruktion av BRP 1970-1994* (Malmöe, From Crisis to Growth, A Long Term Perspective on Structural Change and the Construction of GRP 1970-1994), Malmö.

SOU (Swedish Official Reports) (1998), *Tre Städer, En storstadspolitik för hela landet*. Fritzes: Stockholm, Vol. 25.

PART II

Chapter 8

New York City Career Pathways: Skills Strategies for Low-paid Immigrants

by

Lisa Grossman

Immigrants in New York City (NYC) are integral players in the local economy, representing 46% of the city's existing labour force. Recent immigrants to NYC have lower levels of educational attainment overall than native born residents, however, which presents a barrier to labour market entry and advancement. This case study explores how City University of New York colleges and their partners (including employers, public agencies and unions), are attempting to upgrade unemployed or low-wage immigrant workers' skills through several career pathways models in the health, hospitality and retail sectors.

Introduction

Immigrants in New York City are integral players in the local economy, representing 46% of the city's existing labour force (Fiscal Policy Institute, 2007). Immigrants often face considerable barriers to labour market advancement, and the policies and services available to address these barriers are often fragmented (OECD, 2006). This case study explores how some City University of New York (CUNY) colleges and their partners are attempting to address these barriers and upgrade immigrant workers' skills through "career pathways" programmes. Career pathways are defined as a "series of connected education and training programmes and support services that enable individuals to secure employment within a specific industry or occupational sector, and to advance over time to successively higher levels of education and employment in that sector" (Jenkins and Spence, 2006).

The study begins by assessing the local context for the development of the career pathways strategies and their potential for addressing immigrants' particular needs. The study turns to documenting some well-established career pathway programmes in the health sector. We then describe emerging pathways in the retail, tourism and hospitality sectors before looking at contextualised approaches to teaching Vocational English as a Second Language (VESL) in order to help workers achieve their career advancement goals. The study concludes with an analysis of remaining gaps in the approach, and a summary of these programmes' potential benefits to immigrants. The methodology for the study has consisted of a literature review, programme materials review and interviews with CUNY programme staff, partners, policy makers and experts in career pathways and workforce development.

Assessing the local context

New York City's immigrant population

New York City has a rich history of immigration, and every year new foreign-born individuals and families continue to migrate and settle in its five boroughs. Immigrants account for 37% of the total population in the city, and represent 46% of the total labour force in the city (Fiscal Policy Institute, 2007). Unlike other US cities where migration is dominated by a few major countries of origin, New York City immigrants are incredibly diverse; no group has any clear majority (Orr and Topa, 2006). This diversity extends as well to demographics and socio-economic status, making it very difficult to characterise New York City immigrants as a group (Fiscal Policy Institute, 2007).

Most salient to this study are immigrants for whom low levels of educational attainment, language or other barriers have prevented entry or advancement in the labour market. Educational attainment varies widely for immigrants based on country of origin, but overall, immigrants who arrived to New York City during the 1990's had higher levels of education than their predecessors, but still had lower levels of education than their native born counterparts (Rosen, Wieler and Pereira, 2005). The difference in educational attainment is most extreme at the lowest levels of education: one recent study found that 15% of immigrants had an 8th Grade or lower education as compared to only 5% of the native born population (Fiscal Policy Institute, 2007). Immigrants with higher levels of education may still be at a disadvantage compared to their native born counterparts, since it can be very difficult to get foreign credentials or previous schooling recognised in the United States (Fiscal Policy Institute, 2007; Erisman and Looney, 2007; Kurien, 2008). New York City immigrants tend to work in lower-paying jobs compared to native born workers with the same levels of education (Rosen, Wieler and Pereira, 2005). One national immigrant-serving non-profit organisation, Upwardly Global, estimated in a recent report that there could be 25 000 immigrants with college degrees earned abroad, now earning low wages in New York City (Colton, 2006).

Immigrants who arrived in the 1990s tend to have slightly higher unemployment rates compared to non-immigrants, and this difference is even more pronounced in immigrant groups from certain countries of origin (Rosen, Wieler, and Pereira, 2005). Immigrants can and do participate in unions in New York City in certain sectors, and there is some evidence that union membership can offset the wage disparity for immigrants and native born populations (Fiscal Policy Institute, 2007). One possible reason behind some of these labour market disparities between immigrants and the native born population may be limited English proficiency: a recent analysis found that while most immigrants do master English if they stay long enough, 27% of the city's working age immigrants reported having little or no English skills (Fiscal Policy Institute, 2007). Lower levels of English fluency do appear to be linked with lower income levels among immigrants (Fiscal Policy Institute, 2007 and Rosen, Wieler, and Pereira, 2005).

Fragmented public policy and services for immigrants

State and local policies and programmes that might address the complex workforce needs of immigrants (or other workers, for that matter) are rarely coordinated or integrated to address similar or overlapping workforce development goals (Mazzeo, Roberts, Spence and Strawn, Workforce Strategy Center, 2006). The OECD has found fragmentation in service provision to immigrants in many localities (OECD, 2006). New York City is no exception. Immigrants' education, training and workforce development needs could thus be served through any number of public agencies, private or community based organisations, and education and training providers, as well as through labour unions or employers' own incumbent worker training initiatives. These entities function separately, however, and not as a single system (Fischer, 2007). It must be truly bewildering to navigate these programmes as a recent immigrant or even a long-term resident. In attempt to better coordinate services, the mayor's Office of Immigrant Affairs works collaboratively with providers to address issues of concern to the city's immigrant community, and publishes a directory of the hundreds of community-based organisations which provide free or low-cost services to immigrants.[1]

Immigrants are not targeted directly by most of the major public anti-poverty or workforce development programmes, but instead may access the services available to the general population. Recent immigrants in the United States have reduced options for public assistance when faced with unemployment or underemployment; unless immigrants have resided legally in the United States for five or more years, they are not eligible for various federally funded assistance programmes such as the Temporary Assistance for Needy Families, Medicaid or Food Stamps (Fiscal Policy Institute, 2007).[2] New York State, however, provides greater access to public assistance programmes for recent immigrants through state-funded safety net programmes, although they still cannot access Food Stamps (Fiscal Policy Institute, 2007).

Some mayoral reforms were recently enacted aimed at better aligning workforce development and economic development programmes and policies in the city, and through one of these reforms, responsibility for adult workforce development services was assigned to the New York City Department of Small Business Services. There have been numerous improvements in the oversight and infrastructure for workforce development services in the city, leveraging additional resources and aligning services to better meet employers' needs. However there is still considerable fragmentation overall in terms of connections with other city agencies (Fischer, 2007). Workforce development in New York is largely focused on job placements for relatively "work ready" customers although there have been some recent special projects targeting retention and advancement issues. Job placements continue to be the central priority of the system, driven by the priorities and limited overall funding available through the federal funding source, the Workforce Investment Act (ibid.). Workforce Development services offered through New York City's Workforce One Career Centers (known as One Stops elsewhere) are offered with universal access and should thus be available to immigrants as well as the native born population. There is some anecdotal evidence to suggest that immigrants with language barriers may have some difficulty accessing these workforce development services (*ibid.*).

There is a large network of publicly and privately funded programmes aimed at addressing immigrants' language barriers. English as a Second Language (ESL) and other adult education programmes offered by hundreds of public and private providers are administered by the New York City Department of Education's Office of Adult and Continuing Education, and funded through multiple city, state and federal funding streams. The mayor's Office of Adult Education was established to coordinate the various adult education programmes in the city. The New York City Council also offers some additional funds for ESL programmes through its "Immigrant Opportunities Initiative" (Colton, 2006). All of these efforts combined, however, may not be sufficient to the scope of the task. One recent local study found that ESL programmes were in short supply given the potential demand in New York State, addressing only 3.4% of the potential need for such programmes (Colton, 2007).[3]

Immigrant access to post-secondary education

CUNY is one of the largest service providers for addressing immigrants' workforce development (or other) needs in New York City, and it is considered large by national standards as well. It is the largest public urban post-secondary education system in the United States, consisting of 23 colleges, including 11 four-year senior colleges, 6 community colleges, an honours college and various graduate and professional schools. Nationally, community colleges are often touted as a critical workforce development and post-secondary education provider for the immigrant population. This is particularly true for CUNY where four-year colleges are just as likely to offer workforce development programmes and services as their two-year counterparts.

In New York, four-year colleges also serve even greater numbers of immigrants than do their two-year community college counterparts, overall, according to one study (Erisman and Looney, 2007). The study's authors believe that New York's four year colleges are more accessible to immigrants of traditional college age than is the case in other states, due to the state's own financial aid system. They also explain that native-born students are more likely to attend four-year colleges over community colleges in the state, as well (Erisman and Looney, 2007).

The problem – a lack of adult education for those in work

CUNY and the other public and private higher education institutions in the state serve many traditional college-age immigrants, but could do more to serve the particular focus group for this study *i.e.* adult low-paid workers. New York State has one of the lowest college attendance rates for adults in the country and the rate continues to fall, according to one recent study, which highlighted the relative expense of New York's public college tuition and limitations of the state's financial aid system for working adults (Hilliard, 2007).

There are numerous barriers to attending college for immigrant and other low-wage working adults. One study of community college access and retention found that conflicts with work and family life made traditional community college attendance a major challenge for low-wage working parents. Likewise, low-wage workers with basic skills deficits often require remedial or developmental courses which can extend the time required to complete post-secondary studies, since these courses usually do not count towards degree completion. (Matus-Grossman *et al.*, 2002). Many students do not successfully complete these courses, and among those that do and later enrol in college programmes, many never earn their degrees (Jenkins and Boswell, 2002).[4] Once enrolled in college, immigrants or other working adult college students are often not aware of available supports or services on their campuses or have difficulty accessing them with conflicting work or family schedules. Immigrants may face additional barriers to college attendance, including a basic lack of information about the college application process and financial aid, language barriers, and in some cases, legal issues like immigration status (Erisman and Looney, 2007; Matus-Grossman *et al.*, 2002).

The focus of the study

There are thus many barriers for low-wage immigrants seeking to improve their career prospects through adult study. This is not helped by the increasingly fragmented nature of employment itself, with many occupations and sectors no longer offering a "career for life" or clear ladder towards career progression. Many jobs are temporary, and in today's "hour glass" economy it can be difficult to see how one job may lead to another higher up within the job hierarchy. A new "career pathways approach" which has been developed in the United States in recent years offers a mechanism for overcoming such barriers. When targeted to incumbent workers and in partnership with employers, these pathways may be able to bring career mobility to those who traditionally lacked job training and advancement opportunities, particularly immigrants, through clearly "mapping" out the linkages between education, training and career opportunities, and providing adapted education and training to help people access such opportunities.

Overview of focus sectors

This study explores career pathway programmes developed by the City University of New York in several sectors: healthcare and retail, hospitality and tourism. In New York City, these sectors all share several critical elements

Box 8.1. **Overview of CUNY: An immigrant serving institution**

CUNY is one of the two publicly funded higher education systems in New York State. The other is the State University of New York system which has campuses state-wide, while the CUNY system serves New York City. The CUNY system has a centralised governing body, a board of trustees, a chancellor, and a central administration which sets policies and administers funding. The presidents of each individual college report to the chancellor, but retain a great deal of independence in running their own institutions. CUNY serves approximately 400 000 students annually, with about half enrolled in degree programmes and the other half in adult or continuing education non-degree programmes (CUNY, 2008a).

CUNY experienced a relatively recent growth in its immigrant population during the 1990's and has emerged as a major immigrant-serving institution in New York City, with 48.6% of first year students born outside the United States in 2000, according to one study (Leinbach and Bailey, 2006). According to CUNY's own data, 48% of students have a primary language other than English (CUNY, 2008a).

CUNY has numerous dedicated programmes and services to meeting immigrants' particular needs, including the CUNY Citizenship and Immigration Project which provides citizenship and immigration law services through eight campus based centres, an annual "call-in" event where immigrants can get free legal advice, the "CUNY/NYC Citizenship Corps," which provides legal and citizenship advice in community locations, and a graduate certificate programme in Immigration Law to upgrade the skills of community based providers serving immigrants (CUNY, 2008b). CUNY also offers multiple levels and formats of ESL classes, and targeted job-training programmes to immigrant populations which often combine vocational skills with language instruction; these programmes include some of the career pathway examples described in this study as well as other programmes that prepare unemployed or other interested immigrants for entry-level jobs.

Immigrants are also served through CUNY's academic and workforce development programmes for the general population. Such workforce development programmes have also experienced significant growth as part of CUNY's overall programming (Kleiman, 2004). Career pathway programmes for the most part operate out of the adult and continuing education divisions, with various conscious efforts to connect these efforts to credit granting degree or certificate programmes throughout CUNY.

that support career pathway development, and are well-suited for targeting the immigrant community. All these sectors are high-growth and high-demand, already employ a significant immigrant population, and have potential for career advancement. These sectors are also among the eight high-growth sectors[5] selected by the Workforce Investment Board in New York City. This section briefly profiles each of the key sectors.

Healthcare

The healthcare sector in New York City employed 415 000 workers in 2006, accounting for 43% of the state's healthcare workforce; the sector grew in the city 26% from 1990 to 2006 and far outpaced growth in other sectors (The Center for Health Workforce Studies, 2008). The sector is predicted to continue to grow for many health occupations, home health aides, medical assistants and physicians assistants in particular (Center for Health Workforce Studies, 2008).[6] Certain high-skilled (*e.g.* nurses, nuclear medical technologists, physical therapists) and lower-skilled occupations (*e.g.* home health aides) are currently in high demand, as is the case elsewhere in the United States (The Center for Health Workforce Studies, 2008). The entry-level positions, home healthcare aides in particular, are typically of low pay and experience high-turnover, while the more advanced positions can offer very good wages and benefits (Seedco, 2007).

Of particular relevance to the immigration population is a current shortage for bilingual healthcare professionals in the city (Seedco, 2007). The sector has a longstanding career pathway since many higher-wage jobs require specific education and training or professional credentials; in New York City, the sector is also heavily unionised, which provides incumbent workers who are members with additional education and training benefits and a well-established pay scale. It is very difficult to advance from entry-level low-wage positions to high-skill positions within the sector, however, due to the advanced education and training required (Seedco, 2007). Immigrants play major roles at all levels of employment in the sector; one study found that immigrants accounted for 50% of physicians, 60% of all Registered Nurses (RN's) and 70% of all nurses' aides (Fiscal Policy Institute, 2007).

Retail, hospitality and tourism

The New York City Workforce Investment Board has considered the three sectors, retail, hospitality and tourism, as a "cluster", since the customer service skill set required for many entry-level jobs is transferrable across them (Seedco, 2007). The cluster currently employs more than 1 million workers in the region, and demand is expected to grow nearly 10% by 2012 for both entry-level and mid-level positions (Workforce Strategy Center, 2008).[7] Most entry-level positions in the cluster offer low wages, although many hotels in New York City are unionised, offering higher wages and benefits than is typical in non-unionised settings (Seedco, 2007).

As with healthcare, immigrants are overrepresented in many positions: 54% of all cashiers, 43% of all retail salespersons, 54% of first-line supervisors in retail and 63% food service managers are immigrants (Fiscal Policy Institute, 2007). In contrast to healthcare, the cluster requires much less education for entry-level and some advanced positions, although many of the top-level management positions would require a college degree and specialised skills. Also unlike healthcare, the cluster has no clear career path, although some of the larger employers may have clearly defined internal paths (see Workforce Strategy Center, 2007; Workforce Strategy Center, 2008; and Seedco, 2007).

Designing effective career pathways

This chapter defines and describes the career pathway approach and its potential for serving immigrants' particular workforce development needs. The term "career pathways" has been used in the United States to refer to both 1) education and training programmes that help youth simultaneously prepare for careers and transition into postsecondary education (Hughes and Karp, 2006) and 2) programmes that are primarily focused on forging strong linkages between education and training and career advancement opportunities for adults in the workforce (Jenkins and Spence, 2006). Our focus here is on the second model for adults, although many career pathway models try to integrate both functions (Alssid, 2008). CUNY defines career pathways as "projects focused on industries where additional skills and knowledge help individuals to obtain positions with progressively greater scope, responsibilities and compensation" (Mogulescu, 2008). The CUNY definition includes programmes which "can also help to develop a career path in industries that lack clearly defined opportunities for advancement", and typically include "employers as partners in developing and offering training and education" (Mogulescu, 2008).

Workforce Strategy Center, a national workforce intermediary based in New York, has studied the elements of emerging pathway models (see Box 8.2 below). These programmes ultimately attempt to provide more information to incumbent and potential workers in a sector about what their real options are for career mobility, and what education and training is required to achieve their career goals. They may offer more opportunities for entry and exit than traditional, often disconnected education and training programmes. At the same time, the career pathway approach attempts to make education and training programmes more responsive to both employers and working students' needs.

Documenting the CUNY career pathway models

A number of different pathway models have been developed in the health care, retail, hospitality and tourism sectors. The following section provides an outline of eight such programmes (see Annex 8.A for a summary list) before analysing the mechanisms used for implementation and development.

Overview of the healthcare career pathway programmes

Within the healthcare sector, it is a union and its management partners which have provided a key impetus for the development of the career pathways model. The 1199SEIU Training and Upgrading Fund has contracted with CUNY as well as many other education and training providers to develop several programmes to meet the healthcare union's members' career advancement needs.

Box 8.2. **Workforce Strategy Center's key features of career pathway programmes**

Career pathway programmes typically include many of the following features, according to analysis by Workforce Strategy Center:

- Focus on "industries of importance to local economies".
- Lead to advancement opportunities at every level of employment.
- Improve the "supply of qualified workers for local employers".
- Use labour market and other relevant data to inform every step of the process, from design to programme evaluation.
- "Map" out the linkages between each successive education and training step and connected career advancement opportunity along the pathway.
- Include clear transitions between "remedial, occupational and academic" programmes within and across post-secondary institutions or other education and training providers.
- Education and training that is relevant both in the industry and for future education programmes, often including various modes of experiential learning, and that is designed with adult working students in mind (*e.g.* convenient and flexible).
- May incorporate "wrap-around support services" to address working adults' career and life concerns.
- Often use entry-level "bridge" programmes to help adult learners with basic skills deficits to address those deficits while learning occupational skills and preparing for post-secondary degree programmes.

Source: Jenkins and Spence, 2006.

For example, the Training and Upgrading Fund contracted with CUNY's Lehman College to develop a dedicated programme to prepare union members with foreign nursing or medical degrees who are currently working in non-nursing jobs (*e.g.* home healthcare aides) to become registered nurses in the United States. The programme attempts to address both the nurse shortage as well as provide a concrete path to career advancement for under-employed incumbent workers with language or other barriers. The Foreign Born Registered Nurse Program, as it is known, consists of three months of part-time skill development in maths, reading and writing, and assistance with collecting necessary documents for the qualification process. The programme also includes English as a second language instruction contextualised to the healthcare field.[8] The programme is flexible and designed to accommodate the diverse needs of the participants. Lehman College has worked intensively with nearly 100 foreign born nurses over the past five years. A similar programme provides training for physicians to convert to the nursing profession, given that it is not likely that their credentials will be recognised to practice medicine in the United States.

At the same time, the 1199SEIU Fund has contracted with three CUNY colleges[9] to develop a programme known as "HC4" which is aimed at college-ready union members who require pre-requisite credits before entering nursing or other academic health programmes in the university. The programme aims to help these adult college students adjust to the college experience either as re-entry or first time students by providing them dedicated classes with faculty staff experienced in teaching adult workers. Most of the 700 HC4 participants served each year are racial or ethnic minorities, and female, and a large percentage of HC4 participants are immigrants.

The programme includes closed classes for 1199SEIU members in the pre-requisites required for healthcare degree programmes at CUNY, such as English, Computers, Biology, and Human Anatomy and Physiology. Students earn up to 34 undergraduate credits through the programme, relevant across the CUNY colleges. In view of the fact that students are working, the CUNY staff teach these dedicated courses at convenient locations and times, or even online, outside of the regular academic schedules of the participating colleges. Nursing programmes often have poor retention rates and HC4 aims to better prepare union members to succeed in nursing or other health related degree programmes through successful completion of pre-requisite courses, hiring a dedicated counsellor to support the HC4 students. HC4 has a 91% retention rate in the programme.

LaGuardia's Allied Healthcare Career Pathway. Pathways within the health sector can be relatively complex and multilayered. LaGuardia Community College, for example, has developed a multi-level career pathway programme in the area of health (the Allied Healthcare Career Pathway, see Figure 8.1 below), supported by multiple public and private funding sources. The pathway has a series of different stages. Firstly, in order to address barriers to accessing vocational or academic healthcare programmes, the college offers preparatory/bridge programmes which blend reading, writing and critical thinking instruction in a healthcare context. Each is tailored to a different type of target group. For example the English for Healthcare Workers programme addresses limited English proficiency in a healthcare context, while the GED Bridge to Healthcare Careers prepares participants who do not have a high school diploma to earn a high school equivalency diploma. The Bridge to US Healthcare Careers is targeted to immigrants with medical credentials or sector experience abroad, with language barriers.

At this level, the college also offers "transition programmes" that are more targeted programmes to help incumbent workers already trained for

Figure 8.1. **La Guardia Community College Allied Healthcare Career Pathway**

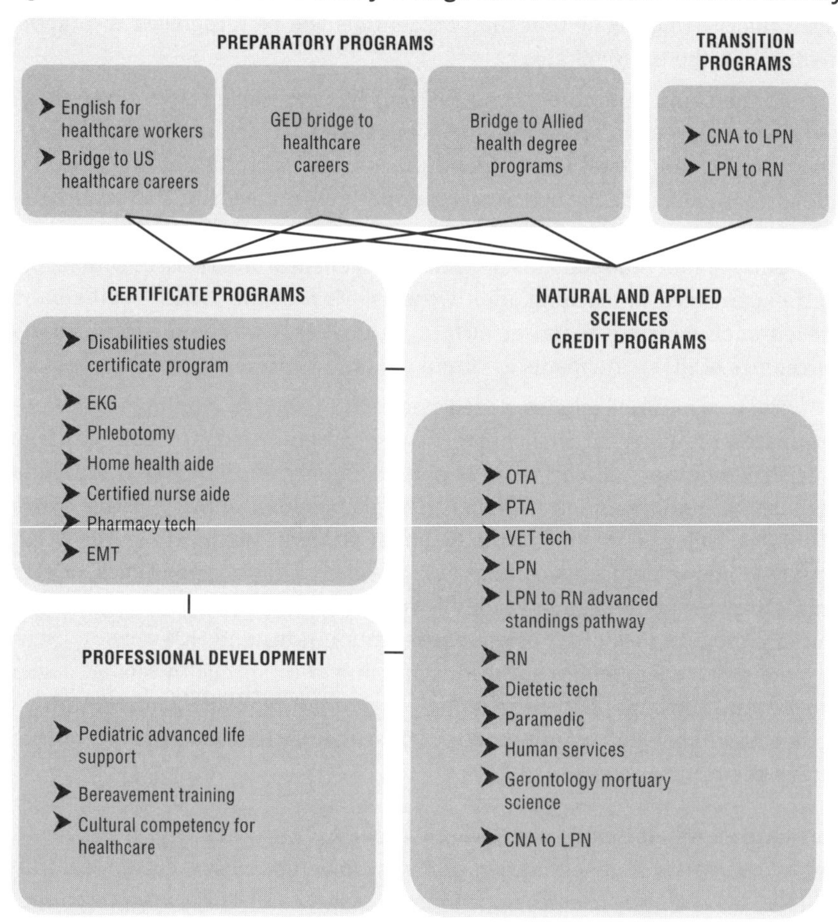

Source: LaGuardia Community College's Allied Health Initiatives, Division of Adult and Continuing Education and Academic Affairs (Natural and Applied Sciences) 2008.

certain occupations move to next step job opportunities. These programmes are often sponsored by workers' employers, the 1199SEIU Training and Upgrading Funds, or public agencies (*e.g.* targeted programmes for welfare recipients) to fill their existing or projected labour shortages. The CNA to LPN programme, for example, is a college preparatory programme that helps incumbent Certified Nurse Assistants to enter the existing Associates Degree programme for Licensed Practical Nurses. Some of these programmes have been conducted for non-native English speakers, to fill a major shortage for bilingual staff in hospitals or other healthcare institutions. The college estimates that about 400 to 500 individuals participated in the past two years, across their various bridge and transition programmes.

The next level along the pathway includes vocational programmes (*e.g.* disability studies for direct care workers). These are specifically designed to bolster the academic skills of adults who have not had much success with education in the past or studied in foreign education institutions, and to prepare them for higher-level vocational or degree programmes.

Finally, for qualified workers, many of whom have graduated from the college's certificate and academic degree programmes in the healthcare field, the college offers continuing education for professional development purposes.

The courses are developed on the basis of agreements with other colleges to ensure a common approach to training, and are again adapted to the needs of adult workers. The college tries to provide additional supports or accommodate adult students with work or family responsibilities, across the Pathway. Programmes are often delivered at more convenient times for workers and parents, or even off the regular academic calendar if necessary. The programmes offer wrap around services such as one-on-one tutoring and career counselling. Work experience is also integrated into the curriculum in many cases – the Basic Emergency Medical Technician (EMT) programme targets low-income women, for example, and combines the occupational training required for entry-level jobs as well as a "Culture of Work" curriculum and assistance with job search.

Overview of the retail, tourism and hospitality pathways

While the career pathways in the healthcare sector have been established for a relatively long time, new pathway programmes are now emerging in the Tourism, Hospitality and Retail Sectors.

Kingsborough's career pathway in tourism and hospitality. Figure 8.2 illustrates the emerging career pathway map for the tourism and hospitality industry cluster which is being developed by Kingsborough Community College's Center for Economic and Workforce Development. This represents the early efforts of the college and its partners to map out the specific education and training required for people to advance their careers across these sectors, as well as the industry-specific certifications required at each level of employment. In contrast to the healthcare sector, which has an established career pathway driven by employer demand, the Kingsborough project is a data driven bottom-up approach by a college to make clear connections between education and training and career advancement where none now exist. The project requires not just employer buy-in, but the buy-in of the college's academic departments as well, where there may be resistance to taking on more of a career development role.

At the same time the college is also piloting a job training programme, Project Welcome. This programme is being developed through partnership working with the New York City Department of Small Business Services, several community based organisations, the college's own Tourism and Hospitality Department, and employers through an advisory board.

Project Welcome mainly targets unemployed and under-employed adults, with about half of the project participants currently being immigrants. Interested participants are screened through a basic intake interview to assess job readiness and basic skills. Three industry tracks are offered: Hospitality Sales and Marketing; Food Service Operations; Hospitality Operations and Management. All tracks include 188 hours of classroom education and training, a Virtual Enterprise programme to apply classroom learning firsthand, and a 100 hour internship. Kingsborough has worked with community-based organisations to roll out Project Welcome and help tailor the curriculum to meet neighbourhood-specific needs. For example, one Project Welcome partner is the Brooklyn-based Williamsburg Works which is engaged in a larger effort to grow neighbourhood job opportunities in food-related small businesses. In order to promote this goal, Project Welcome focused on the culinary arts. Students gain industry certifications in each track and receive job placement assistance through the programme. Typically, the programme lasts about 12-15 weeks. Kingsborough and its partners seek to serve 520 participants over the course of their grant funding.

Figure 8.2. **Draft tourism and hospitality career pathways**

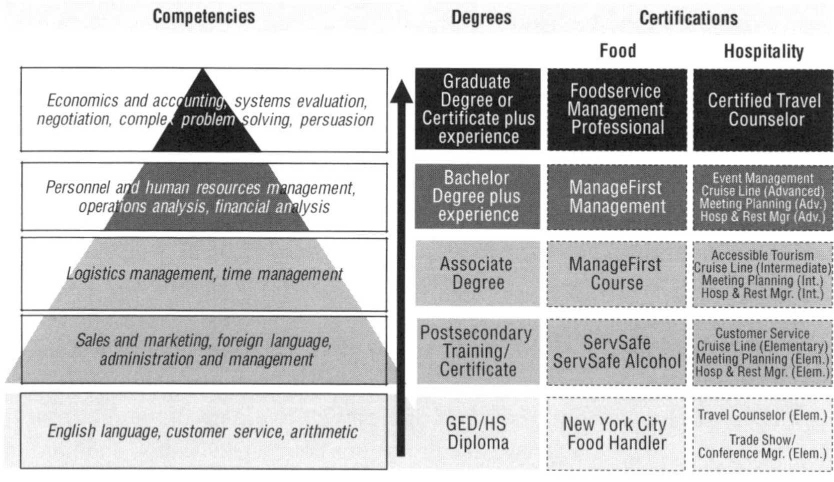

Note: This is a work in progress and the pathway is still being refined through discussions with employers, faculty and other stakeholders.

Source: Kingsborough Community College Center for Economic and Workforce Development (2008).

Both this and the career mapping project are funded by the US Department of Labor, through a Community-Based Job Training Grant and Individual Training Account funds.

Contextualised English as a Second Language Programmes for low-skilled workers in the retail and hospitality industry. In a parallel effort various CUNY colleges are working directly with employer partners to develop English as a second language programmes to prepare workers for career advancement opportunities in retail and hospitality. For example, the LaGuardia Community College has worked with the Sheraton Manhattan Hotel Center to develop a project called Hotel TEACH, again funded by the US Department of Labor. This programme has targeted 22 incumbent hotel workers in non-management positions with limited English proficiency whose work tasks involved little interaction with guests (housekeeping, laundry, etc.). The programme provided 160 hours of contextualised English teaching as well as computer, customer service and "soft skills" required for supervisory-level positions, over a 16 week period. The resulting curriculum was both customised to Sheraton but also provided transferable skills for other jobs or industries. Career counselling was included as part of the curriculum, with a focus on achieving advancement. Students also received MP3 players with voice recorders to practice pronunciation lessons.

In 2006, a consortium of four CUNY colleges[10] won a USD 1 million grant from the US Department of Labor's Limited English Proficiency and Hispanic Worker Initiative for the VESL (Vocational English as a Second Language) for the Successful Worker Project. Each college worked with different employer partners to develop and deliver English as a Second Language programmes for incumbent workers, to prepare them for advancement opportunities. One employer/college partnership was between the Borough of Manhattan Community College and the McDonalds Corporation. McDonalds wanted to improve the language skills of their non-management staff being considered for promotion to the lowest levels of management. LaGuardia Community College developed targeted programmes for two employers: the Duane Reade pharmacy chain, which wanted to upgrade their warehouse staff's language and customer service skills, and Crystal Windows and Doors, a manufacturer with a Chinese workforce with relatively high levels of English who needed language and vocational skills to communicate better in a sales role. The different projects served 265 participants, the majority of whom were of Latino origin, in addition to small cohorts of Chinese, Russian or East European, and other ethnic groups. Participants received up to 160 hours of instruction, typically 8 hours per week.

One direct outcome of the VESL for a Successful Worker project was the launch of a second project for the McDonalds Corporation, The Fast Food, Fast

Track VESL Project, led by the Borough of Manhattan Community College. The second project is funded by a New York State Department of Labor Grant with an additional funds and in-kind resources provided by the McDonalds Corporation. The programme aims to serve 180 incumbent workers with language barriers. Building on a curriculum developed for McDonalds from the first project, the modules will blend ESL, vocational and work experience instructional approaches using materials and scenarios from the students daily work routines. Goals include 85% of programme completers demonstrating increases in English language proficiency, 90% employment retention or advancement, and 85% of the completers receiving wage increases within one year post-completion.

The pathway development process

CUNY colleges and their partners are using different processes to develop and map these pathways over time. In case of healthcare, the colleges have a long history of working with various partners such as hospitals or unions on special projects which over time have evolved into a career pathway model.

> The trick in all of this [career pathway creation] is creating the collaboration, the most difficult part. The partner is the union or the hospital ... then you [also] have the academic department, and more often or not an academic department is rigid in its approach to its subject matter, and then you have the potential student. Each one has very different demands and needs. And then you have continuing education which is really charged with building the bridges between the three constituencies to make it work, Michael Paull, Dean of Adult and Continuing Education at Lehman College (2008).

LaGuardia's approach has been to take on pathway development one sector at a time. Sandra Watson, Dean of the Adult and Continuing Education Division at LaGuardia, estimates that it has taken five or six years to establish their Allied Health Career Pathway programmes, involving both internal collaboration and relationship building between Adult and Continuing Education and academic departments, as well as external work with the industry. They now have an Allied Health Committee which spans both the Adult and Continuing Education Division and the Natural and Applied Sciences Division (the academic department), and meets regularly to collaboratively plan and refine programming.

In retail, tourism and hospitality, the colleges' work to develop career pathways across the sectors is in the very early stages. First the colleges try to learn about the various sectors, reviewing available research or conducting their own. LaGuardia's Center for Corporate Education convened several systematic industry specific forums with employers to study their skill-training and staffing needs. The colleges then embark on pilot projects, often working with specific employers or groups of employers to train incumbent workers or prepare immigrants or other disadvantaged populations for entry-level employment. Through these efforts, the staff is able to learn about the specific needs of their employer partners, as well as the broader needs of the industry. The pilot projects allow the colleges to develop curricula that can be adapted or refined for future programmes.

LaGuardia also established a consortium to support its retail pathway development work, the New York City Sales and Service Training Partnership. The partnership members include five CUNY colleges, the State University of New York's Brooklyn Educational Opportunity Center, business and industry associations (National Retail Foundation Federation, Long Island City Business Development Corporation), employers (Citibank), and public agencies (Small Business Services and the Port Authority of New York and New Jersey). The partnership engages in joint planning and implementation activities, and leverages resources. New partners are brought in as needed when seeking new funding opportunities or to meet specific project needs in the retail sector.

The Kingsborough Community College Tourism and Hospitality Pathway is being developed through a more formal process, with technical assistance from the national Workforce Strategy Center Box 8.3 provides a list of the main steps of the Workforce Strategy Center model, reprinted from Jenkins and Spence (2006). Kingsborough is in the early stages of applying this process to their work.

Partnerships

CUNY colleges have established partnerships as needed for each particular project, or in the case of the 1199SEIU Training and Upgrading Fund or other contract projects, colleges serve as providers on others' projects. Cultivating and maintaining good working relationships to support career pathway development in some cases is the result of long-term investment by all parties. CUNY's long-standing relationship with the Training and Upgrading Fund has evolved over time, for example. In the early stages, CUNY's central administration played a role in brokering the relationship, when the Fund perceived a lot of resistance from the academic departments at individual colleges to serving their non-traditional student populations. The partnership has been mutually beneficial and has led to the development of numerous other programmes along the career pathway, such as a new joint community-based education and training facility operated in partnership with three Bronx-based CUNY colleges. CUNY works with other service providers, like community based organisations, when it makes strategic sense in order to fill a programmatic gap or leverage additional resources.

Box 8.3. The Workforce Strategy Center process for career pathway development

Stage 1. Gap analysis: target industries and jobs that will support individual advancement and growth

- Analyse current and projected supply and demand for labour in region, identifying industries offering jobs with family-supporting wages and opportunities for advancement.
- Assess the strengths and weaknesses of existing education and workforce development services for the target sectors, and identify gaps where needs are currently unmet.
- Consider the return on potential public investments.

Stage 2. Career pathways planning: form a partnership to develop a career pathways plan

- Organise partners, including education and training providers and workforce, economic development and social service entities, to develop the plan.
- Involve employers in mapping the structure of the jobs, job requirements and advancement pathways in the target industry sector(s).
- Rethink partner programmes and services to support career entry and advancement in the target sector(s).
- Identify costs, and develop a funding strategy.
- Develop a stakeholder engagement and communications plan to build broad-based support for the career pathways vision and goals.

Stage 3. Implementation: coordinate the work of the partners

- Establish memoranda of understanding (MOU) specifying the roles, commitments and contributions of each partner, including employers.
- Coordinate the work of the partners, including programme development, marketing and recruitment, delivery of programmes and support services, job development and outcomes tracking.

Stage 4. Continuous improvement: evaluate and continuously improve career pathways programmes and services

- Conduct regular in-process reviews of programme performance.
- Track the employment and further education outcomes of participants at each level.
- Make adjustments based on evidence of programme effectiveness and impacts.
- Regularly re-evaluate the mission, vision and goals.

Stage 5. Expansion: expand the pathways process to involve other partners, populations of participants and sectors

- Apply the pathways model to additional populations or geographic areas, expanding the partnership to include other organisations as needed.
- Replicate the pathways process in other industry sectors of importance to the local economy.

Source: Jenkins and Spence (2006).

Employer partnerships are one of the key elements of any career pathway model, and CUNY's experiences in this area have been variable. CUNY has had some experiences with incumbent worker training (such as for the first VESL for a Successful Worker project) where the employer's initial commitment was not strong enough to sustain the programme. Kingsborough is trying to build their career pathway without full employer commitment up front, and this will be a major challenge as they move forward. Kingsborough and its partners are attempting to gain that buy-in over time, working with employers on their Employer Advisory Board, cultivating new relationships with New York City Department of Small Business Services, which has existing relationships with large employers in the cluster, and through the Project Welcome project.

As far as incentives for engaging partners, the largest incentive CUNY has to offer is free training for employees or clients of employer or community based organisation partners, when that training is funded by an outside source. Even with the offer of free training, engagement varies across partners. In the "VESL for a Successful Worker" project, for example, some individual supervisors did not support workers participation in the free training, changing work schedules to conflict with class sessions, for example. Another challenge for the project was staffing changes over time, where supervisors committed to the project left during implementation. The 1199SEIU Training and Upgrading Fund often prefers working with CUNY compared to private institutions, given the relative low cost of tuition-based programmes. When the demand is high enough for skilled labour, employers are able to offset existing problems in CUNY's own capacity by providing adjunct faculty or facilities. Laboratory space is at a premium across CUNY for its various science and medical programmes, so LaGuardia might not have been able to offer its new radiation technology programme without the use of a partner employer's existing radiation facility (LaGuardia Community College, 2008).

CUNY also partners with various public agencies to support its workforce development efforts. Small Business Services has been a partner on a number of the career pathway projects profiled here, particularly the retail, hospitality and tourism efforts. These can be complicated partnerships, since the agency is both a partner and a funding source, and strives to prevent any conflict of interest between those functions. LaGuardia operates one of Small Business Services' Workforce 1 Career Centers (a One Stop), which allows for a very close connection between the college's career pathway efforts and the city's workforce development services.

Education and training provision

In terms of the education and training offered, the innovation is less in the introduction of new courses, but rather new ways of organising them. The actual education and training provided through career pathway programmes at CUNY may already exist within the colleges, but have not been formally linked together as steps along a career pathway (Chen and Dalsimer, 2008) and/or adapted to meet adult working students' particular needs. For example, the 1199SEIU Training and Upgrading Fund has worked with CUNY and its other partners to develop relatively faster tracks through existing degree programmes for higher-skilled immigrants. In the case of Kingsborough Community College's Project Welcome, the curriculum is also adapted from the college's regular offerings through their academic Tourism and Hospitality programmes, but repackaged in modules to quickly train and place participants in jobs. With the foreign nurse and doctor programmes, Lehman identified the very particular needs of those populations and crafted a programme that addressed their language and basic skills deficits. Dean Paull explained:

> It depends on the population. They define the "bridge". With the foreign trained doctors, we know that the student doesn't understand the culture of nursing, probably has problems with English, and what we try to do is focus on those areas: what does it take to be a nurse, how is the culture of nursing different in New York from their countries; how is it different from being a doctor... and finally, at the end of this bridge, they are taking the NLN (nursing entrance exam) to determine how well they have learned these things. If they score high enough, they go into the nursing programme (2008).

Another way to help adult workers get a jump start on their academic degrees is to grant credit for life experience, including non-credit training or work experience. The 1199SEIU Training and Upgrading Fund is very interested in seeing more of their college partners grant credit for life experience, since their members often bring years of clinical experience. Lehman College has adopted the approach of granting credit for life experience for its Adult Degree programme which serves working adults, and LaGuardia is in the planning stages for establishing formal paths to grant credit for life experience that will support their own career pathway initiatives.

One curricular hallmark of many of the career pathway programmes is the use of contextualised English as a Second Language instruction, where language instruction is based on usage within the industry, or even of the specific employer (Mazzeo *et al.*, 2003). The language instruction is also often blended with specific occupational skills. The curriculum development process for these programmes is labour intensive, since it not only requires an understanding of ESL pedagogy, but requires getting to understand the sector and occupational and language skills required for advancement. Both the Hotel TEACH and both VESL programmes with McDonalds, for example, involved months of qualitative research to design the curriculum. Developers and instructors met with human resources, management and staff at all levels, shadowed potential students on their jobs, reviewed corporate training manuals and other written materials that students would come into contact on a daily basis at their jobs. They also identified existing curricula or standards that would be relevant to both English language learners and to their sector. In the case of Hotel TEACH, the curriculum was adapted in part from the Equipped for the Future standards developed by the National Institute for Literacy for adult basic education and have been used previously for retail and customer service training, but not for English language learners

Career pathway curricula often attempt to incorporate industry-relevant credentialing as well. In healthcare, even low-wage entry-level positions require certification or credentials. For example, Certified Nurse Assistants must complete a state-approved training programme and pass certain exams to be allowed to work in hospitals or nursing homes in these relatively low-wage positions. Many of the 1199SEIU Training and Upgrading Fund and CUNY healthcare programmes include a component to prepare students for the various required entry or credentialing exams (*e.g.* the Foreign Born Registered Nurse programme includes preparation for the NCLEX nursing licensing exam). In the retail, tourism and hospitality sectors, industry certifications are also part of the career pathway programme design. One particular concern for some immigrants in career pathway programmes is that not all industry certifications may be realistic goals, depending on English proficiency. Some of the VESL for a Successful Worker projects piloted using the National Retail Foundation Federation's customer service and sales certification, but few of these pilot participants were successful, and the testing experience was traumatic for those that did not succeed. Even though the VESL projects were successful in producing measurable gains in participants' language skills, the industry certification tests were not considered appropriate for English language learners except at the most advanced level.

Data and information

According to the Workforce Strategy Center model, Career Pathways ought to be data driven, and analysis has to be an ongoing process, incorporating employer feedback.

> We find that too many workforce initiatives are designed on broad labour market projects alone... how do you then take that analysis and have conversations with real employers, to find out exactly what people you are looking for, how has the economy changed suddenly... that won't come through in the initial analysis. You need on the ground conversation, and then hopefully those on the ground conversations lead to better relationships with employers to hire and influence curriculum (Julian Alssid, Director of Workforce Strategy Center, 2008).

The use of data and industry information occurs in many forms in the CUNY career pathway efforts, to varying degrees. The 1199SEIU Training and Upgrading Fund does its own tracking and research for accountability and programme management purposes. The Fund regularly consults its employer partners to identify their emerging employment needs and then develops new programmes to address these forecasted shortages.

Where possible, the colleges try to draw on existing data sources, although they have also commissioned their own small studies to better inform their work. Kingsborough's work with Workforce Strategy Center and their partner, Economic Modeling Specialists, Inc. involved a regional labour market analysis of the tourism and hospitality sectors, to design their pathway and Project Welcome. This analysis included identifying occupations which pay more than USD 15/hour at the entry level, the education and training required for those positions, and potential routes for advancement. In the retail area, LaGuardia Community College's Center for Corporate Education conducted industry forums in retail and hospitality which generated data to inform the design of the VESL projects. The partnership also commissioned a survey of sector employers to better understand their staffing and skill training needs.

Budgets and funding streams

Outside of 1199SEIU's Training and Upgrading Fund's significant training budget for its own career pathway efforts, the budgets for the various CUNY pilot efforts range between USD 500 000 to USD 2 million per pilot project. The HC4 project is supported through approximately USD 800 000 per year in tuition payments from the 1199SEIU Fund to serve 700 students per semester, and the union's Training and Upgrading Fund provides dedicated counsellors for the programme. Kingsborough's three-year Project Welcome and the related Retail, Tourism and Hospitality Career Pathway project are funded through a US Department of Labor Community-Based Job Training Grant for USD 1.6 million, with an additional USD 210 000 in Individual Training Account funds from the New York City Department of Small Business Services. The LaGuardia Hotel TEACH project had a much smaller budget for the two year project of just under USD 500 000 from a one-time federal grant from the US Department of Labor High Growth Training Initiative Grant for the Hospitality Sector. The consortium of CUNY colleges that operated the various VESL projects described in the study had budgets of USD 700 000 for the new McDonald's project, with funding from the New York State Department of Labor and McDonalds Corporation, and a budget of USD 1 million in federal US Department of Labor grant funding for the VESL for a Successful Worker project which served multiple employers. The VESL for a Successful Worker also received various in-kind or financial resources from their employer partners, including space, materials, release time or completion bonuses.

Much of the funding is dedicated to capacity building or curriculum development since the actual training delivered is often on a relatively small scale. The largest projects serve several hundred participants, with smaller pilots serving tens of participants, directly. Compared to CUNY's overall budget of approximately USD 2.2 billion, these programmes represent a very small fraction of that larger funding pool (City University of New York, 2008).

There is no "career pathway" funding stream, much less a single funding stream for workforce development activities in New York State, although local advocates recently called for the establishment of such a fund in testimony to the state's Board of Higher Education (New York City Employment and Training Coalition, 2008). The funding streams for these programmes are typically separate from the full-time equivalent (FTE) model used to support traditional academic programmes, and in New York State, there is no general state postsecondary education funding available to support non-credit workforce development programmes directly, although community colleges can access some state workforce training dollars (Van Noy *et al.*, 2008; Hoffman, 2008). The career pathway projects in this study all rely on very different funding sources, which are often one-time project specific grants or contracts. Sometimes colleges are able to continue their work in particular areas by raising new funds, as is the case with the second VESL project for McDonalds, and in other cases, the programmes cease to operate when the funding runs out.

At the local level, CUNY's central administration provides small amounts of seed funding through its Workforce Development Initiative grant programme, which has recently adopted a focus on career pathway development. Small Business Services has contributed funds for some of these initiatives, often helping their college partners leverage available state or federal funding. Small Business Services used Individual Training Account dollars to support training for the unemployed through Project Welcome; these funds are most often targeted to individuals and not on a contract basis, so these dollars are not likely to be a reliable source of contract funding for CUNY colleges in the future[12].

Colleges tap into some federal funding sources, such as the one-time grants they have used to seed the various pilot projects described in this study (*e.g.* Kingsborough's work is funded through the US Department of Labor Community and Job Training Grant programme). Renewable sources of federal funding are also available for career pathway efforts, such as the Carl D. Perkins Vocational and Technical Education Act (VTEA), which are passed through the state's Department of Education and fund LaGuardia's Bridge to Allied Health Careers programme (see Figure 8.1). These are, however, relatively small and limited streams, and require reapplication annually; LaGuardia has seen its overall Perkins VTEA allocation shrink annually, from USD 1.9 million down to USD 1.3 million over the past three years. CUNY also draws down some private foundation dollars. LaGuardia's new GED Bridge for Business, a parallel project to the GED Bridge to Healthcare, is funded in part by the MetLife Foundation. In addition to the direct funding that 1199SEIU Training and Upgrading Fund provides for many health pathway programmes, the fund also draws down additional grant funds from public or private foundation sources for employer-specific project work.

LaGuardia's approach to funding these efforts mirrors the institutional funding structure they have put into place for all their Adult and Continuing Education programmes. They pursue blended funding streams for every effort, so that if one source of funding diminishes, they will use other sources to continue a successful programme. The three streams they rely on are CUNY's tax levy funds; fee based funding; and grant funding from various public and private sources. The tax levy option is one way to institutionalise and sustain some of the individual CUNY college's career pathway efforts. Some colleges have also experimented with offering some career pathway programmes on a tuition or fee basis, although it has proven very difficult to recruit self-paying students.

Accountability mechanisms

Each CUNY project relies on different data sources and tracking mechanisms, largely driven by funder accountability requirements. Individual colleges have been working to create databases and collecting data, often at the same time they are engaged in programme start-up activities. Kingsborough recently developed a database to track outcomes, for example, with some consultation with the New York City Department of Small Business Services. These data collection efforts are in their early stages, and often occur on parallel tracks among the individual college partners, even when working on the same project. Overall there appears to be a limited existing infrastructure to support data collection and analysis for the projects.

Formal evaluations are also not typically conducted of these pilot efforts, with a few noteable exceptions. As part of Hotel TEACH, LaGuardia Community College contracted with an outside evaluator, The Commonwealth Corporation, to conduct a formative evaluation of the first phase of the project. 1199SEIU Training and Upgrading Fund hired CUNY to do a longitudinal study of the HC4 programme, to better understand how the union's workers outcomes compared to other populations at CUNY. The Fund conducts its own research on the various programmes it funds, as part of its own accountability process to its Board of Directors. LaGuardia is exploring ways to establish data collection mechanisms and hire outside evaluators to document the outcomes of its emerging career pathway programmes, and has made this a capacity building goal in coming years.

Outcomes to date

Overall, the outcome information suggests these programmes are effective in achieving their initial goals, but as mentioned, there are few comprehensive evaluation efforts underway to understand their real impacts on career advancement. 1199SEIU Training and Upgrading Fund conducted one study of their nursing programmes in which they found that nurses who earn their credentials while working their way up the healthcare career pathway have better retention in their jobs than nurses who were trained without healthcare experience prior to enrolling in college. Initial results for the HC4 programme since it began in 1999 include findings that HC4 students typically earn higher grades in some courses than non-HC4 union members and other CUNY students (Ebenstein, Dale, and Croke, 2007). HC4 students are also more likely to continue on to higher-level courses than the non-HC4 groups (Ebenstein, Dale and Croke, 2007). As of spring 2007, 82 of the 1 034 HC4 participants had earned CUNY academic degrees, with most in nursing, usually at the Associate Degree level (Ebenstein, Dale and Croke, 2007). There is also some early evidence to suggest that Latino students who participate in the HC4 programmes do better in nursing programmes than non-HC4 Latino students.

CUNY is able to track enrolments and graduations from nursing or other professional programmes, but one major challenge in measuring outcomes for career pathway programmes is that it can take a very long time for individuals to achieve career advancement goals. While the Fund offers some fast-track programmes for eligible members to earn high-demand degrees, like nursing, low-skilled immigrants or other members starting out on the bottom steps of the pathway have a very long road ahead of them. It is estimated that starting out in a GED-prep programme with the ultimate goal of becoming a nurse, and attending school part-time can easily take ten years.

The emerging retail, tourism and hospitality programmes shared some early outcomes from these pilot projects as part of the study. They have very good completion rates and have seen some evidence that these approaches lead to promotions, enrolment in further education, or job placements. Kingsborough's Project Welcome has served approximately 200 participants in the first year, exceeding original targets – indeed, demand exceeded the slots available. First year outcomes include an 80% retention and 75% job placement rate. At least ten students have enrolled in the Kingsborough degree programme. LaGuardia's Hotel TEACH had impressive outcomes for its small pilot, as well. 90% of the 22 participants completed the programme, and 80% of the completers increased their English skills at least one level. The programme reported high attendance with most participants attending 100 or more hours. Students also demonstrated improvements in computer and hotel industry skills. Twenty-five per cent of the completers received promotions or entered management training programmes within Sheraton. More would have been eligible for promotion but chose not to accept management level jobs because the higher-level positions were not unionised and they did not want to lose their union benefits (Goldberg and White, 2006).

Borough of Manhattan Community College and its CUNY partners were still evaluating the outcomes from the VESL for a Successful Worker project during this study, but early analysis suggested that 85% of completers improved at least one level in their standardised language test scores. Twenty-seven per cent of the completers moved up three levels in their test scores. Programme staff believe at least 10% of completers have already enrolled in ESL classes at participating colleges and several students have enrolled in college degree programmes. Programme staff estimate that only about 10-12% didn't finish the various programmes, and some of those non-completers had positive advancement outcomes without the full programme, such as enrolment in other college programmes, raises or promotions, or better jobs (Dail and Hoffman, 2007).

Institutional outcomes

Another set of outcomes worth exploring further are those on the institutional level. The comprehensive and supportive approach the 1199SEIU Training and Upgrading Fund takes with supporting members to achieve their career advancement goals has in turn influenced the delivery of education and training services in their partner institutions. CUNY is considering ways to institutionalise the HC4 model across the CUNY system, for all students pursuing health career majors, particularly the cohort model and the additional supports and counselling available to the union members.

LaGuardia's Adult and Continuing Education Division is approaching career pathway development pilot as a way to bring about institutional change; this work is supported at the highest levels of the institution, including by the college's President. Developing an allied healthcare career ladder was one of the college's goals in its strategic plan two years ago, and that level of institutional focus and support has been a huge factor in developing the pathway. The resulting Allied Health Career Pathway (see Figure 8.1) has taken more than five years to build, but that process has brought about better working relationships between the academic/credit-granting and continuing education/non-credit divisions, leveraging of new resources, and better outcomes for both divisions.

Kingsborough Community College is trying to build off Project Welcome's approach to curriculum development for the academic programmes at the college, by making the academic curriculum more responsive to industry needs. The curriculum review process usually only occurs every three years, but they are learning from the Project Welcome experience that the industry changes at a much faster pace.

Future plans

There are various plans to further develop career pathway initiatives at the local, state and federal levels.

Local level

The 1199SEIU Training and Upgrading Fund is now turning to look at new shortage areas in healthcare and working with CUNY or other education providers to address these, such as the emerging shortage in respiratory or radiology technicians.

The CUNY colleges have plans to build on their pathway pilots in various sectors, to attempt to reach more of each industry's incumbent workforce and to build better connections between their non-credit workforce development work and related credit academic programmes. LaGuardia plans to pursue several new funding opportunities to move towards their longer term goal of establishing the New York City Sales and Service Training Partnership as a separate operating entity from the college. Lehman and 1199SEIU Training and Upgrading Fund are also working with other cities, even other countries, to export the HC4 model. CUNY's Central Administration also tries to promote the career pathway approach internally, by reinforcing the message that workforce development or continuing education programmes "should always have a next step" in mind.

At the city level, the Mayor's Office of Adult Education has listed pathway creation, in terms of making basic education courses prepare students for college, as a potential part of its long-term vision for strengthening connections between adult education and career and postsecondary opportunities (2007). The Mayor's Center for Economic Opportunity, which provides new funding for demonstration projects and evaluation on poverty reduction, has seeded efforts to improve services for immigrants (the Language Access Program), and various career pathway efforts that may serve immigrants' workforce development needs.[13]

Seventeen million dollars in Center for Economic Opportunity funding is also allowing Small Business Services to pilot a number of new sector specific and retention and advancement initiatives and enhance existing initiatives, including an expansion of the Business Solutions Training Funds programme to include ESL projects, adult literacy and numeracy classes, work readiness training, and three future sector-specific Workforce 1 Career Center. The New York City Employment and Training Coalition which represents the interests of local education, training, and workforce development providers, has also been promoting the career pathways approach, through forums, testimony in state hearings, and through an annual awards programme which recognises promising practices or individuals in the workforce development community. The LaGuardia healthcare pathway model was recognised by this annual award programme in the programme's Encouraging Career Advancement category.

State level

Likewise, there is a great deal of interest in sectoral approaches to workforce development in New York City and New York State, The New York State Department of Labor is embracing the approach on a project by project basis. In addition to funding the Fast Food, Fast Track VESL project described in this study, the state recently hired Workforce Strategy Center to work with the New York City Workforce Investment Board and Small Business Services to map out career pathways in the city's transportation sector (Alssid, 2008). Small Business Services and the Workforce Investment Board are also embarking on several additional related and high profile initiatives, including the New York State Sector Policy Academy sponsored by the National Governors Association and the New York City Sectors Initiative, coordinated by Public/ Private Ventures.[13] New York State leadership have not embraced the approach to the same degree as their counterparts in other states (*e.g.* Washington, Arkansas) which have adopted state level career pathway promotion policies, however, and New York State does not have yet any specific policies to support the approach (Mazzeo *et al.*, 2006).

Conclusions

The career pathway model appears well-suited to helping immigrants in low-wage jobs or with low-skills overcome various labour market or educational barriers, in a number of ways. The multiple entry and exit points along a pathway responds to the very diverse skill levels and needs of immigrants, from those needing some combination of language, occupational and/or other basic skills to access entry-level employment, to incumbent workers needing additional skills or education to advance to higher-level positions. Fully "mapped out" pathways can provide information that many immigrants lack about both the US educational system and the labour market, to allow for more informed decision-making.[14] The mapping process can also highlight opportunities with other employers or related industries, where similar skill sets are required, and provide immigrants who are over-represented in low-wage work with an avenue for advancement outside of their current employer.[15]

For immigrants who already have college or professional credentials, career pathway programmes may help them more quickly move into jobs they are already qualified for instead of starting over in the US education system. The additional support services and flexibility built in to accommodate working adults can potentially help immigrants overcome additional barriers they face in completing education programmes. Over the course of interviews with many CUNY staff and instructors, one common theme was their belief that the "bridge" programmes that are often the entry or transition points in a pathway model are a concrete way to help immigrants with low-skills or low levels of education address their skill deficits, acquire job skills, and overcome past negative experiences with education, giving them the confidence and basic skills to re-enter the educational system.

However the career pathway work at CUNY faces some considerable challenges moving forward, and the overriding challenge for any of these efforts will be in bringing them to scale. Many of the current pilots are finding they can serve larger numbers of participants than they had once thought, although the numbers are marginal compared to the potential demand. CUNY has taken other pilot projects to scale, such as some of their youth projects. Their pre-college experience programme, College Now, which started out as a pilot now serves more than 30 000 city high school students each year.[16]

The chief obstacle to sustaining what has already been implemented, much less going to scale, is lack of reliable funding sources. As described previously, these projects are largely funded with one-time grants and some institutional resources, and thus sustainability is likely to be a real challenge. The public sector has played a small role but the career pathway approach has not yet been widely adopted or promoted in New York at the state level despite promising levels of interest. Similarly, the colleges continue to work on getting full buy-in from individual employers or the full sector to sustain and promote these approaches. While the healthcare work has been very employer driven, the emerging work in retail, tourism and hospitality is mostly being driven by the colleges themselves. Individual programmes are working to build that support through programme-specific partnerships or industry-wide approaches, like the New York City Sales and Service Training Partnership at LaGuardia. The individual employer partnerships described in this case study are a good start, but it will take a great deal more buy-in for employers to get proposed new credentials recognised as industry-approved paths to career advancement, outside of the health sector.

As mentioned in earlier, there are also no systematic data collection or evaluation mechanisms in place to understand the outcomes from these programmes and communicate their results more broadly. More of an emphasis on evaluation may prove helpful in justifying future investment by public or private sources. Evaluation of these efforts is no small task, however, given the complexity of training workers for advancement which may take them to different jobs in different employers or to any number of further education and training programmes. Understanding career advancement as a goal has been challenging for the various CUNY programmes, and their pilot projects are teaching them valuable lessons in this area. Through Hotel TEACH, LaGuardia learned that future versions of the programme will require clearer understanding of individual workers' goals up front so that they are able to dedicate limited training resources to workers who are interested in advancement, and not just interested in free ESL training. In the Hotel TEACH case, fewer workers received promotions than could have, because many workers did not want to lose their union membership by moving from unionised positions to non-unionised management opportunities. 1199SEIU Training and Upgrading Fund had had similar experiences with members who are reluctant to move to potential advancement opportunities within the same or different employers if the potential new job title is not organised by 1199SEIU.

There is also a risk that these programmes are leading to "creaming effects". The limited resources and slots available for participants have led many of these programmes to place very strict requirements for entry. Evaluation could shed light on whether these programmes are having real impacts on participants' advancement goals, or whether they are actually serving populations that might have eventually achieved those successes on their own. It would likely be very difficult to design an experimental evaluation given limited scale and the complexity of the approach, although many in the career pathways field are interested in seeing that occur.

The career pathway approach may also have some more fundamental limitations for serving immigrants or other workers. While improved communication skills in the various VESL programmes can make an immediate difference in job performance for participants in their current jobs, and may help some get promotions, it is likely to take a very long time to move to the higher paying rungs in many industries. As mentioned previously, outside of customised fast track programmes in the healthcare sector, it can take many years for someone with low educational attainment to move from entry-level healthcare jobs to become a credentialed nurse, and many individuals who start on these pathways will never reach their goals. These efforts are usually of a small scale, and thus are not likely to serve the full demand that exists in the labour market and among the underemployed.

However, the career pathway process is a promising experiment, which could be particular valuable if up-scaled further. The participating colleges, in particular, generally consider that while their career pathway mapping projects are ambitious, the process is worth it if it leads to concrete changes in how colleges operate, how responsive they are to industry needs and how flexible they are in serving adult workers.

Notes

1. The Mayor's Office for Immigrant Affairs directory of services is available online: *https://a069-webapps3.nyc.gov/dsial/IMG_Listing.aspx.*
2. Note that this case study was limited in focus to immigrants with legal status to work and remain in the United States; immigrants without legal status to reside here are faced with numerous other barriers to self-sufficiency or career mobility, beyond the scope of this study.
3. Erisman and Looney (2007) also cite interviews with the New York City Immigration Coalition that report a similar shortage of ESL services in the city.
4. Adelman, Clifford (1998)."The Kiss of Death? An Alternative View of College Remediation." National Center for Public Policy and Higher Education and National Center on Education Statistics, "Remedial Education at Higher Education Institutions in Fall 1995", US Department of Education as cited in Jenkins and Boswell, 2002.
5. Their selection is supposed to drive policy, allocation of funds, and other key workforce development decisions. Individual Training Account vouchers, funded through the federal Workforce Investment Act, can only be awarded to individuals pursuing training in these high growth sector areas, for example.
6. These figures are based on New York State Department of Labor data analysis as cited in the Center for Health Workforce Studies report.
7. These figures are from private industry analysis conducted by Economic Modeling Specialists, Inc. for Workforce Strategy Center, for Kingsborough Community College.
8. Lehman College has identified ESL instructors who have medical backgrounds or team teaching approaches to make sure both skill sets are involved.
9. Lehman College in the Bronx, College of Staten Island, and New York City College of Technology in Brooklyn.
10. Three community colleges: LaGuardia, Kingsborough and Borough of Manhattan Community College, and one senior college, New York City College of Technology.
11. For more information on requirements to become a CNA in New York State, see the Department of Labor's website at *www.Labor.state.ny.us/workforceindustrydata/olcny/certnurs.asp.*
12. Another potential future resource is the New York City Business Solutions Training Grants, a total pool of several million dollars for incumbent worker training from Small Business Services.
13. See the CEO website for more information: *www.nyc.gov/html/ceo/html/home/home.shtml.*
14. Erisman and Looney (2007) cite lack of information as a major barrier for immigrants in accessing and succeeding in postsecondary education programmes.
15. Workers can overcome limited mobility in one industry by moving to another that values their same skill set but has better advancement opportunities; mapping out these cross-industry moves is sometimes called a "crosswalk". For an example, see Greg Shrock and Judith Kossy (2007), "Career Pathways and Crosswalks in the Hotel, Retail and Restaurant Industries", Chicago Workforce Board and the Joyce Foundation.
16. *http://collegenow.cuny.edu/whatiscn/historyphilosophy/.*

Bibliography

1199SEIU (2007), *New York City Region*, retrieved March 2008 from 1199 SEIU United Healthcare Workers East, *www.1199seiu.org/members/regions/nyc/index.cfm*.

1199SEIU Training and Employment Funds (2007), HC4 Program Brochure.

Alssid, J. (2008), Workforce Strategy Center Update, 1 May.

Bailey, T and E. Weininger (2002), *Educating Immigrants and Native Minorities in CUNY Community Colleges*, Community College Research Center, Teachers College, Columbia University.

Borough of Manhattan Community College (2007, 2008), Quarterly Project Reports to the US Department of Labor on the VESL for a Successful Worker Project.

Center for Economic and Workforce Development, Kinsborough Community College (2006), proposal to the US Department of Labor for the Community Based Job Training Grant.

Center for Health Workforce Studies (2008), *The Health Care Workforce in New York, 2006: Trends in Supply and Demand for Health Workers*, School of Public Health, University at Albany, State University of New York.

Center for Immigrant Education and Training (2007), *Hotel TEACH Curriculum*, retrieved March 2008, from LaGuardia Community College, *http://ace.laguardia.edu/ciet/hotel_teach_curriculum.htm*.

Chen, L., and A. Dalsimer (2008), Instructors, Adult and Continuing Education Division, LaGuardia Community College.

Christopher Mazzeo, Sara Rab and Julian Alssid (2003), "*Building Bridges to College and Careers: Contextualised Basic Skills Programs at Community Colleges*", Workforce Strategy Center.

City University of New York (2008), *CUNY 2008-2009 Budget Request*, retrieved March 2008, from CUNY Administration, Budget and Finance, *www1.cuny.edu/administration/budget/final_request_09.pdf*.

Colton, T. (2006), *Lost in Translation*, Center for an Urban Future and the Schuyler Center for Analysis and Advocacy.

Colton, T. (2007), *Update: Still Lost in Translation*, Center for an Urban Future.

CUNY (2008a), *About CUNY*, retrieved March 2008, from CUNY, *www1.cuny.edu/about/index.html*.

CUNY (2008b), *CUNY Citizenship and Immigration Project*, retrieved March 2008, from CUNY, *www1.cuny.edu/about/citizenship.html*.

Dail, L. P. and C. Hoffman (2007), Contextualized ESL: Lessons Learned from a US DOL-funded CUNY Demonstration Project, Presentation for CEANY Conference.

Ebenstein, W., T. Dale and E. Croke (2007), Profile of CUNY-1199 Health Careers College Core Curriculum (HC4) Participants, *Powerpoint Presentation*.

Erisman, W. and S. Looney (2007), *Opening the Door to the American Dream: Increasing Higher Education Access and Success for Immigrants*, Institute for Higher Education Policy.

Fiscal Policy Institute (2007), *Working for a Better Life: A Profile of Immigrants in the New York State Economy*.

Fischer, D. J. (2003), *Labor Gains*, Center for an Urban Future.

Fischer, D. J. (2007), *Work in Progress*, Center for an Urban Future.

Goldberg, C. and G. White (2006), *Hotel TEACH Formative Evaluation*. Commonwealth Corporation for LaGuardia Community College.

Hilliard, T. (2007), *Working to Learn, Learning to Work: Unlocking the Potential of New York's Adult College Students*. Schuyler Center for Analysis and Advocacy and the Center for an Urban Future.

Hughes, K., and M. M. Karp (2006), *Strengthening Transitions by Encouraging Career Pathways: A Look at State Policies and Practices*, Community College Research Center, Teachers College, Columbia University.

Jenkins, D., and K. Boswell (2002), *State Policies on Community College Remediation: Findings from a National Survey*, Education Commission of the States.

Jenkins, D. and C. Spence (2006), *The Career Pathways How-to-Guide*, Workforce Strategy Center.

Kingsborough Community College (2007), Kingsborough's Project Welcome holds first graduation,1(3). *Currents newsletter*.

Kleiman, N. S. (2004), *CUNY on the Job: The City's New Workforce Workhorse*, Center for an Urban Future and Workforce Strategy Center.

Klein, H. (2007), "Welcome" development at KCC – Popular Hospitality and Tourism curriculum exceeds expectations, *Courier-Life Publications*.

LaGuardia Community College (2008), *Application for the New York City Employment and Training Opportunity Award*.

Leinbach, T. and T. Bailey (2006), *Access and Achievements of Hispanics and Hispanic Immigrants in the Colleges of the City University of New York*. Community College Research Center, Teachers College, Columbia University.

McDonalds Corporation (2006), *"Our People"*, *Annual Report*.

Matus-Grossman, L., S. Gooden, M.Wavelet, M. Diaz and R. Seupersad (2002), *Students' Perspectives on Juggling Work, Family and College*. MDRC.

Mazzeo, C., B. Roberts, C. Spence and J. Strawn (2006), *Working Together: Aligning State Systems and Policies for Individual and Regional Prosperity*, Workforce Strategy Center.

McDonalds Corporation (2006), "*Letter to Shareholders*", *Annual Report*.

McDonalds Corporation (n.d.), *Worldwide Corporate Responsibility Report*, retrieved, *www.mcdonalds.com/corp/career/hamburger_university/our_college_degree.html*, accessed March 2008.

Mogulescu, J. (2008), Dean *Request for 2007-2008 Workforce Development Initiative (WDI) Proposals, Internal Memo Draft* , CUNY, 25 February.

New York City Employment and Training Coalition (2008), *New York City Workforce Weekly*, 2(6).

New York City Mayor's Office for Adult Education (25 October 2007), *Summary Report of the Adult Education Visioning Retreat:Growing into the Future – Keeping Students at the Center*, *www.nyc.gov/html/adulted/downloads/pdf/vision_retreat_report.pdf*, accessed March 2008.

OECD (2006), *From Immigration to Integration: Local Solutions to a Global Challenge*, OECD, Paris.

Orr, J., and G. Topa (2006), Challenges Facing the New York Metropolitan Area Economy, *Current Issues in Economics and Finance, Second District Highlights, 12(1), Federal Reserve Bank of New York* .

Research Foundation of CUNY (2007), *The Fast Food, Fast Track VESL Project: Language Skills for Career Mobility Grant Proposal to the New York State Department of Labor.*

Rosen, R., S. Wieler and J. Pereira (2005), New York City Immigrants: The 1990s Wave. *Current Issues in Economics and Finance: Second District Highlights, 11(6), Federal Reserve Bank of New York* .

Saks, M. (2007, October 22), "College Programme Helps Adults Looking to Switch Careers", *New York Daily News* .

Seavey, D., S. Dawson and C. Rodat (2006), *Addressing New York City's Care Gap: Aligning Workforce Policy to Support Home and Community Care,* New York City Workforce Investment Board.

Seedco (2007), *Seedco Industry Review Consultant Services.* New York City Workforce Investment Board and Department of Small Business Services, New York City Sectoral Research Project.

Troppe, M., M. Clagett, R. Holm and T. Barnicle (submitted), *Integrating Employment, Skills and Economic Development: A Perspective from the United States,* OECD, Paris.

US Department of Labor Employment and Training Administration (2005), *President's High Growth Job Training Initiative, LaGuardia Community College, Hotel TEACH, www.doleta.gov/BRG/pdf/Hospitality_LaGuardia_Community_College_Hotel_TEACH_6.28.05.pdf,* accessed March 2008.

US Department of Labor, Employment and Training Administration (2008), *The Community Based Job Training Initiative Fact Sheet, www.doleta.gov/Business/PDF/cbjt_overview.pdf,* accessed May 2008.

US Department of Labor, Employment and Training Administration (2008), *The President's High Growth Job Training Initiative Fact Sheet, www.doleta.gov/business/PDF/1%20-%20HGJTI%20overview.pdf,* accessed May 2008.

US Department of Labor, Employment and Training Administration (2007), *Workforce Innovation in Regional Economic Development Fact Sheet, www.doleta.gov/wired/files/WIRED_Fact_Sheet.pdf, accessed* May 2008.

Van Noy, M., J. Jacobs, S. Korey, T. Bailey and K. Hughes (2008), *The Landscape of Noncredit Workforce Education: State Policies and Community College Practices,* Community College Research Center, Teachers College, Columbia University.

Workforce Strategy Center (2007), *Draft Analysis of New York City Metropolitan Labor Market and Recommendations for Developing Career Pathways.*

Workforce Strategy Center (2008), Kingsborough Community College Career Pathways, Presentation.

York, T.C. (2008), *HHC – Who We Are.* Retrieved March 2008, from New York City Health and Hospitals Corporation, *www.nyc.gov/html/hhc/html/about/about.shtml.*

ANNEX 8.A1

Overview of the CUNY Career Pathway Programmes

Table 8.A1.1. **CUNY career pathway programmes to help immigrants or other workers advance**

Healthcare sector		
Programme	Description	CUNY colleges/partners
Foreign Born Registered Nurse Program/Foreign Trained Physician to Registered Nurse Program	Eligible healthcare workers in non-nursing jobs with foreign nursing or medical doctor credentials receive contextualised ESL instruction, test preparation assistance and other support to become credentialed nurses in the US. The physician's programme involves additional undergraduate education in order to meet nursing programme requirements.	Lehman College under contract to the 1199SEIU Training and Upgrading Fund
Health Careers College Core Curriculum (HC4)	Eligible healthcare workers take dedicated pre-nursing undergraduate courses and receive additional supports to prepare them for existing CUNY nursing or other health degree programmes.	Lehman College in the Bronx, College of Staten Island, and New York City College of Technology under contract to the 1199SEIU Training and Upgrading Fund
LaGuardia Community College's Allied Healthcare Career Pathway	Continuum of education and training programmes with multiple entry and exit points to prepare new and incumbent workers for healthcare careers.	LaGuardia Community College's Adult and Continuing Education and Natural and Applied Sciences Divisions

Table 8.A1.1. **CUNY career pathway programmes to help immigrants or other workers advance** *(cont.)*

	Retail, tourism and hospitality sectors	
Programme	Description	CUNY colleges/partners
Project Welcome	Job training programme to prepare unemployed or under-employed workers for careers in tourism and hospitality sectors. Also includes project to develop and map out a career pathway for the sectors.	Kingsborough Community College's Center for Economic and Workforce Development and the Tourism and Hospitality Department; Workforce Strategy Center; New York City Department of Small Business Services; community based organisations and employers.
Hotel T.E.A.C.H	Pilot Vocational English as a Second Language (VESL) programme to prepare incumbent hotel workers for management positions.	LaGuardia Community College's Center for Immigrant Education and Training ; Sheraton Manhattan Hotel; Advisory Council including industry and government representatives from the LaGuardia Workforce 1 Career Center (a WIA-funded One Stop).
VESL for the Successful Worker Project	Pilot projects offering customised VESL customer service training programmes to incumbent workers for different employers including McDonalds Corporation, Duane Reade Pharmacy, and Crystal Windows and Doors. The colleges also developed a general curriculum to disseminate nationally.	Borough of Manhattan Community College, LaGuardia Community College, New York City College of Technology and Kingsborough Community College; New York City Department of Small Business Services; various employers and employer associations.
The Fast Food Fast Track VESL Project	Building on the VESL for Successful Worker Project curriculum developed for the McDonalds' Corporation, further VESL customer service training will be provided to incumbent McDonalds' workers who are eligible for promotion to management positions.	New York City Sales and Service Training Partnership members including CUNY colleges (Borough of Manhattan Community College, New York City College of Technology and LaGuardia Community College); McDonalds Corporation and its Owner Operator Council; New York City Department of Small Business Services.

Glossary

Generic skills: Generic skills are those that apply across different jobs and occupations. They are sometimes known as core skills, key competences, transferable skills and employability skills. They can include basic skills such as literacy and numeracy, people-related skills and conceptual/thinking skills. In today's economy, generic skills are becoming particularly important, as more and more workers need to communicate with a significant number of different people in their working lives, innovate and problem-solve, and deal with non-routine processes.

Knowledge-based economy: "The knowledge-based economy" refers to the fact that know-how and expertise are today becoming as critical to many economic sectors as other resources (land, technology or raw materials for example). This process is driven in part by the development of new technologies (known as "skill-biased technological change"), which permit the rapid circulation of information, while at the same time replacing more manual tasks with automated processes.

Life-long learning: The continual acquisition of knowledge and skills throughout somebody's life. The OECD (1996) points out that it is no longer feasible within today's constantly changing economy to survive with a "front-end" model of education and skill formation just for young people – learning must instead be a lifelong process.

Low-skilled equilibrium: This refers to a situation where a low-skills level within the local population is matched by a low demand for skills by local employers. This is a particular problem facing rural areas where companies may survive at a low level of productivity which does not require the strong utilisation of skills. A vicious circle can develop as it does not pay individuals to remain in education if local companies are not seeking higher-level skills. Likewise, managers will be reluctant to raise their level of productivity and better utilise skills if there is a lack of well-educated workers within their locality. The term was first coined in the United Kingdom by Finegold and Soskice in 1988.*

* Finegold, D. and Soskice, D. (1988), "The Failure of Training in Britain: Analysis and Prescription" in *Oxford Review of Economic Policy*, No. 4, pp. 21-53.

Receiving countries: The country that an international migrant moves to (the country of immigration).

Secondary education: Secondary education is generally the final stage of compulsory education, provided by a high school, secondary school or gymnasium. Upper secondary education (ISCED 3) corresponds to the final stage of secondary education in most OECD countries.

Sending countries: The country of origin of an international migrant (the country of emigration).

Skill: A facility or capability that is acquired or developed through training or experience.

Skills ecology: This refers to the diverse set of skills issues which affect any particular locality, including skills demand within particular economic sectors, the concentration of skills within the current workforce, variations in skills supply between different areas and neighbourhoods, etc.

Skills gap: A situation where members of an existing workforce are found to lack the skills required to perform their roles effectively.

Skills shortage: A situation where a vacancy cannot be filled because of a lack of applicants with the required levels and types of skills to fill it. This can be distinguished from a "labour shortage" where a post cannot be filled for other reasons – *e.g.* because of a lack of applicants overall, or because other factors, *e.g.* pay structure and conditions – deter people from taking jobs.

Skills upgrading (or upskilling): This refers to workforce development initiatives that specifically target incumbent workers, *i.e.* the existing workforce. The aim is often to promote employment sustainability and career progression for low-paid workers while better meeting industry needs.

Tertiary education: Tertiary education (IESED 5A and B) is the educational level which people precede to after completing school education (*i.e.* education provided by a high school, secondary school, or gymnasium). Such education is usually provided by colleges, universities, institutes of technology and polytechnics and may lead to a vocational diploma or academic degree.

Technical skills: Operational capabilities necessary to perform certain job specifications.

Vocational training: Vocational education prepares participants for direct entry into a specific occupation, industry or trade.

Workforce development: This is a term used to describe activities which increase the capacity of individuals to participate in, and contribute effectively to, employment, either through training or other forms of public assistance.

OECD PUBLISHING, 2, rue André-Pascal, 75775 PARIS CEDEX 16
PRINTED IN FRANCE
(84 2009 07 1 P) ISBN 978-92-64-06662-5 – No. 57015 2009